Adventure After

Adventure After

A Journey in Search of ME

Trudi Remer

Copyright © 2021 by Trudi Remer

All rights reserved. No part of this publication may be reproduced, distributed or transmitted in any form or by any means without permission of the publisher, except in the case of brief quotations referencing the body of work and in accordance with copyright law.

The information given in this book should not be treated as a substitute for professional medical advice; always consult a medical practitioner. Any use of information in this book is at the reader's discretion and risk. Neither the author nor the publisher can be held responsible for any loss, claim or damage arising out of the use, or misuse, of the suggestions made, the failure to take medical advice or for any material on third party websites.

978-1-913590-39-0 Paperback
978-1-913590-40-6 Ebook

The Unbound Press
www.theunboundpress.com

Hey unbound one!

Welcome to this magical book brought to you by
The Unbound Press.

At The Unbound Press we believe that when women write freely from the fullest expression of who they are, it can't help but activate a feeling of deep connection and transformation in others. When we come together, we become more and we're changing the world, one book at a time!

This book has been carefully crafted by both the author and publisher with the intention of inspiring you to move ever more deeply into who you truly are.

We hope that this book helps you to connect with your Unbound Self and that you feel called to pass it on to others who want to live a more fully expressed life.

With much love,
Nicola Humber

Founder of The Unbound Press
www.theunboundpress.com

To Todd, Jim and Rose Remer:
without experiencing your unconditional love
I would not be who I am today.

Foreword

"You who have made me see many troubles and calamities will revive me again; from the depths of the earth you will bring me up again. You will increase my greatness and comfort me again."
Psalm 71: 20-21 ESV

Trudi is a relatable individual and the personification of contradictory. She embodies love and loss, familiar and foreign, fragile and strong, fearful and fearless. Trudi is one of the most resilient people on the planet, a designation that she detests. She would have rather skipped the events of her life that shaped who she had to become.

Trudi was born into in a happy household led by spiritually and emotionally strong parents. Trudi's partner-in-crime, Todd, was both her childhood mentor and her loving adversary. Then, her life's trajectory changed in an instant. Occasion after occasion, the losses of Trudi's life scaffolded upon one another like a cruel pyramid of sorrow. For years, one step forward was met with two, or more, steps backward. Trudi attempted to build her own family only to be disappointed time and time again when those around her could not relate to, or accept, her truth.

Trudi's journey takes her from the depths of loss, through the fog of grief and self-discovery, to the peak of peace. In a unique blend of faith, independence, and vulnerability, Trudi forged her own path. Her setbacks, tenacity, and, ultimately, redemption, are lifelong lessons that she packed into four decades. Woven into the fabric of these pages are guideposts to a necessary element of life – mortality.

~ Renee Boelcke

Intro

I looked down at my cell phone and the clock read 6:24 p.m. as Aunt Karen's name popped onto the screen. I knew at that very second that this was the call I had been dreading for years.

Now, I could start my story here. I intended my story to begin here. Friday, January 27, 2012, my world completely collapsed. I thought to myself, *My life is forever changed*. This was not the first time I had uttered these words. Here I was again. Alone in my grief.

I know I need to go back to the beginning. I need to explain the dynamic of my family so you can understand the gravity of my loss. When I tell you that my mom died that Friday, you might understand. Truthfully, you probably will not. She wasn't the first in my family to die, but she was the last member of my immediate family. I was now what I had feared the most: all alone.

My birth name means "maiden of strength." I don't find it coincidental that I have lived up to the power of my name more than my parents ever could have intended.

Welcome to the story of my journey. I will not only share my family with you but also who I became after all the grief I experienced. After my mom died, I bribed myself to handle all the hardship. Once I accomplished all the responsibilities necessary, I would treat myself with an adventure overseas.

Several times, I was asked why I was writing a memoir. There never was a clear answer other than it was time. After the words flowed out of me, I realized it was going to be published the year I turned 44-years old. This was significant to me since I realized shortly after my mom died that the average lifespan of my family was 44 years old. It was synchronistic to me.

The more I learn about human condition, the more I realize

how connected we are to one another. I am not sure what you will take from reading this, but I know that somewhere within these pages, you will see a part of yourself.

I constantly questioned if life would ever get better. If you have been knocked down time after time, or if you have ever felt alone, I want you to know that you can create your own life exactly how you want it. Your life is a beautiful journey in all the ebbs and flows. While there are moments that are downright hard, it is in these moments that your soul is growing to who it was always meant to be.

Some names have been changed for my own personal reasons. While others may have interpreted this differently than I did, this is my best recollection at how it unfolded.

PART 1

1

Looking back, I grew up in a picture-perfect family, not that I ever thought about it this way. It was the only family I had ever known. I never thought about how great life was because we lived in the moment. I honestly thought this was what everyone's home life was like. We were a happy little family, a dad, a mom, a boy, and a girl. Like I said, picture-perfect.

My mom and dad were madly in love with each other. My older brother, Todd, was four years and a week older than me. It was fun having close birthdays. Since our parents also had similar birthdays with my dad being three days older than my mom, they always had separate birthday parties for us.

Not only were we a tight-knit family, but we also had close relationships with all four of my grandparents, who lived near us in a northern suburb of Detroit, Michigan. My dad's parents were our next-door neighbors. Adding even more sweetness to our family history, both sets of grandparents had been in the same social circles for years, so my mom and dad had been friends before they ever started dating.

Both my mom and dad came from devout Lutheran backgrounds. My mom's parents went to Immanuel Lutheran Church. My dad's parents went to Trinity Lutheran Church. The two churches were six miles apart. Both had grade schools, but as Immanuel only went up to sixth grade, my mom started to attend Trinity when she was in seventh grade. This is when she was placed in my dad's class. How adorable that they met when in grade school! Eventually, they went to Utica High School together which was right by my dad's childhood house.

Having both grown up in the Christian faith, it only made sense that my parents would have a Christ-centered life. My mom decided at a young age that she wanted to devote her career to becoming a Lutheran school teacher. After she graduated from Concordia college, she had a student teaching position in Florida. While she was there, her and my dad's relationship started to deepen. My dad enlisted in the Marines after high school and went overseas to serve the country in the Vietnam war. When he was on leave, he headed to see my mom in Florida instead of going home to Michigan to see his parents. The rest is history. After my mom completed her student teaching assignment, she ended up receiving a call to be a teacher at Trinity Lutheran School. In the ministry, instead of calling it a "job offer," it is referred to as "a call from God."

I mentioned how my dad's parents were our neighbors. My dad had purchased the land from my grandparents so that he could build a house for his family when my parents were going to be married. Todd and I loved being spoiled with having our grandparents live right next door. All we needed to do was run up the hill to see them.

Not only was it great having my grandparents next door, but this meant that we would get to see all our cousins when they came to visit my grandparents. My dad was the middle child of nine children. This meant that I had a lot of cousins. I ended up being the tenth grandchild of what would eventually be twenty of us grandchildren! Like my dad, I was the middle one. My grandparents were always so proud to have all the grandkids around playing.

Even though my paternal grandparents lived next door to us, we were closer to my mom's family. My mom had one sister, Karen. My aunt Karen married my uncle John and they had two children, Brian and Jenni. My maternal grandparents, parents, aunt and uncle, Brian, Todd, Jenni, and I would hang out regularly together. Brian was a year older than Todd while Jenni was a year older than me. Playing together was always easy since we were similar in age and had the same interests.

Life was simple and perfect.

2

I had just returned home from spending a week at camp with Jenni. My brother was going to be heading out on an adventure himself. He was going with the church youth group to the Smoky mountains for all types of fun activities. Since he was going to be gone for my eleventh birthday, plus it was his birthday the day he was leaving, my mom decided that we should exchange our birthday presents. I grabbed my gift for him, and Todd brought his gift for me to my bedroom. We sat on my bed to give them to one another. I don't recall what I got him – probably some action figure, just not sure if it was Star Wars or some wrestling action figure. Whatever it was, I am sure it was very '80s. When I opened my gift, it was a purple organizer where I could hold my craft supplies I used for making friendship bracelets. This was perfect, since I needed something to have everything organized. We hugged and thanked each other for our gifts.

A few days later, I was heading over to my best friend Teri's house who lived just down the street. As I was leaving my house, a car pulled into our driveway. I noticed it was the head Pastor of our church. We greeted each other as he made his way to the front door. While I knew the Pastor, seeing him weekly in the pulpit, it was strange for him to come to our house in the middle of the day.

When I got to Teri's house, I was reminded that it was her mom's birthday. Birthday celebrations were in the air as we'd just celebrated Todd's, and mine was in another three days. Shortly after I arrived, the phone in the kitchen rang. When Mrs. Imig answered it, she walked out of the kitchen and into their family room to talk on the phone. I did not understand it at first, but something about her body language told me that this wasn't a call to sing "Happy Birthday." After several minutes, she came back into the kitchen to hang up the phone. She told me something had come up with Todd and my parents needed to head out of town to go be with him. Aunt Karen was on her way to get me as I would be staying with them for the next several days. This was something out of the ordinary.

While we waited for my aunt to come get me, Teri and I went outside to play on her swing set. As we swung on the swings, we guessed what may have happened to Todd that my parents had to travel down to see him. One of the theories we came up with was that he may have broken his leg. What in the world would he do if his leg was broken when he wanted to learn how to drive a car? This would mean he wouldn't be able to start learning how to drive.

About an hour later, Aunt Karen arrived in her blue minivan to get me. I said my goodbyes to the Imigs and got into the minivan. I was happy that Jenni had come along so she could keep me company, but there was awkwardness hanging in the air. It's like I could sense something was incredibly off, but my aunt was not saying anything about why my parents left. I really couldn't understand it, but I knew it must be serious for my mom and dad to leave without saying goodbye. Trying to avoid the weirdness that I was experiencing, I focused on filling the quiet space with mindless ramblings.

When we got to my aunt's house, Jenni and I sat down to watch a movie, Spaceballs. This was one of my favorite movies to watch with Todd, so as every scene happened, I'd recall what Todd thought about this and that. Uncle John and Brian had been out in the fields, and when they came in, Brian immediately went into his bedroom and shut the door while Uncle John went to make himself a drink. Aunt Karen asked for us to turn off the television and for me to come sit on the couch next to her.

Truthfully, I should remember this moment. I should remember exactly how my aunt told me the devastating news of my brother's death. But I don't remember the details. Mostly, I remember how incredibly hot it was that August day. She told me that Todd had an accident – he'd fallen off a mountain and died. My aunt said all of this with anguish written all over her face. Not knowing what exactly to do at this moment, she hugged me tightly. To say I was shocked is an understatement. Mind you, I was ten years old at the time, turning eleven in three days. I had no concept of death. All four of my grandparents were still alive and this was the first major death I was experiencing. Trying to wrap my head around what it meant to have a dead brother was incredibly overwhelming. I was not prepared to deal with the heaviness of these emotions. To top it off, my parents weren't even there to console me.

I'm not sure I cried. Or how much I might have cried. I know that I wrestled with how heavy this felt to me. It was in these first moments that I started to create a narrative to forget my brother's existence. He was gone, and so forgetting him would help minimize my pain. I wanted to make sure that I wasn't feeling pain. Moments ago, we were watching one of his favorite movies, sharing his thoughts and humorous comments. And now he's gone? We'd never be able to have these moments again. It was overwhelming. I sat there, stunned. The less I said, the tighter my aunt squeezed me. It was one of those hot, sticky Midwest summers where you're constantly sweating from the humidity. The more she hugged me, the more I wanted to run. It was a lot for me to take in. Not only was it sticky, but the smell of stale tobacco lingered in the air. I know this is the moment that made me dislike hugs. For me, it feels that it's not a genuine exchange, but rather one person needing comfort from the other and taking it in the exchange of a hug.

My maternal grandparents showed up shortly after my aunt shared the news with me. They walked in and gave me a hug, too. The room was unbelievably quiet. It felt as if everyone was staring at me. Checking to see how I was doing. Looking inwards for what they were thinking and feeling. This news had just shaken our entire family. The mood was somber.

I was scared. I was what I can see now as traumatized. He fell off a mountain? He's dead? What does this all mean to my world? Do I cry? Do I just sit here in silence? Why won't they stop hugging me?

I chose silence. I had nothing to say. What could I say? Looking back at this very moment, I know that I didn't understand this, the gravity of what my world was going to be for years to come. My birthday was in three days and now I needed to go to a funeral. What a sick twisted joke this was. When it got too overwhelming for others, they would hug me. Did not they understand that it was the last thing that I wanted? However, being in a state of shock, I did not know how to ask them to stop touching me.

The next couple of days that I spent at my aunt and uncle's house are a blur. Also, my first encounter with my parents arriving home is hazy, too. I cannot even fathom what it was like for them to have to identify the body of their fifteen-year-old son. A ranger had gone down to check if Todd was still alive and ended up staying overnight with Todd's body before the rescue mission was able to bring up his body. My mother spoke of this often, how she appreciated that Todd was not alone after the fall. I have never given much thought to what it was like for my parents to travel down to the Smoky Mountains. What they went through as individuals, parents, and partners. It must have been an excruciating experience for both. I imagine my mom was openly sobbing while my dad went back and forth between crying and supporting her. What has been shared with me is that the youth group that was there experiencing this loss in their own way was amazed by the love my parents poured into them. While devastated, they were so compassionate to the other children.

One thing I remember clearly in the aftermath of Todd's death was having to call all my friends to cancel my birthday party. We were supposed to be going to a Detroit Tiger's baseball game to celebrate my 11th birthday. However, now I was going to my brother's funeral. When one of my friends asked why I was cancelling, I remember sharing that my brother had died. She completely stumbled over her words as she didn't know how to respond to that answer. I awkwardly got off the phone. When I finished all the calls, I was so grateful to stop having that conversation. I couldn't believe that I had to call everyone to let them know. Little did I know that this would only be the beginning of constant awkwardness.

The pain.
The anguish.
The heartache.
The trauma.
The overwhelm of the unknown.

3

To this day, my 11th birthday is one that haunts me. I will never forget it. I already confessed to you that I don't remember many details from my childhood. Therefore, when I say that it is one that I will never forget, what I am talking about is that sinking feeling of it not being about me. My birthday was supposed to be a celebration of the day I was brought into this world, but now it was all about my brother. My dead brother. It now was a day of pain and sadness.

The first day of my brother's wake was on my birthday. I laid my eyes on my brother's lifeless body for the first time, and also witnessed my mom touch his dead body. This freaked me out to my core. Her wails of devastation haunted me. She even bent down to kiss his face. She was examining the side of his head that was not easily seen by people. With my lack of knowledge on how bodies are viewed in a casket, he was facing the opposite way. Due to the injuries sustained in the fall, a special casket was used for the body to have his left cheek facing towards the public.

My mom remarked how they had done a good job of staging

his body and that he looked good. What I saw was that they used a lot of makeup to help his body closely resemble what he looked like in life. Commenting about how a deceased body looks is something I will never understand. I'm not sure if it stems from my trauma of seeing Todd this way, but to this day I will never understand why people talk about how a dead body looks good. They look dead to me, and there is nothing good about that.

My father, who up until this point in my life I'd only witnessed being an extraordinarily strong man, was also crying alongside my mom. This was a lot for me to take in. First, this was the first dead body I was seeing up close and personal. Second, it was my brother. Third, the reactions of both of my parents. I'd never seen my parents in this light before. Watching my mom crying. Observing my dad trying to hold back the tears but letting out a sound I had never heard come from him before. Lastly, it was my birthday and here I was, looking at my brother laying in a casket. Too many emotions that I did not know how to process. My age and life experience up until this point had not permitted me to understand the gravity of what I was witnessing. My parents had always been the ones to comfort me, but now I was seeing them in utter anguish. I wanted to run. But I was way too young and had nowhere to go.

It was devastating, to say the least.

After viewing the body without any other people besides close family, others started to arrive. I was told that I didn't need to stay with my parents, who decided to stand by the casket to greet everyone who came by to wish their condolences. People were arriving so quickly that a line started to form that went out past the door into the room and down the hall. I went to find my cousins or other children who were my age.

My oldest cousin on my dad's side was smoking in a room off to the side of the viewing room. This was back in the day where it was normal to smoke inside buildings. He was showing all of us younger cousins how he could make circles of smoke when he exhaled. I found it gross and fascinating that he was doing this, but what was my other option? Go stand by the casket? As I was surrounded by my cousins, I told them jokingly that it was so nice of everyone to come out to celebrate my birthday with me. No one said a word. A part of me wonders if this moment is the reason that when I am greeted with silence, I tend to think the absolute worst.

When my two younger twin cousins arrived to pay their respects, I watched them each put a single red rose in my brother's casket. Why this sticks in my mind is beyond me, but it does. I do attribute the fact that it has taken me years to appreciate receiving flowers, especially red roses, to this memory. Anytime I smell lilies, I am reminded of a funeral home. On one of my birthdays as an adult, I received both a bouquet of long stem red roses and another bouquet of mixed flowers. When I walked into the room, I was transported back in time to my 11th birthday with the smell of being in that funeral home. I ended up needing to give the flowers away as it was too triggering for me to handle, being my birthday.

The viewing for my brother was two days long – two days that blend together in my mind. There were so many people there for both days. My mom and dad created a scholarship fund in memory of my brother and asked people to donate in lieu of flowers. The entire time we were in the funeral home, there was a heaviness that lingered. People talked quietly and whispering was common. The only times there was happiness and laughter were when I was playing with my cousins to avoid the heaviness around me. We were scolded for having a good time, which truly was not helpful. Could they not get that these were adult feelings, too heavy for us kids to have to deal with?

The third day was the funeral. If I thought there had been a lot of people at the wake, the church had even more people. It was packed with people on that hot summer day to support our family and to say their final goodbyes. The funeral was held on 8-8-88. At the beginning of the year, my mom had wondered what we would be doing on that day. She never dreamt that she would be burying her own son.

A few of the songs that were played for his service were "Children of the Heavenly Father" and "I Know My Redeemer Lives." The other song that stands out is his 8th grade graduation class song, which was "Lift High the Cross." My mom never sang any of these three songs again. Mimicking her reactions, it took me a long time to sing them myself. During the sermon, there was a passage from Isaiah 40:30-31 which reads, "Even youths grow tired and weary, and young men stumble and fall; but those who hope in the LORD will renew their strength. They will soar on wings like eagles; they will run and not grow weary; they will walk and not be faint."

As the service ended, the attendants from the funeral home closed the casket. I witnessed my mom break down crying, her body convulsing. My dad tried to support her, but he himself was struggling to remain calm. It was a lot to take in, seeing my protectors as devastated as they were, while feeling whatever it was that I was feeling. My body tightened in this uncomfortable setting. Talk about having no capacity to know what to do for them or myself. I took it all in and internalized it like only an eleven-year-old could.

We followed the casket down the aisle and watched it be lifted into the hearse. We were then escorted to sit inside a car which seemed like a limo to me, directly behind the hearse. We watched every single person who was in that funeral walk out of the church and to their car. This went on for the longest time. While we waited, a little girl handed me a teddy bear through the window. I'd never met her before, but later we became connected. She, too, had lost her brother at a young age. I hugged the teddy bear tight as it was something soft to hold onto. It was nice to have something small to give me comfort during this incredibly uncomfortable moment. What I didn't know at the time was this was the very reason she had given it to me. She wanted me to have something soft to give me a little bit of comfort. To this day, I have that stuffed animal and it has given me comfort many times.

There was a procession from the church to the cemetery where the committal would be taking place. Once we left the church parking lot, we had a police escort leading the way followed by the hearse and then our car. As we went through various lights, police cars were there to stop traffic as the massive procession of cars made their way. I had never been in a procession before, but this seemed larger than what I imagined it would have been. It seemed like an hour before we arrived at the cemetery since the cars drove slowly there.

Once we arrived at the correct spot in the cemetery, we waited for all the pallbearers to carry the coffin. The pallbearers placed my brother's coffin on a platform above a recently dug out ground. There were four green chairs placed directly in front of the coffin. This was the topper of the last several days. Seeing his body was awful. Now I was witnessing it above ground before it would be lowered and placed there forever. My mom did not want me to sit on one of the chairs since she thought my grandmothers should sit there. I had no idea where they wanted me to go so, I stood near them while they sat. The committal was done as another little mini ceremony as the funeral was concluded.

These last five days felt like eternity. However, this was just the beginning.

4

Life after Todd's death was difficult. It's hard for me to feel as if I'm speaking poorly of my parents. I want to acknowledge here and now that I believe that my parents did the absolute best they were capable of doing during this time. They were in mourning. However, I need to honor myself by being truthful about my experience as a grieving child whose entire world completely crumbled the day my brother died. I understand I hadn't fully developed enough to be able to handle the maturity of the new paradigm I was forced into.

Piecing this back together, it did not surprise me that I was unable to find a lot of information for the year after my brother's death. I started to write a diary a year after his death, but that first year is a complete blur. However, I can remember how lonely I was. How isolated I felt. How incredibly scared I was. How it felt to me was that my parents had each other, but I had no one. Todd was my sibling and partner in crime. Now I was grieving someone that I desperately wanted to talk to. He had been my protector for years, so it was strange not to have him there anymore.

My parents, whom I never recalled fighting before, were now always in some type of disagreement behind closed doors. One of the things I heard my mom yelling at my dad about was his use of alcohol. I had seen my dad drink before, but he now had a shorter temper. I am certain that his way of dealing with his grief was to drink. Since my mom did not drink, this caused constant tension between the two of them.

Heaviness loomed in the air. I hid in my bedroom a lot. The way the house was designed meant I looked directly into my brother's room before I could veer off into my room. It took me over a year before I was able to go into his room. After his death, all his birthday gifts sat unopened on his bed.

Our family had always been on the go before, and now this was no longer the case. We stayed home a lot more and didn't hang out with the usual family or friends like we used to. I believe that it was hard for my parents to be around other families who had children around the same age as Todd. It just magnified what they were missing. I always felt as if I was walking on eggshells, afraid to say or do anything.

One moment stands out to me where I learned quickly not to speak Todd's name around my mom. Shortly before his death, Todd and I both got yelled at for something that neither one of us took responsibility for doing. One day, my mom and I were sitting in the car in the garage and I let her know that it wasn't me who did it. Her body reacted in a way I took to mean I should never bring up Todd's name again. It was not until years later that I was able to see this from a completely different viewpoint. This was my mom reacting in her grief at the mention of his name. While I never meant to hurt her by sharing this information, my young brain wanted to clear the air that I was not the guilty party. This quick moment in time was seared into my memory in a way that stuck to me. It wasn't safe for me to mention his name. I spent a lot of energy trying to keep myself from ever uttering his name to my mother.

This event caused me to believe that Todd was the golden child. And if he was the golden child then it must mean I was only the consolation prize. I had severe survivor's guilt. I watched my parents grieve day in and day out for Todd. It seemed as if they didn't recognize that I was there, alive and suffering. When people die: they no longer can mess up. Therefore, they become saint-like since the bad things that happened fade into the distance as you remember the good memories. Even though we all knew that Todd was never perfect to begin with, in his memory it was as if he was. To my immature brain, this became a truth at my core.

My mother struggled with understanding how Todd's accident could have happened. For her, if she could make it make sense, maybe then she would not lie awake wondering why. There had been talk that he was goofing around, and this didn't sit well with my mother. Todd was an intelligent, levelheaded kid. She was discussing this with her best friend, Donna, when it was brought up that Todd had fainted the week before at church. Maybe this is what happened to cause the fall! This was a little bit better to understand for my mom and was what I was told when I asked about it. Even though I have asked those who were physically there when he died, the story my brain goes to is the one I was told as a child. The outcome is still the same. The story I retell is that when Todd turned to head back from the overhang at Charlies Bunion, he fainted and fell off the mountainside. As a young child, I envisioned him falling back with his eyes closed. How it happened doesn't change the outcome and everything that transpired for me after his death.

While I was learning how to deal with life in complete sadness, I would find the article clippings my mother saved from the newspapers. Todd even made the local news days after his death. There was a helicopter crash that happened when they were trying to recover the body. It seemed as if it was a bigger deal to the newscasters that the helicopter crashed than my brother dying. No one was killed in the crash, yet they kept talking about it. The pilot had not been careful in maneuvering it. The media also had no clue how to pronounce our last name. Even my name was spelled wrong in some articles. I found some of the quotes made by teachers or pastors insensitive to my family who would read them. The way I read their words sounded as if they blamed Todd for being careless on that mountainside.

One of the details that always comforted me was hearing that Todd never screamed as he fell. This was always important for me to know. that my brother fell but did not scream meant to me that he did not experience the terror of falling.

Since I have various clippings of articles my paternal grandparents saved, I wanted to share one of them with you so that you can read the details recorded of the accident. Since this is where I discovered most of the information surrounding his fall, I find it fitting for you to learn the details from it, too.

> **Utica boy killed in mountain fall - Macomb Daily/ Friday, August 5, 1988**
>
> While exploring near a cliff on a hiking trip Wednesday in the Great Smoky Mountains National Park, a 15-year-old boy lost his footing and fell 800 feet to his death from "Charlie's Bunion", one of the highest sections on the Appalachian Trail.

Rangers confirmed that Todd Remer of Utica died upon impact in the rough terrain about four miles northeast of Newfound Gap, a popular site for tourists. He was with the Trinity Lutheran youth group on a week-long camping, hiking, and rafting trip in Sevierville, TN, near Knoxville, said the Rev. John Messman, Trinity Lutheran Church associate pastor.

A park spokesperson said rangers were called at 12:30pm shortly after Remer and an unidentified friend had ventured ahead of the rest of the group and the accident happened. Nine youngsters and five adults were on the trip.

Search efforts Wednesday were hampered by severe storms and dangerous territory and it took eight agencies seven hours to locate Remer. A ranger stayed the night with the boy all night and the rescuers set out at 9am Thursday to recover the body. The boy's parents, Jim and Rose Remer, were in North Carolina near the site of the accident Thursday and could not be reached for comment. Remer also has a sister, Trudy, 11.

Meanwhile at Trinity Lutheran, church members united in prayer for the Remer family and the youth group which is expected to make the 650-mile trip back to Michigan today. Messman said that nearly all 3,800 church members have been notified of the accident and the general feeling is one of disbelief.

"It's all a very distant thing right now", he said.

Remer was a straight "A" student at both Trinity Lutheran School and Lutheran North High School in Utica where he would have been a sophomore this fall.

"He was a very responsible and positive type of student," Messman said.

Remer was the valedictorian of his eighth-grade class at Trinity

> Lutheran School where his mother is an assistant principal and seventh grade teacher. He served as an acolyte at church service, was an athlete and played tuba in the school band.
>
> "He was a joy to have in class. He would always be there to help set up or tear down. You could ask him to do something and he did it. You could always count on Todd to get things done. He's a tough kid to lose." said Lutheran North band director Dean Kratz.
>
> "We do not know what the Lord's will is. It's hard to understand sometimes," he said.

My parents attended a grief group. I've heard that they would have me stay at my grandparent's house, but I do not recall this. At some point when they would go to their meetings, they started leaving me in the house by myself. I enjoyed the time by myself, but it also scared me to be all alone now. My brother used to be my babysitter when my parents went out, so it was strange to be in this huge house on my own. As I said, I started to think my dad and mom had each other to share their pain with and I did not have anyone. I was on my own, not really understanding how life can change so drastically. They would try to get me to talk about how I was handling the loss of Todd, but I had already learned from that experience in the car that it was not safe to mention Todd's name. I was always so concerned about causing them pain, so I did whatever it took to make it appear as if I was doing okay. Any time they would ask me how I was doing; I would respond that I was doing fine. I'm not sure if they believed me.

The sadness was always present in our home. Our home used to be filled with love, laughter, and joy before Todd's death, but now it was the polar opposite. My parents now fought regularly, and my mom cried often. We still went to church every single Sunday to the 8am service. My paternal grandparents would always greet us when we arrived. After the service, we headed over to the cemetery to view Todd's grave and then we would go to breakfast with my grandparents.

What fascinated me, but not in a good way, was how my grandparents would tell us about all the funerals they had been to that week. While I understand that this is the world they lived in, it infuriated me that they did not display any sensitivity to who they were speaking to. I dreaded Sundays. It is safe to say this was a very dark time in my life. Being a young child going to the cemetery to stare at the ground was the absolute worst. I was uncertain as to what we were supposed to be thinking or doing as we were looking at the grave. About a year after his death, we stopped going every single week. At some point we stopped going altogether as a family. I was grateful when we reached that stage.

One day while I was doing my chores, I came across a photo in my mother's sock drawer. It was a photograph of Todd's body in the casket. This took me by surprise. Why was there a picture taken? Did my mom look at it often? I felt uncomfortable asking her these questions, so I just put it back in her sock drawer. It really disturbed me that she had this in her possession.

My parents made it a point to try to find me some support like they had. I was put into a children's grief group called Rainbows. It was also for children who were dealing with their parents' separation or divorce, as well as death. We met in the library of my grade school. However, there were no other children who were dealing with a death in their immediate family. On a rare occasion, another student would be dealing with the death of a grandparent. It felt as if no one who could understand what I was feeling and going through. I noticed myself struggling to share because it could possibly get back to my mom and also because no one could relate to my loss. Safety did not exist for me in this environment. Fortunately, I didn't have to go to Rainbows for too long. I am not sure if there were not enough students or if my mom realized I wasn't getting anything out of it.

My parents got me involved in counseling. It was an opportunity for me to share whatever I needed to talk about. When I first met my counselor, I remember thinking he was incredibly cute. However, this was the only time I looked at him since I spent every session looking down in my lap while he would ask me various questions to try to get me to open. He did his best to reassure me that all our conversations were confidential, but I struggled to believe this. Since the church and school were affiliated with the counseling center, I didn't trust that he wouldn't share whatever we talked about with my parents, specifically my mom. After a few sessions, I confessed to my mom that I never talked during my session with the counselor. She was angry that she was wasting money to have me sit there and not say anything. Needless to say, she stopped making me go. It was the right decision at the time, but I never realized how much this would impact me later in life. I can see now how I rarely trusted anyone in my life to support any of my emotional needs. I was terrified and climbed farther into the abyss of aloneness.

Todd was smart, athletic, and social. Not only this, but he was the first-born son. I felt like Todd became a saint to my parents. It created a larger gap for what he was post death to me in the living flesh. The "I am not good enough" mentality really played heavily on me during my childhood.

While I know deep down that everyone did their best, even me, I still was getting lost in the mix of emotions. I can't tell you how many times I heard the phrase, "The death of a child is the absolute worst." How was that supposed to make me feel? I'll tell you how it made me feel: as if my pain was nowhere near as agonizing as my parents'. This could not be farther from the truth. My parents had matured to the point where they could understand this. I was still young, still mentally developing. One thing that drives me crazy is always having to single out who has it worse. We all had it bad. Losing a loved one is hard. Saying one type of loss is the hardest minimizes others' feelings towards their own loss.

My parents amaze me. One of the statistics they heard in their grief support group is that 80% of marriages end in divorce after the death of a child. They stayed together and supported one another. While I am sure this was not the easiest thing to do, they continued to communicate and give each other the space to grieve how they needed to grieve. I am grateful that their marriage was strong and they relied on each other and God to help them through their journey in grief.

I suffered from survivor's guilt. I really felt as if my parents were left with the wrong child. Watching the grief they experienced made me question if they would have cared if it were me who died instead of him. Their extreme focus on their own needs also made me question why they didn't pay attention to me. I was jealous that they had each other to lean on and I had no one. I was missing my partner in crime. It was in these moments that I took on the expectation to live into his image. To be the good kid. Often children will act out, but the role I took on was to be their good child now. I thought that taking on this role would help them not feel any extra pain. They already had so much to bear. A part of me lost the innocence of being a kid because "in the blink" everything could change. This was a phrase my mom constantly said throughout my childhood.

I alternated between feeling alone or smothered. While I hid in my bedroom, it felt as if no one cared about me. Then there would be moments where I was unable to do something because my parents feared something bad would happen to me. I never knew which side would show up. I spent my youth walking on eggshells, hoping to cause the least number of waves.

As we went through the first year after Todd's death, we experienced all the firsts. When it came to holidays, it felt heavy. We had spent a lot of time with my cousins, but this year it was different. When we walked into my maternal grandparent's house, it felt as if we had taken the joy out of the room. A heaviness came with us everywhere we went. It was good for me to see Jenni and Brian as I had not seen them much since the funeral. I was happy to get to play with them.

Before the first Christmas season came, my mom sat me down to ask if I needed a Christmas tree. This has always been a cruel memory. She asked my opinion, but being real, how was I to say, "Yes, I want a Christmas tree"? I could tell that it hurt her to think about putting it up. I love my mom dearly and I do know from the bottom of my heart that she meant well, but this act damaged me. This allowed me to create and perpetuate the narrative that my needs were not important. That happiness was not something I could have when she was hurting. How was a traumatized eleven-year-old girl able to stand up and selfishly say I wanted to have a Christmas tree or any joy in my life? I never said a word to her about how damaging this was.

I realize I have not shared the details of that day back in August of 1988 beyond the basics. This has been done on purpose. One of the things that personally frustrates me is how we are culturally conditioned to ask people who are in grief how their loved one died. Why does that matter? Does it cure your curiosity bug? Do you feel better now that you know the details of my anguish? Because it does not feel like you asked for my benefit, but rather your own. It has been a painful thing to repeat this story over and over again. Especially when I had not completely processed it myself.

There were moments when I would meet new people, and they would ask if I had any siblings. At first, I was not certain how to answer this question. In the beginning, I would say that I had a brother. When they would ask more questions, I would eventually need to say that he had died. Then, for some reason, everyone would always ask HOW he died. This has always felt invasive to me. Why do people get so caught up on the death part? Why do they always assume they deserve to get to know how someone I deeply loved died? Plus, I did not feel comfortable sharing an incredibly painful moment in my life. After a while, I would start to not even acknowledge my brother ever lived so I did not have to deal with the insensitivity of others. This sent me down my own inward spiral of guilt over not acknowledging Todd's existence. It became a habit to take an internal check to see if I was willing to have the conversation and acknowledge Todd or not. Sharing this truth makes me angry.

I am committed to making a change in how we speak to those who have experienced loss. I personally don't feel there is any reason to ask how someone died. It takes away from the way they lived. How we die is such a small blip in comparison to the life that we have lived. We can be remembered as a fighter, but that is still more about how someone LIVED their life.

5

While home life was incredibly hard, life in the classroom wasn't much better. I entered the sixth grade after Todd's death. My teacher was my mom's friend and co-worker. It felt like I was under a watchful eye. One day during lunch, the teacher asked me to come out into the hall with her. She shared that she wanted to give me a heads up that in the intriguing story she had been reading to us, one of the main characters was going to die in the upcoming chapter. She gave me the opportunity to decide if I wanted to be in the room or not while she read the chapter. She had already asked my mom if she needed to refrain from reading this book to the class because of this, but my mom gave her blessing to have the book be read.

Upon hearing that there was going to be a death, I was once again taken back into my shock. Quickly, I needed to decide to be present. I was enjoying the book, so I wanted to hear what happened. As she read the chapter, I could feel my face starting to get warm, wondering if others were looking at me. They did not turn their heads to observe me, but it was too late. I already assumed my classmates thought of me when the teacher read the chapter with the death. True or not, it was another area where I just did not feel like I fit in.

A little over a year after my brother's death, my family headed to the high school for a special service where they were honoring my brother on All Saints Day. My parents donated memory banners, an altar cross, and refurbished chapel furnishings in his memory. There was an unknown girl who turned and said to me, "I know how you feel." I don't recall who this girl was, but I know that I then sat through the entire service thinking to myself, "You do not know how I feel. Did you lose a sibling suddenly?" This was another example of people saying things they believe are comforting yet are anything but. Even if this girl knew exactly how I felt, my relationship with my brother was my relationship with my brother. Whatever her relationship to her deceased loved one was her relationship to her loved one. It is not helpful to ever tell someone that you know exactly how they feel. While I know that it is coming from a genuine place, you are taking a moment and making it about you and your loss rather than allowing one to have their own experience. Listening is helpful versus sharing your story. This still bothers me over thirty years later. Even if you have experienced a death, you really do not know how I feel.

It was a year after the death of my brother, and the girl who got me the teddy bear at the funeral had bought me a journal to write my thoughts in. Our families got to know one another after Todd's death. She too lost a brother. I now had one friend who I was able to be with the pain and agony of going through heavy emotions. She was comfortable with the pain because she understood it. Her brother's death was not sudden and while that is a different experience, it is still a loss. I was happy to know someone else who felt the heartache that I did. Who watched her parents grieve openly in the privacy of their own home. She watched her parents put on brave faces when they were with people, as if everything was okay. Basically, she was a gift in my life. Someone who got me. When our families got together, we would go off and play and our parents could have grown-up conversations. What I discovered is that our families connected because the leader of the youth group who was there when Todd died was related to the mom. The mom knew she could step in to support my mom in this tragedy. That is why the little girl I had never met brought me that teddy bear at the funeral. She knew how scary it was to deal with all these heavy emotions. Once again, she was so thoughtful to give me things that I have to this day that meant the world to me during such a dark time.

When I moved into 7th grade, this meant I was finally the age when I would have my mom as a teacher. The way my grade school was set up is that it went from kindergarten until 8th grade. We did not have a middle school like most of the public schools. When we reached 7th grade, we would rotate between the 7th and 8th grade teachers for specialized subjects. Our homeroom teacher would teach their specialty along with religion and literature. My mom was not assigned as my homeroom teacher, and it was nice to have her teaching partner instead. Thankfully, my mom was well loved by most students who attended the school, but she was still my mom.

While my mom taught social studies as her specialty, we also had her for sex education for the girls. This was incredibly embarrassing, having my mom be the one to talk about the female body with all the other girls in my class. I could never say it verbally, but this was hard for me. I saw my mom at home and then all day at school. I had no separation from her in discovering who I was without having a watchful eye over me.

At some point during this time, my dad started working at the church as a janitor. My dad was not a big talker. He was the strong, silent type. He was proud to always do any job he had with integrity – both of my parents were hard working people. While he seemed to work more in the afternoon and the evenings, it was challenging to have both of my parents around all the time.

Trinity was expanding the grade school as well as the church. There was now a space between the church and school where they were going to have a small atrium. My parents donated their time along with the landscaping in honor of my brother. A statue was going to be added into this area that was crafted for the church. It was a statue of Jesus being surrounded by little children. It was then called "Children's Garden." The statue would be the focal point with a walkway from one entry point to another door. Several of the congregation members worked at various stadium events in the concession stands to help raise money towards the cost of the statue. My dad used his talents to create the design for the landscape within the garden. The dedication was done around All Saints Day, two years after my brother's death. My dad spent long hours working on laying the brick, adding the retainer walls, and bringing in all the trees and shrubs. My mom and I helped with getting the work done to make it look beautiful.

The newsletter my grandparents saved says this about the dedication of the children's garden:

> *On November 4th at Trinity Lutheran Church Utica, the Children's Garden was dedicated. A statue of Christ and the Children is surrounded by a walk and a garden of shrubs, trees, and other plantings. The Garden was given in memory of Todd Remer by his parents, Rose and Jim Remer, and his sister, Trudi. The garden and walk are the work of the hands of Jim Remer as a living Memorial for Todd. The Stature of Christ and the Children was given by members and friends of Trinity, which included some members of the L.F.A. #57. Todd was a member of L.F.A. #57 as are his parents, sister, grandparents and many other members on the family tree.*

As I entered 8th grade, my mom had been asked to become an 8th grade homeroom teacher. I wondered why it needed to be changing when I was going into 8th grade – it seemed as if they could wait one more year for me to graduate from Trinity. I ended up having her as my homeroom teacher for 8th grade. But, it really didn't matter who I had as a teacher since they were all close friends with my parents. My parents had a card night once a month with both of her teaching partners and their wives. In my younger years, their daughters babysat me and Todd on those card nights. Most of my parents' friends belonged to the church and several were her coworkers.

My mom led the 8th grade students on a class trip to Washington DC every year. When my class went, my dad came along as a chaperone. I got to see the Vietnam Memorial with my dad. He fought in that war but never spoke about his time over there to me. Watching my dad go up to that wall made me see him in a different light. He was quiet and sorrowful as he approached the wall. My mom was his rock, his support at this moment. This was opposite of what I was used to seeing at home. Yes, both of my parents loved and supported each other, but in this instance, it was like I was able to see those early days of their romantic relationship. This was a somber moment. However, I am so glad that I was able to witness this moment with them.

While on the DC trip, my mom always planned fun activities for us to do. One of the evenings there was a dance. I know that my mom loved being able to have both my dad and I there for her favorite thing she did with her students. My mom also loved slow dancing with my dad, and she took the opportunity to dance with him here. These were the sweet moments to me, witnessing the great love that my parents had for one another.

It was DC tradition to get everyone in the class to stand on the steps in front of the Capitol for a class picture. This photo was my mom's treasure and she would post it in her classroom so you could see the students throughout the years. One of the favorite parts of this photo is that she and the other 8th grade teacher were always at the top on both the left and right side of the picture. The camera was a slow-moving landscape shot, so after the photographer captured them on the left side, my mom and the other 8th grade teacher would duck out of sight and run to the other end to be captured a second time. With technology today, I know this is not that impressive, but back in the '80s and '90s this was a big thing. The year I went, my mom stood by my dad on one side and the 8th grade teacher stood by his wife on the other side.

During one of the Christmas celebrations with my dad's extended family in downtown Detroit, a photographer was taking photographs of all the individual families. When it was our turn – my dad, my mom and me – the photographer said, "What a beautiful family of three." He had no idea what we had been through and how harsh that was to hear. Upon hearing this, my dad broke down, crying uncontrollably. The reference to the three of us being a happy little family was too much for him to handle. The rest of the family did what they could to help my dad out, but he was embarrassed that he had broken down in front of his family.

6

Once I graduated from Trinity Lutheran School, I went to Lutheran High North for high school. I thought that I would be able to have freedom as I would no longer be around both of my parents all day long. However, I had forgotten that the Lutheran community is a close-knit group. My mom had various connections from when she went to Concordia college, which specializes in Lutheran teachers and pastors. She had built relationships when Todd had been at Lutheran High North for a year. My first week, I walked by one of my mom's friends, the wife of my mom's 7th grade teaching partner. How did I forget that one of my mom's closest friends was a teacher at the high school? While I was no longer a teacher's kid, this did not mean that I was not being watched. I get that I am probably being incredibly dramatic, but to me it felt like I was always under a watchful eye. If not my mom, my mom's friends were always making sure that I was behaving.

After my freshman year, there was a large national youth gathering in New Orleans for all the youth in the Lutheran Missouri Synod. These events happened every three years and you needed to be in high school to attend. Most of my friends from the church youth group were going, and I wanted to go too. However, this was really confronting for my mother. Not only was I the same age that Todd was when he went on the trip, but also it was the same week he went. It was too much for her to deal with emotionally, so I would not be able to go.

My mom and dad had always let me go to church functions, so it felt unfair that because of timing, I would not be going. I was angry, but what was I going to do? This was what my parents had decided. I was angry, but I had also been taught that as a good Christian daughter, you need to honor thy mother and father. I understood as best as I could, but this seemed to be such bullshit to me. Once again, their grief won out. Once again, I was suffering because of Todd's accident. This just continued to perpetuate my belief that I was in Todd's shadow and always would be. While my parents were doing their best, it did feel that they forgot that I was still alive. It was suffocating to live in that shadow.

As a consolation prize, my mom decided that we would do other adventures. We did the first trip as a family: my mom, dad and I went to visit my dad's sister, Carol, in New York City. During the day, we went to various sights all over the city. My aunt was used to the walking pace of NYC, but my parents and I were not. We tried as best as we could to keep up with her, but my aunt was so fast, weaving in and out of people. The following day, my mom came up with the idea of tying a balloon to her so that we could still see her as she speed-walked. We went to see Cats on Broadway and sat in the front row. I was a little creeped out when one of the actors came up to me and pretended to purr and rub their head on my shoulder. I loved the experience of seeing a live production, but the play itself, not so much. Overall, it was a fun family trip where we witnessed my aunt in her element. I would always see her during the holidays at my grandparent's house, but it was nice to see her as the strong independent woman she is.

On the second trip, just my mom and I visited one of her college roommates in California. We took a day trip to Yosemite National Park, which was stunning. This was my first opportunity to see a national park. I had been jealous of my brother since he had gone with his best friend's family to see several national parks the summer before he died. In retrospect, I am happy he had that experience, but now I was able to see a glimpse of some of the beauty around the states.

The third trip I ended up going on that summer was to Toronto. It was a true girls' trip, with my mom, other women friends of my mom, and my friend Rosey. Rosey and I had been through grade school together, but since we never seemed to have the same homeroom teacher, we didn't become close until we entered high school. We both were highly active with the church youth group, so this is where we started spending a lot of time together. We traveled to Toronto, went shopping, and went to a theater production of *Joseph and the Amazing Technicolor Dreamcoat*. My mom became obsessed with this play when Donny Osmond started to perform in the cast. Not only had she loved the play, but she was obsessed with Donny Osmond.

After all that, about three weeks before the national youth conference, my mom asked me if I wanted to go. I immediately said yes. However, I was slightly hesitant to say so, since I knew how much she didn't want me to go. She told me that she and my dad had reconsidered it, and if I wanted to, I could. This made me so happy since I really wanted to attend with my friends and go to New

Orleans. We traveled by bus from Michigan down to Louisiana. It was a long ride, but we set up various euchre tournaments. Overall, it was an incredible conference. On the way back on the bus, everyone sang "Happy Birthday" to me, as it was my 15th birthday. I am sure that my parents were nervous, but it felt like a relief to make it past my 15th birthday.

At the beginning of my sophomore year, my parents pulled me into the kitchen to tell me something. As my dad was standing there, he broke down and started crying. It was rare to see my father cry, but when he did, I always knew that it was serious. He told me he received the news that he had malignant cancer. He'd found a lump under his right arm which he had checked out. They also found another lump on his neck. The plan was that he was going to have surgery to remove the tumors and then start chemotherapy to eradicate the cancerous cells in his body. I did my best not to show it, but I was terrified of what this meant. God had already taken my brother; we could not lose my dad too. There in the kitchen, we all cried as a family.

My dad's surgery was successful. The next step was to start chemotherapy. He would stay in the hospital for a few days each time he had a treatment. For some reason, my parents did not make me go see him on his first several trips. When I went to see him in the hospital for the first time, it ended up being the worst time for me to go. I entered the room as my dad had run to the bathroom to vomit. He did not make it to the bathroom before he ended up throwing up all over the floor. I had never seen my dad appear so weak. He was always a strong, sturdy man, and seeing him this way was devastating. While it was hard for me to witness him this way, I know that he was embarrassed. I never went back to see him while he was getting chemo. My only trip to see him in the hospital had been the worst reaction to the chemo.

After his chemo treatments, he would sleep a lot on the couch downstairs in the basement. There were a couple times that seeing him reminded me of seeing Todd lying in that casket. I would sit and stare at him while he was lying there so I could see if he was breathing. If it became too intense for me, thinking he was not breathing, I would touch him to make sure that he was still alive. There was always such a relief that rushed over me when I would realize that he was only resting.

After going through six months of chemotherapy, he was tested to see if he had any cancer still in his body. The doctors were happy to report he was in remission. While this was fabulous news, we were told that it was the first step in watching his cell counts. Once he passed all the necessary markers, they declared that he was in full remission. His body was cancer-free. My parents and I all rejoiced that this period was over! I was happy to have two healthy parents.

The year I started Lutheran High North, they added a girls' soccer team to their sports program. I was so excited to get to try out to play for the team. This was a great opportunity to meet more of the girls in my school. I had been playing soccer for years recreationally, so I was overjoyed to get the opportunity to play during high school. My dad would come after work to the home games – he was so passionate about sports that he would scream to cheer me along. It was a little bit embarrassing, but I was really touched that he came out to support me.

After I had gotten my driver's license, there was a little bit more freedom in my world. I was able to go places without needing to be driven around by my parents or one of my friends' parents. It was around this time that my mom's eyesight was starting to go, but this was not something she acknowledged to me. She had me start driving us to places more. I had thought this was because she wanted me to practice. Eventually, when I expressed how upset I was that she never came to any of my soccer games, it came out that she was unable to see well. She told me it was already dangerous that she was driving to work with blurry vision, but she justified that she could drive to work since she was not taking any main roads and it was only a mile away from the house.

She went to see an eye doctor to see what was wrong. Eventually, she had surgery in one of her eyes for cataracts. Once her eye was healed, the other eye needed to have surgery on it too. This was part of the process of getting her to look at her health. She was a diabetic but had not done anything in years to regulate it. When I was born, she was diagnosed as having gestational diabetes. After I was born, my mom had made a conscious decision that she was not going to do anything to manage her diabetes. She knew at some point she would pay the consequences but decided it was not a concern for her at that time. About 15 years later, her decision was catching up with her.

My parents had taken a trip to Cancun, Mexico. While they were on the trip, they had taken a boat tour where my mom had hung her feet over the boat, resulting in the balls of her feet getting sunburned. The sunburn was so bad that the padding blistered, which meant she couldn't walk until it healed. When they got home, she had to get medical attention for her feet. The doctor told her she needed to start taking insulin since her blood sugar was off the charts. Finally, she started to manage her diabetes and her health, as she was now unable to continue ignoring it.

7

I was so excited to go to college because it meant that I would finally have a new sense of freedom. This was by far a new step in going beyond what Todd had. He started at Lutheran High North, so he was still present there, but going off to college really was a new chapter that I was navigating. I only applied to one college and was accepted: Central Michigan University (CMU). My cousin Brian had recently graduated from there and his sister Jenni was going to be a sophomore. CMU was about two hours from home, so this seemed like the perfect distance to have my own space to figure out who I was. The other part that excited me was that it was going to be my first time going to a public school. I didn't know what that meant, but I was excited for the new experience.

When we arrived on campus, my parents and I headed in through the front door of the dormitory to locate my room. After we passed the front desk, a girl followed us all the way to my new room. Turns out it was one of my roommates, Renee. I was the last one of the four of us to arrive. One of the girls started asking me if it was okay if she and Renee had the bigger room, since they were the sophomores. I was confused as to why I was being asked this when my cousin Jenni ran into the room screaming. Quickly we all learned that Jenni had put a piece of paper on a bed in the larger room to claim it for me. It was thoughtful, but I had already planned on sharing the smaller room with my other freshman roommate. Jenni was disappointed her genius plan had not worked but greeted me and my parents with a huge hug.

The two of us freshman had decided prior to arriving that we would each have high lofts so we could use the space underneath for our desks. Since my dad was a skilled craftsman, he made my bed by hand rather than buying a kit. As we were trying to put it together, my parents and I continued to bicker the way we always did, only now it was strange as other people were observing us. After I settled into my room, my parents left. It was the newfound freedom I had been looking for.

Jenni was our next-door neighbor. She introduced us to her roommates and several of her friends. Since I had always been close to her, I was excited that we were now adults going to college together. I always looked up to Jenni. She was smart and athletic. I loved having her as my family. In a way, I considered her to be a sister to me. It was going to be great having her around.

Renee and I realized early on that we were both raised in the Lutheran faith. The synods were different, but overall, the beliefs were remarkably similar. She had gone to a private school like I had. However, she had lived an hour away from her parent's house on a campus. It was the next level of a private school, but I appreciated that she had a similar background as me. I started to realize we had a lot in common.

The summer before I left for college, I'd gotten into my first serious relationship. This was with a boy from the public school that my friend Robin from my high school job went to. We tried to see if we could maintain our relationship while going to separate colleges but learned why most long-distance relationships end within a couple months. We connected over Christmas break where I ended up losing my virginity to him. I was happy that he was my first sexual experience even if we were never getting back together.

Growing up in a Christian home, you are told you need to save yourself for marriage. With my newfound freedom, I knew that I could do what I wanted. However, choosing my own path wasn't always easy. I was open to exploring what sex was like, but I had not been prepared for the emotional side to having sex. In a way, I was using sex to find love.

I started smoking cigarettes right before college. A bunch of us, including Robin and her boyfriend Blake, spent the summer partying together before we all went our separate ways to college. The day I tried a cigarette, I was hooked. After the boyfriend and I had broken up, Robin, Blake, and two of Blake's friends came up to visit me at college. Blake's friend brought marijuana with him. I'd tried a couple times in high school but had never gotten high. That evening was a different story as I was incredibly stoned for my very first time.

At college, there was a new sense of freedom to learn who I was without my parents watching every single movement I made. I was experimenting with alcohol and taking it way too far. I would drink to the point where I was blackout drunk. I was fortunate to be surrounded by people who were able to make sure I was safe. It was alarming, though, how often I would drink to the point of not remembering. Students were able to see a campus counselor. I did go to a few sessions to acknowledge what I was going through. I didn't go for a long period of time, but it was nice to be able to talk to someone not connected to my family.

When I started attending CMU, my plan was to get an accounting degree. However, after my first accounting class, I decided it wasn't for me. It was incredibly boring. The professor was also very bland. I had always known that I wanted to do something in business. I ended up following in Renee's footsteps by getting a hospitality degree. Having it as a specialty meant I would still be getting the business degree. As a bonus, it sounded fun to be in the travel and food industry.

During my sophomore year of college, my dad started college too. So not only was my mom an empty nester, but she also lived solo for a couple years while my dad was getting his golf management degree. He had various jobs while I grew up, but my mom really encouraged him to go to school. My dad had been a landscaper, so it made sense for him to blend his love of greenery and golf. He had taken our camper and made it into his own little home while he was attending Michigan State University. Since the winter can get incredibly cold, he put up paneling to help keep the floors warmer by not allowing the wind to blow beneath the camper. My mom and I were so proud of my dad for graduating from college. The best part was he was now getting the opportunity to do what he loved for work.

Most students live on campus for two years, but I put in a request to live off campus with Jenni, Renee and another girl, Samantha. I loved that Jenni and I were going to be living together. The apartment was furnished and had four bedrooms. Jenni had started to date someone from the volleyball club, so she was not there too often as she was at his place.

One day, I really wanted to smoke weed but was nervous to do it in the house since I did not want Jenni to know. Samantha told me that I could smoke in her room. After I had gotten high and the smell of weed permeated through the apartment, Jenni got home. She busted into Samantha's room and yelled at us. Samantha took the blame, but Jenni yelled at me, too. Jenni had no problem with alcohol, but she had an issue with weed. This is where she and I differed. I had more control over myself when I smoked weed, rather than blacking out when I drank. However, I was terrified she would tell my parents, so I made sure to never smoke in the apartment again.

I decided to get a part-time job as a cashier in a department store. I befriended a couple of my coworkers, who both happened to be gay. This was my first time being friends with someone who was gay. It was not condoned in my religion, but I personally did not care about their sexual orientation. One of them was named Toby.

About five miles away from the college was the Isabella reservation, home to the Saginaw Chippewa Tribe. There was a casino there called the Soaring Eagle Casino, so I went to check out the blackjack tables. I started playing more often than a college student should, and figured the best way to stop going as a patron was to start working there. The job was a full-time position, so I had a forty-hour work week along with classes to attend. Toby, from the part-time job, now worked at the casino, which made this the second place we worked together. Once we reconnected at the casino, we started to hang out a lot more often.

One day when I was working at the casino, Renee showed up. The look on her face told me something was very wrong. This was back before cell phones were a thing, so she came to find me to inform me my mom had been in a bad car accident, and I needed to call my dad immediately. I was on my way to my lunch break when she found me. Her telling me the news didn't sink in, so I thanked her and went on my break. The entire time I sat in the breakroom I was in shock. The last five minutes of the break, I realized that I needed to leave for the day. I called my dad to find out what was going on and he told me Mom had been airlifted to the hospital. I'd never heard my dad sound as scared as he did until this moment. A few days later, I was finally able to talk to my mom on the phone.

My mom had been on her way to see her parents when she had a reaction to having low blood sugar. She went into a fog while she was driving and drove past my grandparents' street. Somehow, she went through their small town. Outside of the city limits where the road was turning into open country roads, she blacked out. This caused the car to head into oncoming traffic where she had a head-on collision with another vehicle. Thankfully, no one was killed in the accident. My mom had to be airlifted to the nearest hospital due to the impact she sustained during the accident. Her body had a long black and blue bruise from where the seat belt had been. There is no doubt in my mind that this prevented her from dying in the accident. It took months for her to heal.

Renee was my best friend during college. Both of us were welcomed into each other's families. I considered her mom and dad as second parents while she did the same thing with mine. Our mothers would send us care packages from which we developed a love of rice pudding.

Jenni ended up moving out of the apartment after a year. Renee, Samantha, and I stayed in the apartment and added another girl to the place. While I missed having Jenni around, it ended up being nice, feeling like I could be myself without having to worry about being on good behavior. I loved Jenni, but it was becoming apparent that we had different interests in life. Her life circled around her boyfriend.

At the casino, I met a man who pursued me. However, he was married. He told me they were separating, but honestly, I am not sure now if his wife ever knew this. Sadly, I craved attention and was easy prey. He and his wife ended up getting divorced. We dated for two years. Not my proudest moment, but karma paid me back with him cheating on me too. A friend of his was there when I confronted him about cheating. His friend became my future husband, since we started dating the following day. My future husband witnessed my fiery passionate side from the get-go.

My relationship with my future husband was drama-free. My ex-boyfriend and I constantly fought so it was refreshing to date someone who was sweet on me. When we started dating, I did not anticipate this relationship lasting past my graduation. However, it was nice to be appreciated for just being myself. Renee never liked the married man. However, when it came to my future husband, she shared with me that it was nice seeing how happy he made me. In the back of my mind, I worried that my relationship with my future husband might be a rebound.

My maternal grandparents decided to throw a party in honor of their 50th wedding anniversary. It was hosted at a hall close to their home. It was an honor to witness their love. When we took pictures of the family, I was upset that my parents would not let my now-ex-boyfriend in the picture since we were not married. In the end, I am glad they made that decision. My parents danced to all the slow songs. Most of the songs were country songs that I had listened to while growing up. To this day, I can see my dad singing to my mom the words to "Forever and Ever, Amen" by Randy Travis. It was a sweet moment to witness the love that my parents had for one another.

We needed to complete an internship to graduate with a hospitality degree. The summer between my junior and senior year of college, I found a company where I would be able to get credit for my internship. Our advisor had recommended that we go outside of Michigan to complete this. Renee was headed to Colorado, and I went to South Carolina. I wanted to be near the ocean. My mom went with me to drive down to Myrtle Beach since she didn't want me diving across the country by myself. The company offered us a place to work and provided us with housing and a small stipend. When my mom and I arrived in Myrtle Beach, there were tons of people on motorcycles who took over the town. As soon as I checked in, they let my mom and I know that there were two weekends a year this happened, but it was not how the town typically was during the summer. I drove my mom to the airport so she could board her flight home.

The internship was a unique experience. There was a large group of us from all over the world. While we each were given different locations to work, they also provided activities for all of us to bond with one another. There was a bar across the street that several of the interns would go to for happy hour and karaoke. I was not a huge karaoke fan, but I went to hang out with everyone. I did not go out as often as most, since I spent a lot of time talking to my boyfriend, who I missed. While I was there, the Detroit Red Wings won their second championship. I watched as Konstantinov was pushed in his wheelchair onto the ice. He had been in a car accident that had ended his career four days after their first championship. It was a huge moment for Detroit fans, but when I looked around, I realized I was alone in my excitement.

Both of my parents made trips down to South Carolina to see me while I was there. My mom came about halfway through the internship. We took a day trip down to Savannah, Georgia. My mom, being a social studies teacher, chose the tour we took, and we went to see Fort Pulaski. We checked out the downtown area of Savannah too, which is rich with history. My dad came down at the end of the summer to help drive me back to Michigan. When we were leaving the town, I started to cry as I was sad to have this chapter end. I noticed he was teary eyed seeing me. It was endearing to have this sweet moment with my dad.

I had the pleasure of getting to see several hockey games with my parents and friends. My dad loved to sit in his recliner chair to watch the Detroit Red Wings. Even though he was sitting in the chair, he was moving constantly as he watched them play. He would yell their first names and do his best to coach them through the television. I found it adorable to see him enjoy himself. My mom's best friend Donna had a hookup where we were able to get seats on the ice. Several people went with me on various trips to Joe Louis arena. Renee loved watching my dad enjoy the game too. She almost found him more entertaining than the game as he was telling the guys where they needed to be on the ice.

Renee took a job with Hyatt Hotels in Chicago. I was sad to see her move that far away, but I knew that being in the hospitality industry meant we needed to move out of state. I had traveled to Chicago to visit her on spring break.

We were all growing up and moving on.

8

My mentor from the hospitality program always encouraged us to move away from home upon graduation. Initially when I heard this, I thought she was crazy. However, as I continued to open my mind to new possibilities, I understood what she was saying. Where I grew up in Michigan is not a typical area that you'd considered as a travel destination. With Renee in Chicago, I started to look at moving there. Knowing it was a little over five hours to drive from Detroit to Chicago made this a perfect option for me. I ended up being offered a position as a management trainee at Hyatt Hotels. I was thrilled to get a job offer in the industry I'd gotten my degree in. This also elated my mom and she bragged to everyone about me having a position in my field. Another reason Chicago was a good option was that Hyatt's headquarters were located there. This meant I could grow within the company without having to physically move.

Before I made the move to Chicago, there was about a month

after graduation until I started the job. Living again with my parents was incredibly challenging. I needed to tell them everywhere I was going and what time I would be home. While I understood that they worried about me, it was hard to live in these conditions again. I had enjoyed being able to do whatever I wanted. My mom and I started to butt heads again living under her roof. We had a moment where my mom politely told me that while she loved me dearly and I was always welcomed home that I would not be able to live with them for an extended period. I completely agreed with this, and I appreciated that we both enjoyed having separate lives.

One of the perks with my new job is I was able to move into the hotel while I searched for an apartment. It was not an open-ended offer, but it gave me a bit of time to find a place to live. My mom came out with me to help me move and stayed with me in the hotel as I started my job. She enjoyed getting to see my new surroundings. It was wonderful to have her with me as I started this scary new adventure. Now I was finally on my own.

I found a place that was decent, but the rent was a lot more than I expected it to be. The suburbs of Chicago had a higher cost of living than the college town I lived in. This made sense, but it was a moment of sticker shock at first. I had not realized what the true cost would be.

My future husband and I decided that we would continue to date as we were in love and did not want to end it. This was a little tricky as I was moving to Chicago. The tentative plan was that once I moved, he would follow me and live with me. This was an internal conflict for me, growing up Christian. It was frowned upon to live with someone before you were married. I knew that my parents would be angry, so I decided to keep it secret from them. This was hard for me because it went against how I was raised. I knew their stance would be that I was living in sin, but it was not realistic for me and my future husband to have our own places. Since we were committed to seeing where our relationship was headed, I chose him over the wrath I knew I would get once my parents found out.

About a month after living in the Chicago 'burbs, my future husband and his cat, Circe, moved in with me. I loved having him with me. Even though I knew at some point that I would have to have an uncomfortable conversation with my parents, I was happy that we were together again.

Being in the manager in trainee (MIT) program, I was able to spend at least a week in every department in both the food and beverage division along with the rooms division. It was designed so that you could figure out where in the hotel you were interested in working. I thoroughly enjoyed working in all the food and beverage departments over the room departments.

I chose to go in the route of the food and beverage department. There was an assistant manager position in the In-Room Dining department that I interviewed for and got. After six months, I transferred to the restaurants department.

Shortly after moving there, my parents came out to visit me. At this point my future husband was living with me. I decided to lie by saying that he was in town to visit me. We made sure that all things of his were hidden so they would not know. However, my parents knew I was lying to them. While they were there, they would not have the uncomfortable conversation in his presence. They asked later if I was lying to them. They were disappointed in me that not only did my future husband live with me, but now I was lying to them. They questioned if I had learned anything in my childhood. At some point, we got past this hurdle as we both wanted to maintain our relationship, but I always knew that they did not approve of me living in sin.

We decided that we wanted to get a playmate for Circe, so we went downtown to a shelter to adopt another cat. The moment I held Abby I knew that she was destined to be my girl. She instantly cuddled with me and started rubbing her whiskers on me. We adopted her that day. We took her home to meet Circe and it took a little while for them to warm up to one another. Circe gravitated towards my future husband and Abby gravitated towards me.

As a way of connecting with one another, we started to smoke weed on a regular basis. I'd always preferred smoking weed to alcohol as it was something that I felt I could control myself. The worst thing that happened for me by smoking was that I would eat too many snacks or sweets.

After a year of living in the apartment, we moved to a nicer place – we even had a washer and dryer in the unit. It cost a little bit more than the last apartment, but it had more amenities and space. It was close to work and was even off the same road, but 20 minutes south of where we had been.

Life was looking pretty good!!

9

My future husband's proposal was lackluster. I had given him a deadline of when I wanted us to get engaged, and I am sure that he felt the pressure of my demands. He put my engagement ring in the middle of a pizza. On the box cover he wrote, "Will you marry me?" The moment fell flat. We were engaged, though, and I couldn't wait to share the news with my parents. Even though they congratulated me, I could tell that they were not as happy as I wanted them to be. I found out later that he never asked my parents for my hand in marriage. This was something I had wanted him to do to show respect to my parents. It made sense that they were less than thrilled with him.

With the internal dilemma of living with my future husband, I knew that the way to set things right was for us to get married. This would justify my living in sin. No one told me that this was what needed to happen but my own guilt. I wish I hadn't believed this. It set me on a path that may not have been for my highest good. It never allowed me to think that this relationship could end.

While I thought I loved him, I'm not sure that I ever knew what love was. We had similar interests, but we did not have a lot of the same values. Being only 23 years old, I was not in touch with myself enough to realize I was making a poor decision. I am certain that being high all the time didn't help me think things through. My determination to make living in sin right only had me focused on getting married. The part of being married "until death do us part" did not factor into my mind. The impact of Todd's death unconsciously taught me that people do not stay.

We would be getting married in my home church back in Michigan. My future husband went along with this even though, as a proud atheist, he was incredibly uncomfortable being in a church. How I didn't see this as a red flag is beyond me. It was the first time in my life where I was around someone who did not suffocate me with beliefs. I never challenged him in being an atheist since I didn't want to hear how we wouldn't be compatible for the long term.

I found my wedding dress rather quickly. Renee was with me when I found it, and my mom came out to see what I had chosen. Since I lived in Chicago, my mom went to see different venues in Michigan where I could have my reception. She chose the reception hall where her and my dad had their reception.

My mom and I were on the phone one day as we were getting closer to the wedding, and she asked me if I was sure I wanted to go through with it. I was stunned that she had asked me, and I reacted by saying yes immediately. Final payments were due for the various vendors. She finished it off by saying there was no turning back after that moment. I have thought of this moment often. It always bothered me that she said this. I know she said this because this was her thought process. However, it really made me feel as if I was now stuck with no way out. This played on the energy I had grown up in. What if I had wanted to change my mind? My mom's question and statement meant that if I did want something else, money would be lost. It made it feel as if money was more important than my own happiness.

Renee was my maid of honor. She planned my bachelorette party, which was held at a spa. We had champagne, cheesecake, and massages. It was perfect. I was never the one to want to get dressed up to go clubbing with plastic penises. My other bridesmaids along with a couple friends attended. I asked Jenni and two of my former roommates from my senior year in college to be in my wedding.

The wedding day wasn't what I pictured it would be – not that I had a specific picture in mind. However, I did think that it would be a special day for my mom and I, going through all the preparations together. However, my mom was running around all morning, so we really didn't see each other. All my bridesmaids were invited to my parent's house to have their hair done. Right before the ceremony, my mom came down briefly to see me, and I realized that I'd barely seen her all day. I was sad that as close as we were, we did not have a moment where she bestowed her wisdom on me. She headed to the church to be seated as the ceremony was about to start.

In anticipation of the wedding, I kept saying, "Today is the day I get married." It was never about getting married to my future husband, but rather all about me. It was as if all was right in the world, having the social status of being married. I was a little nervous about the ceremony since he had been uneasy with a church wedding.

As we lined up in the narthex (antechamber) of the church, my dad and I had a moment where we both made the other cry. When my dad looked at me, he got choked up. I then started to cry and turned from him as I did not want to break down. My dad was not one to say much, but his facial expressions gave him away. We then stood there not looking at one another as neither one of us wanted to start bawling. I was always his little girl. He had always been so proud of me, and I loved having his unconditional love.

My future husband didn't invite many people to the wedding – only his mom and stepdad. His best man had a family emergency that came up right before the wedding. My cousin Brian, who was only going to be an usher, ended up stepping in as a groomsman. Despite this, there were about 300 people in attendance. It ended up being more of a party for my parents than a wedding for us, but I was happy to have my family there to celebrate.

For our honeymoon, we wanted to go to a warm location where we could stay at a Hyatt hotel. We decided on Scottsdale, Arizona, as it would be a perfect temperature to lay by the pool. When we arrived, we got several drinks at the bar for the first night. The next morning, we ordered room service. It was shortly after we ate that my future husband got sick. He ended up being so sick that for the remainder of the honeymoon we stayed in our hotel room so he could be close to a bathroom. We believed that he got food poisoning from the breakfast.

He told me to go to the pool without him, but I didn't since it was our honeymoon. It didn't feel right to leave him. Instead, I stayed in the room and pouted that this was the worst vacation ever. We were married for less than a week when I questioned if I'd just made a major mistake. We had never traveled together other than to visit family or friends, and I was shocked to discover on our very first trip that he was not a good traveler. I was ready to head home since our honeymoon was a boring disaster.

10

When I got back to work after the wedding, all my co-workers asked me how the wedding and the honeymoon were. I was so embarrassed, feeling the honeymoon was a waste, that I just answered with a quick, "It was good." I was starting to understand that I made a mistake but had no idea how to get out of it. The best choice for me was to dive into my career.

Renee had moved to a Hyatt hotel that was a little bit more private than any of the other Hyatt's. It was a hotel that was associated with the McDonald's headquarters. The hotel supported many people who came in for different classes at Hamburger University (yes, that really is the name of McDonald's training facility). She shared there was an Assistant Manager position in the Banquet department. While this would be another lateral move, it would be awesome to check out the opportunity to learn another area within the food and beverage department. I would be able to see Renee on a more regular basis. I had not taken the time to develop any other friendships since I focused on my career and my husband.

I was offered the role at The Lodge shortly after the wedding. It was a slower pace than the previous hotel I worked at. Since it was a smaller hotel, there were fewer guests. It was a private location, not well known to the public. There were two large banquet rooms on the premises that were booked for various events.

As I was driving into work on a Tuesday morning, I was mesmerized by how stunning the sky looked that day. It was crystal clear blue with white, fluffy clouds. I was happily walking through the building saying my good morning greetings to my coworkers. As I made my way through a lower hallway, I walked past the stewarding office. The manager came out frantically saying he had just heard Howard Stern say one of the towers of the World Trade Center had been struck by an airplane. Shocked at what he said, I was unable to comprehend how a plane could have hit a tower. Immediately, I knew that this could not be an accident, but I also could not understand how this was possible. I needed to find a television to see this for myself.

When I located a television, there were other guests surrounding it as we all watched in horror. There had been few camera shots of the north tower being hit, but there were several replays of the south tower being hit. We all stood there in horror watching and rewatching the towers being crashed into. I stood there helpless, watching the towers burning. How were the people in the building going to get out? As I was wondering this, the south tower collapsed before our eyes. It seemed as if this was a nightmare, but it was devastatingly real. As the second tower crashed to the ground, I wanted to cry for all these innocent lives who were lost that day.

This certainly brought up similar emotions to what I experienced upon learning of Todd's death. It was completely different, but that feeling of shock and disbelief was one I could never forget. I thought of my aunt in New York and prayed for her safety. This was horrific for our nation. I could not believe that in my lifetime I witnessed something so horrifying.

Shortly after the towers collapsed, I called my husband. I woke him up to share the devastating news. The nation was grieving all who perished that day. My heart ached for the families' of those lost.

Several of the hotel guests had flown to Chicago. They were trying to find out how they would be able to travel home. I am sure that they realized that planes had been grounded and they would need to find another way to get home. It was a challenging day since not only did we want to help our guests, but we too were impacted by what we had just witnessed.

On the drive home, the skies were eerily quiet. Since I lived by O'Hare, I had tuned out the sound of the air traffic. However, that day it was so strange to notice how quiet the surroundings were. The day that started out with white, fluffy clouds now was a moment of a heavy, dark cloud over the nation. The days following September 11th were filled with such grief. It was the first time I remember the news being on all the time. It was a dark time rewatching the tragic attacks. They were showing how people were jumping out of the buildings before they collapsed. This was hard for me to stomach since Todd falling was always something that had haunted me.

A month after the 9/11 attacks, I was escorted down to the Human Resources office. Renee would not make eye contact with me as I passed her desk. The Director informed me I was being let go. I was being given a severance package along with being paid out any vacation I had accrued. I was shocked and devastated, and the tears started to flow. After I gathered my things from my office, I walked out of the building. Renee followed me out the door and to my car. I really did not want to talk to her since I was so embarrassed that I had been fired. Even though it had nothing to do with me, I was experiencing a lot of shame about having to tell my husband and parents that I was now unemployed. She asked if she could sit in the car with me for a moment to talk to me. I couldn't say no to Renee since she had been with me through a lot.

Renee tried to comfort me with her words of wisdom. However, I was unable to take any of it in since I was embarrassed. I was not ready to discuss it since I was stressed with needing the income to survive. Even though my husband had a job, I was the one who we relied on for a steady income. I had no idea how we were going to make ends meet. I was overwhelmed and could not listen.

One thing I heard was she told me that I had my husband at home to support me. Hearing this made me freak out internally even more. All those doubts I was feeling were now at the surface, questioning how he could support me. Years later, we talked about this moment, and I shared with Renee how I got stressed out when she told me that I had my husband. Renee told me I started crying harder when she said it. It was funny years later, but at the time it was not funny at all. I knew in my mind I thought, "Fuck."

My world was starting to crumble. Or so I thought. What was I going to do with a hospitality career when the world was uneasy about traveling? There was so much uncertainty going on. It would not be easy to find a job when most companies were laying off rather than hiring people. It was a scary time for me.

I knew I needed to start collecting unemployment. Initially, I felt guilty about it, but my mom told me that this was the reason why unemployment existed. It was to help cover bills while one looks for a job. My dad had also been let go from his job. Not only did my dad and I get the emotions the other was feeling, but we were able to support each other during this time. To bring a sense of lightness to our conversations, we would talk about the Detroit Red Wings. They had an amazing season that year in which they ended up winning the Stanley Cup.

My mom did her best to be supportive to me and my dad. However, she had a hard time relating to us. She had the same job for over 25 years. We never openly discussed it in front of her, but it was challenging talking to her since she did not understand what it was like to be let go from a job. She lived in her little Lutheran bubble. It was one of those secretive bonds that we had together. He could tell me something about work and I got it. During this time, my dad and I would bond over the Red Wings games to help take our mind off how bad we were both feeling being out of work.

My usage of marijuana was now a daily habit. I was waking and baking during this time. I knew that I had nowhere to be, so I was using it to cope with my depression over not having a job. The only thing I needed to do was apply for a certain number of jobs needed to collect my unemployment. There were very few places that were hiring so I did not get my hopes up.

I reached out to my former advisor to get her thoughts on what would benefit me most in my career. I contemplated going back to school to get a secondary degree. It made me realize that accounting would be a better career move as it would not be as volatile an industry. She encouraged me to get my MBA. I'd never considered getting my master's, but this made sense. I researched local universities who had a good business program. After touring a couple campuses, I chose a Catholic university.

I started at the beginning of the year, which helped me from going into a depression. All the classes were at night since most of the students were working during the day. This worked for me as I have always thrived best at night. Since I wanted to excel in my studies, going back to school helped me slow down my marijuana intake.

It was time to start a new chapter in my life.

11

My unemployment was about to be exhausted. Right as I was about to lose benefits, I interviewed with a company that ended up hiring me. The company was a startup who specialized in private aviation catering, looking to expand into the Chicago market.

It was a step down for my career, but the income was much needed. The major benefit to the position was the ten-minute commute to work. I would be delivering the catered food to various airports. It ended up being a great position since it was mindless and gave me the opportunity to learn the Chicagoland area. I enjoyed not having to manage anyone but myself. It was a great balance to have this job alongside studying for my classes.

A week after I started, we were sent to have our drug tests done. I had been anxious about this, as I knew that I would not pass it. I researched a way to find out how I could pass the test. I drank one of the detox drinks that would have your pee test clear. However, one guy that I worked with kept stalling when he wanted to go. It meant that I had gone to the bathroom a couple times too many. A couple days later when I was home from work, my company phone chirped. We had been given walkie styled phones so that we did not need to call one another. Unfortunately, I had thought I had passed the test and had gotten high. When I heard from my manager, I knew this was not good. He told me that I needed to come by the main office the next day. My stomach dropped since I knew that I more than likely failed the drug test.

The following day, my prediction had been confirmed. I had

failed the drug test. Then what he said next surprised me. He informed me that he was going to give me thirty days to have my system cleaned out and I would be retested. I couldn't believe that I was allowed another opportunity to take the test. He made sure I knew I'd better not fail the drug test again. I was incredibly relieved because I would have been mortified to have been fired for weed. He had said that he was personally vouching for me since I was a good worker and did not want to let me go. I was grateful that he saw what I had to offer to the team. It also gave me an insight that he was a partier back in the day. I stopped smoking and upped my water intake to ensure that any traces would be gone by the time I retested. There were no doubts, and I knew that I had passed the second time.

The president of the company came into town to see how our operations were running. While on this visit, he asked me to have a conversation with him in his office. He did not sugar coat that he was completely against the manager's decision to allow me to test again. He clearly told me that he was going to be keeping an eye on my performance as there would not be a second chance anywhere. I understood the anger he expressed but knew I would not give him a chance to have me fired. Knowing that he would not be in Chicago often, I let him have his peace with the threat. He never came back to our office since he moved his family down to Florida.

I was grateful to have this lucky escape.

12

When I would call my parents to catch up with them, they would let me know what was going on with the family. My grandma had been tired more than usual and they were concerned about her health. After months of getting tested to see what was going on with my grandma, they realized that she had mesothelioma which is a cancer caused by asbestos. I called my grandmother to see how she was doing and feeling. On our call, she was in high spirits and told me that she was going to beat this. She was going to start chemotherapy treatment to give her longevity for the remainder of her life. There wasn't a cure for mesothelioma, but she managed to prolong her life by getting treatment. Beyond chemotherapy, she had been taking shots to manage her red blood cell count. The fluid in her lungs was the deadly part of this disease. She eventually passed away. I never had the opportunity to get back home to Michigan to see her before she died.

My husband and I headed back to Michigan for the funeral. My grandpa was incredibly distraught. They'd been married for over 60 years. All my dad's siblings were able to make it to the funeral. This was the first funeral since Todd's death. The wake ended up being in the same room where Todd's had been. Since my grandpa wanted to allow for people to stop by to pay their respects, the wake was two days long. This ended up not being necessary since there wasn't nearly the same amount of traffic to give their condolences. Since Todd was young and it had been unexpected, more people had come to support my parents. Unfortunately for my grandpa, there were not as many people besides the family who came to give their love.

My husband spent most of his time in the backroom where he could smoke. When my grandpa was overwhelmed or needed to step away for a moment, he had a cigarette with my husband. During these conversations, my husband and my grandpa bonded with each other. This warmed my heart since I had witnessed my grandparents' dislike of some of the in-laws, so I was happy that my husband was well-received by my grandpa.

While we were at the funeral home, I started to notice how strange the conversations people had with one another. Some people whispered, some talked a little too loud, people shared weird personal details. It was all strange. It made me realize that this must have happened for Todd's funeral, but I had never realized since I was too young. Being back in the same room fourteen years later stirred up a lot of emotions I thought were no longer present. This was the dreaded space where I saw my first dead body, my brother. Having walked back into this room meant seeing another family member's corpse. I had to face my trauma which I had not yet healed, nor even knew I needed to heal.

13

Shortly after my grandmother's funeral, I decided that I no longer wanted to smoke weed. Nothing had happened other than I had grown tired of constantly smoking. I was tired of feeling foggy and airy all the time. I stopped cold turkey. Almost four years of smoking daily and I was just done. As the days passed by, I started to realize I was able to think clearly.

A week later, I arrived home after my Thursday night class. My husband asked me to sit down since he needed to share something with me. Immediately I was on edge. I sensed I would not like whatever it was that he had to say. Slowly he began to share with me that he had been served papers requiring him to take a DNA test. A girl he had a one-night stand with years ago was claiming he was the father of an eight-year-old boy. To say I was stunned is an understatement. I asked him if he ever had any suspicion if he was a dad. This is when he told me that she had accused him when she was pregnant. He never believed that he was the father, so he did nothing about the accusation.

This really got under my skin. The fact that he had known this child was possibly his, yet he did nothing to find out terribly disappointed me. It was a huge character flaw, showing total lack of responsibility. I could not wrap my head around how he wouldn't want to know. What was he avoiding by denying the child and himself the opportunity to know each other?

When he shared this news with me, he said that he would be leaving me. That if he were the father, he knew he would owe back child support and did not want to place that burden on me. Once again, the way he was processing this was completely different from how I would have handled it. I'd always known we had vastly different values, but this was really showing the gap in how we handled conflict. I wasn't okay with leaving. I believed in working things out.

I called my parents to share what had transpired. I was terrified to tell my parents that we were thinking of separating. However, on that phone call my mom and dad shared this was not something you leave a relationship for. My mom told me, "You know there are way worse things that can happen," referring to my brother's death. They asked me if we still loved each other, and I said yes. By the end of the call with my parents I had changed my tune and knew that this was something that we would be able to get past.

However, this was not the case for my husband. He was worried that the test results would show that he was the father and it would change everything. We got the results, and it was confirmed that he was indeed the father. This meant he was now responsible for child support and back child support. In his mind, he'd already decided that he wanted to leave. It was our two-year anniversary and I had begged him to stay in honor of our commitment to one another. After the day of our anniversary passed, he left. He packed minimal items to move to Indiana to be near his mother and his friends. I was heartbroken and sobbed hysterically when he left. He left Circe with me as he did not want to split up the two cats.

Going into work the following day was a challenge, but I knew that I was now the only one responsible for all the bills. This left me with no other choice but to go to work. The distraction was very needed. Fortunately, I did not have to interact with many people throughout the day. It was easy to focus on driving around, delivering the catering orders. When he left, I was lonely since I had not built any friendships to lean on.

He called me while he was living in Indiana to tell me how much he loved me. He expressed sorrow for leaving. For the first several weeks, it gave me comfort as it provided hope that, somehow, we would figure out a way to get back together. However, as time went on, it was becoming clear that he was not taking responsibility anywhere in his life. First with his son. Second with me. Why profess your love and live hours away for no real reason other than not wanting to hurt me? It did not give us the opportunity to work on it together. We were each doing our own thing.

By the end of Memorial Day weekend, I realized I was done. There was no point in continuing a marriage if one party of the union was not there to work together. He never made it a priority to come back to Chicago to work on it with me. He was starting his life over and I told him I wanted a divorce. Thinking I was being bold, I let him know that I wanted him to take responsibility for the first time in his life and file for the divorce for the two of us. He then started the process of filing for the divorce.

Work ended up changing during this time, too. We had been at two commercial kitchens but had dropped down to one. Then the owners signed a deal with a private kitchen next door to our office to start preparing the food for our orders. It made more sense as most of the deliveries were at Midway airport and the new kitchen was closer than where the O'Hare kitchen was. I was grateful for the change as it helped me keep my mind off the mess of my home life. What ended up being a blessing is that the owner of the private kitchen had an assistant, Johana, that was around my age.

Besides just changing over to the private kitchen, the manager of the catering company was going to be moving onto the next market where the company would be expanding. This meant that there was an operations manager position opening up. I expressed interest, since I wanted to get back into a management position. There was an older gentleman that worked with us who also wanted the position. However, I ended up getting it. He was older than me and was less than pleased that I got the position. I understood his anger as best as I could but was overall pleased to be given the opportunity. This meant that my hours were longer.

I decided I wanted to find a church that I could call my home church. With my husband out of the picture, I felt free to find a church community that fit me. After trying out a couple different locations, I found one that felt like a right fit. It also helped that they had a Saturday evening service. This would be perfect for me as I would be able to attend without worrying about having to get up early on Sunday.

As I was doing my best to move forward, I decided to try out speed dating. What I loved about the setup of speed dating is that if you didn't enjoy talking to someone, you could move onto the next person after three minutes. It would either be the quickest three minutes or the longest. At the end of the night, you would report those who you would be interested in connecting with. If it was mutual, you would get their email address to connect on your own.

The end of the year was quickly approaching, and I still hadn't heard anything about the divorce getting finalized. I wanted to make sure that I started 2004 as a single woman. I called my husband to see what the status was, and he stumbled over his words. I put the pressure on to let him know that he needed to make sure that the divorced happened by the end of the year or I was going to have to come down to Indiana to make sure that it happened. If he did not want to see my rage, it would be in his best interest for him to ensure that it got finalized. He promised me that he would find out what he needed to do to make it happen. I thanked him and waited to hear that I was officially a single woman.

14

My parents and I had not seen each other for most of the year. I'd not had the chance to drive back home after my grandmother's funeral. This was the longest time we had gone without seeing each other. Knowing that I was going to have to work on Christmas Day as we were a 24/7 business, I decided I would head home to Michigan the weekend before Christmas. When I got into town, my mom's best friend Donna was throwing her annual Christmas party that my parents would be attending. My mom asked me to meet them at the party. When I got there, she surprised me with front row tickets to see the Detroit Red Wings the following day with my dad. Donna's husband had season tickets so every so often my mom would spoil us with tickets to have quality father daughter time.

After the hockey game, my dad did the sweetest thing ever. Since my dad knew that I was obsessed with Kirk Maltby, he suggested that we go around to a couple of places the players were known to hang out after the game to see if we could happen to meet him. I was so excited that I didn't realize how late it was and that he needed to go to work early the next morning. All that my dad cared about was having this quality time with me. Once I realized he was scheduled to work, I thanked him for being so thoughtful and said we could head home. It was such an endearing moment with my dad, who was always thinking of my wants.

Earlier in the year, my parents and I had planned a time for them to head out to Chicago to visit me. We scheduled it for when the Detroit Red Wings would be in town playing the Chicago Blackhawks. It just so happened that it was the weekend after Christmas. While it had been a long time since I had seen my parents, it was fabulous to get to see them two weekends in a row. My mom decided that instead of attending the game herself, she would forgo her seat so that my dad and I could get better seats. It was a win for all of us. This was the first game my dad watched in Chicago. The Blackhawk fans chanted "Detroit Sucks" the entire game. He was so angry at their poor sportsmanship. I tried to let my dad know that this was normal here.

My parents headed home Monday morning. It had been a wonderful time for the three of us to spend back-to-back weekends together. This was the best time we'd had as a family in many years. I am not sure, but I have a strong suspicion it had a lot to do with them being happy I was no longer with my soon to be ex-husband. When I hugged my father, I noticed he had tears rolling down his cheek. I was touched by witnessing his love for me in a sweet innocent way. I hugged him again tighter and said, "It's okay daddy, I will see you really soon." We all got in our cars and drove to our destinations. I was so grateful that my parents and I had this quality time together. I did not realize then how much I would appreciate these moments for the rest of my life.

Two days later, my phone rang late at night. When I answered, it was my mom. She did not sound like herself. All she could manage to say was, "Dad is with Todd."

Holy shit! How was this even possible? Even through the shock, I understood she meant Dad had died. We did not talk long. She was devastated. I was devastated. I could not believe I needed to head home to bury another family member. Why? Why was this happening to us again?

15

I got off the phone with my mom and sobbed. How was this real? My dad had just been here in Chicago with me and my mom.

How was I losing another family member? I knew I needed to focus on getting a flight into Michigan. My mom said to find the quickest flight home. The cost did not matter; she wanted me home with her immediately.

I found a flight into Detroit the following afternoon, as I knew with it being so late at night there wouldn't be any flights immediately. A friend was able to give me a ride from the airport to the house. When he picked me up, I was silent for the entire ride. I was in disbelief. Most of my friends had not lost a single family member and here I was on my second major loss, at only 26 years old. This seemed completely unfair, having to go through the process of grief again.

When I walked into my parent's house, my mom was on the telephone. My maternal grandparents were sitting at the dining room table with my mom. My grandmother got up to hug me. The look on her face showed the anguish that she was feeling. It felt as if it was directed at both her daughter and me. I knew that she had loved my dad as a son, but it was written all over her face how awful she felt for us to have to go through this. My mom finally got off the phone and came over to hug me. I could feel her despair. I had seen her anguish over Todd, but this was a whole new level of devastation that I was witnessing.

Next, the whirlwind of all the funeral arrangements needed to be organized. This was why it was so important for me to get home right away – my mom wanted my help. We headed over to the funeral home as soon as she got off the phone. My mom had called ahead to let the funeral director know that we would be there shortly after my arrival, and he greeted us when we walked in. We started to work out the details. She wanted the viewing to be two days long because she believed with the extended families along with those from the church and school, it was necessary.

The funeral director led us back to a room I'd never been in before, despite having spent a lot of time in this funeral home as a child. Inside this room, there were so many different caskets to see – it was time to choose the coffin. The prices displayed were a little bit overwhelming. Was I to base the choice of coffin on the price? It was super odd, and I understood why my parents never let me see this room before. When I came across a wooden casket with a cutout of Jesus with his disciples at the Lord's Supper, I knew immediately this would be perfect for my dad. When I looked at the price, it was one of the more reasonable prices I'd seen in the room. I showed my mom and she agreed that it would be perfect. We would need to bring back to the funeral home the clothes that we wanted his body staged in and a picture so that they could make him look like himself. At the end of the meeting, the financial commitment was laid out, including how the payment needed to be received within 30 days. This caught me off guard, but my mom signed the paperwork with no hesitation.

This was the first New Year's Eve I went to bed early. Why would I want to celebrate the new year, when I was starting the year by burying my father? However, I was grateful to be able to spend these couple of days with my mom. She shared with me what had happened to Dad. He had come up from downstairs where he had been playing his computer game to let my mom know that he was ready to go to bed. My mom was in the den when she heard my dad's body hit the ground. He was there one moment and gone the very next moment. She called 911 to see if he could be resuscitated. When she rode in the ambulance with my father, the paramedics were administering CPR, but she knew that he was already gone. She said that they would have broken ribs to get his heart beating if there was a chance that they could revive him. She said he had peed, which let her know he was gone. I had never known that body fluids were released when someone dies, but it made sense. In a way, I found some peace in knowing that he never suffered. It was those of us who remain that do the suffering.

We went to the cemetery to get his burial plot ready for his body. As we went, I realized how much I did not understand what my parents had to do after my brother's death. When land was purchased for my brother, they bought four lots all together for the entire family. Therefore, we only needed to buy a vault for my dad's casket to be placed in. I did not realize there was something besides the land that needed to be purchased. A casket, land, and a vault made me realize that burying a body is incredibly expensive. And this did not include the addition of the headstone.

While we were sitting there, my mom asked me if she should pay for hers now rather than later. I was taken aback by the question and told her that she could do whatever she thought was best. I guess that the rates of the vaults go up in price so she was thinking she would split it out over the years. The cemetery attendant met us at where the plots were so we could verify the placement of my dad.

We headed over to the church to meet with the head pastor. Here, my mom wanted to share stories of my dad that could be used for the sermon. She wanted to also prepare the service for him with different scriptures and songs. A guy I met at the speed dating event gave me the suggestion of a song that I had not heard before. It was called "I Can Only Imagine," by MercyMe. I asked for it to be played for his service. The pastor let my mom know that the school would be closed on Monday for the funeral. They knew that several of her colleagues would want to attend to support her. This really meant a lot to my mom that they would be canceling school in honor of my dad and showing their support for her. She had given so much of herself to the church and the school and this was appreciated deeply.

When we headed over to the funeral home for the start of the wake, we had a private moment with my mom, my dad's dad, my maternal grandparents, and all my dad's siblings who had arrived in town. The first hour was to give us a moment to see the body before others came to pay their respects. When I walked up to see my dad's body, there was something that did not look right. I was uncomfortable seeing dead bodies, but I had a feeling it was more than that. Later, I found out that my mom had given the funeral home a picture of him from over twenty years prior. He was made to look like he had in my childhood rather than what he had recently looked like. My mom touched his body and kissed his face, and this creeped me out. I was never ever going to touch a dead body. This made me have flashbacks to seeing my mom touch Todd's body. This was the third time I'd been in this exact viewing room to bury a close family member. Being only in my mid-twenties, this seemed as if this was higher than the average person.

People started to arrive to give my mom their condolences. My mom was trying to step away from greeting people to use the restroom, but people kept greeting her, making it challenging for her to walk away. By the time she got into the restroom, she had waited too long. Donna had come to find me to tell me my mom needed me. She led me to the restroom where my mom was in a stall. My mom was embarrassed and asked me to please go get her some fresh garments to change into. Thankfully, the house was only five minutes away, so I was able to go and come back rather quickly. My mom had been so focused on the people that were showing up that she forgot to take care of her personal needs.

Once again, the conversation came up about how my dad's body looked good. I am not sure if it is that people are just so uncomfortable with the awkwardness of looking at a dead body that they always comment on how the body looks. I get that people do not want to tell the grieving family that this is weird, staring at a corpse. However, why do we go with how they look good? It looks dead. It is a body decomposing right in front of us. Once again, I witnessed how the side conversations around the funeral home were completely inappropriate. Death is taboo in American culture and people tend to think of their own mortality when someone they know dies. We are not taught how to be comfortable in the uncomfortable. We then start talking awkwardly to pretend that we are comfortable which shows up as simply weird.

My grandpa was the first to ask me about my soon-to-be ex-husband, asking me where he was. I had not been openly sharing with everyone that we were divorced since I wanted to have the papers in hand. I told him that we were in the process of a divorce. My grandpa shared he really liked my soon-to-be ex-husband as they had talked a lot at my grandmother's funeral.

Both of my parents were the godparents to my cousin Brian. My mom was elated that Brian was going to be flying in for the funeral – so happy that it felt as if she cared more about him being there than me. I know this was not true, but she was thrilled that he could be there to support her. I know that my mom had a special bond with Brian, so I was happy that he was able to be there.

So many people came to see my mom to give her condolences. Some of my friends from various points in my life had stopped by to give me support. When a few of my friends from college had come in, I snuck out of the funeral home to have a smoke as I was beyond stressed. I had tried to quit smoking, but with the death of my dad I started again.

In memory of my dad, we asked people to donate to the Todd Remer scholarship fund in lieu of flowers. The scholarship was to help assist those who could not afford the tuition to the Lutheran high school.

As we walked into the church for the memorial service, my grandpa, my mom, and I walked in as a trio. This was one of those moments when I realized how unique this was. We were three generations connected to my dad. A parent, a spouse, and a child. And we had all lost our partners in crime: my grandpa and mom lost their spouses, and I lost my sibling. All out of order deaths. I cannot for one second pretend that I was not bitter. I was.

The service for my dad was beautiful. It started with the song "I Can Only Imagine." It was the perfect song for my dad. There is a part of the song that goes, "When that day comes, and I find myself standing in the 'Son'." This helped me visualize what it must have been like for my father when he woke up in heaven. It was as if you could hear a pin drop, but you could hear some people crying.

The Lutheran high school brass ensemble accompanied the organ for some of the songs. My mom had always loved the sound of the trumpets playing. The sermon was a beautiful tribute, showing the impact my dad had on all our lives. Part was directed towards me and how my dad demonstrated Christ's love by the way he shined his love onto me. One of my vivid memories of my father was witnessing him sitting in his recliner reading the Word of God out loud. This was one way he showed me how he was a devout Christian.

My dad had been born and raised in Trinity Lutheran Church and School. He'd been baptized, confirmed, married, and now buried all at the church, a lifelong member.

Being January when it could snow, my mom decided that she did not want to have a procession to the cemetery, so they had the committal at the end of the service. A few people went to see the body lowered into the grave, but most went to the luncheon in the fellowship hall.

While the service was a beautiful tribute to my dad, now was when my mom, grandpa started our own individual processes with grief. My grandpa struggled with his grief since my dad had been spending more time with him since my grandmother had died. My mom was devastated to lose her soulmate. I traveled back to Illinois to grieve him alone. Processing the loss of my dad was challenging since I had built my adult life in a different state. For years, I hadn't physically seen him on a regular basis, so in my mind I did not need to believe that he was dead. While I could feel the loss of my ex-husband, it was easy to intwine both of their absences.

It was time to grieve again, whatever that ended up looking like for me.

16

The year following the death of my brother and the one following the death of my father have both been rather hazy. I honor this as a time of deep mourning. When I was going through it, every single moment was challenging. It was a day-by-day process. I see this as a part of the grief cycle of someone that you love deeply. My mom repeated the phrase, "No major changes for a year" for her own benefit when it came to making any major decisions. Hearing her say this impacted me. This meant staying in the apartment I shared with my ex-husband for another year. I was coping the best way I knew how. Some days the grief was heavy and some days I was able to do things without having to be so diligent about getting it done. Also, I was going through the separation and divorce.

When I returned home to Illinois, I found out I'd received the divorce papers in the mail. The divorced had been finalized on the same day as my father's death. I had wanted it completed by the end of the year, so I was happy that it was finalized.

I rarely acknowledge my first marriage. With it not being my proudest moment, I tend to forget that it ever happened. Since I'd considered my father's death to be more important, I did not process the loss of a failed marriage. I usually forget that I was going through both the loss of my dad and the loss of a relationship, even though it was a different type of loss with my ex-husband. We had been separated for several months beforehand. I'd started the process of grieving that relationship. Therefore, when my dad died, I put my loss of a spouse on the backburner.

A few people had asked about my ex-husband at the funeral. I told them we'd gotten divorced. The normal response was a head tilt which I perceived as their pity. Some would comment how hard it must have been to have lost two important men in my life. This is another one of those things that people assume about. If we have gotten a divorce, there more than likely is a reason. It's rude to assume that I'm sad about it. If they would have asked me if I were happy about it, they would have learned that it was a good thing that we went our separate ways.

My mom and I were now talking a lot more on the phone. She'd always tell me that I knew how she felt, but this always felt flat for me. My divorce was completely different than her losing her husband and love of her life of 32 years. They'd been through a lot together. They were committed to one another. He died. He did not leave her. It was so different. We were able to relate in some ways, but that was related to our family. We had loved the same people, but they were different relationships.

My mom was devastated. She would share openly with me about how hard it was for her. She had a hard time talking to others since no one else in her circle had lost their spouse. My parents had been a couple hanging out with other couples. This meant that she needed to find a new group of people, but my mom was too reserved to do this. Also, she was in her thickest of grief. I was one of her support avenues.

I started a new semester shortly after returning from my dad's funeral. As I sat in class, I was overwhelmed with emotions of loss. It took a lot to focus on instructors during their lectures. It seemed so insignificant in comparison to the life of a loved one. I no longer was carefree. It was a challenge to manage my emotions, classes, job, and social life.

When I traveled back to Michigan, I started to call it my mom's house rather than my parent's house, which felt strange. I felt guilty not acknowledging my father since he was the one who had built the home. I felt that if I called it my mom's house to new people I met, they would think my parents were divorced. However, it did not feel right to call it my parent's house. It was a small thing that was more challenging than I thought it would be.

I wanted to ensure that I processed my grief differently than I had for my brother's death. I reached out to the pastor at my new church for support. He met with me in his office a few times. I was grateful that he gave me a safe space to cry. One Sunday during his sermon, he was highlighting the Stephen Ministry that the congregation had to serve their members. I asked him about being paired with someone who had gone through loss. The Stephen Ministry is someone who has gone through training to provide high-quality, one to one, Christ-centered care to those in the congregation and the community experiencing life difficulties.

I was working late in the office doing paperwork and listening to MercyMe live in concert. The lead singer was sharing how the band had eight deaths happen in the month of December and January. The lead singer had been trying to write a song that would be able to help others during a loss, but he was struggling to connect to the true emotion of the song. Then his brother-in-law, who was 20 years old, suddenly died. I was taken aback when I heard him explain this next bit since it was exactly how I was feeling:

> *I had felt my heart had been pulled out of my chest and cut into pieces. You know I sit here every night and talk about how God is greater than anything and He can fix anything. But I felt a hurt and a pain that crippled me. And for the first time in my life, I thought I just do not know if God can fix this. And deep down and ultimately, I know He can, but that is what I was feeling at the time. I could not move. And needless to say, that song that I could not remember what it felt like to finish. I finished pretty quickly.*

The song he sang was called "Homesick." I was meant to hear this song at that very moment. It felt like more than a coincidence that the day his brother-in-law died was the first day of my dad's wake. The timing and the emotions he conveyed were exactly what I needed at this time. While I loved the song "I Can Only Imagine," "Homesick" was my experience.

Mother's Day was approaching, and I called my former mother-in-law. I knew that she was no longer technically family, but I was thinking of her and wanted her to know. When I talked to her, she told me my ex-husband was dating a new woman. This did not bother me, but it did shock me to hear. Then she said, "I'm hoping the third time's the charm."

Being completely naive I asked her, "You want him to get married a second time so that he can get married a third time?"

She replied, "Oh, he didn't tell you that either?"

Immediately I was irate. Not only did my ex-husband lie to me about having a child, but he lied about being married to another woman. He had gotten married while he was in the military. It was a different woman than the mother of his child.

The owner of the kitchen knew that I was going through a lot with both my divorce and my dad's death. He asked his assistant Johana to befriend me. Johana invited me to come hang out with her and a couple of her friends. As time progressed, we regularly went to a dive bar across the street to play pool or throw darts. Johana and my other friends Julia and Vanessa checked out a martini bar for ladies' night one Thursday and it quickly became the place where we would start our evenings.

After hanging out with the girls for a while, Julia, who was separating from her husband, and I talked about getting an apartment together. I had been torn about leaving my apartment since it was the last place I had seen my dad. However, it was also the place I had lived with my ex-husband. I knew it was time for a fresh new start. We found an apartment farther south of where I'd been, but still off the same road. Ever since I moved to Illinois, I moved farther south each time, but it was always right off the same major road. As I was preparing to move, there was a note on the bulletin board from someone giving away his furniture for free. It was perfect to completely start fresh, furniture included.

17

My mom asked me if I would be interested in going to Europe with her. There was a trip that she had wanted to take with my dad, so now she asked me about going. Of course, I said yes to this opportunity. I knew this trip would be good for her soul, as she was a social studies teacher and one who loves adventure. It would be fun for us to have some mother daughter bonding time where we could focus on something besides grief. It was a tour of the Eastern capitals of Europe with an additional trip to walk in the footsteps of Martin Luther. My mom's cousin's husband organized this trip for those in his church who were interested in attending. He was a pastor of a different Lutheran church. Besides seeing Europe, I knew my mom was most excited about following in Luther's footsteps. Martin Luther was a monk in the Catholic church that disputed the indulgences of the Catholic Church. He posted the Ninety-Five Theses on the door in Wittenberg. His work led to people following his teachings and they called themselves Lutherans.

We flew into Warsaw, Poland to start the adventure. The first place we went was the Chopin Statue at Lazienki Park. As we continued to walk around the grounds, we saw a peacock walking around and displaying its beautiful tail feathers. This was my first time I ever saw a peacock in person. It was stunning to see the feathers on display.

We traveled by bus from city to city. There was a lot of time in the bus, so I had prepared by bringing a couple books to read. As we left Warsaw, we headed to visit Auschwitz concentration camp. The drive had been sunny on the way, but as we approached this area, it became dreary and started to drizzle. It became silent. I could feel the heaviness that hung in the air. I am not sure if I never comprehended what Auschwitz was before seeing it with my own eyes, but it is a feeling I will never forget.

Seeing the displays of the mass quantities of shoes, luggage, and other items was incredibly disturbing. Seeing all these personal items of those who were murdered let me understand the gravity of what happened on this land. It became incredibly clear why it felt so heavy and dark over the concentration camp. So many lives were maliciously executed there. We visited the quarters where people lived. We even saw the gas chambers and the crematoria. I cannot think of this place without my heart aching for all the lives that were unnecessarily taken from innocent people.

While it was not the capital of Poland, we still made our way to see Krakow. We visited different cathedrals, museums, and castles. My favorite spots to see are always outdoors, such as the town squares or the parks. We made our way over to Budapest. My mom had been looking forward to spending time in an ancient bath. She wanted to sit in the baths and get a massage. Unfortunately, due to the timing of when we were there, she was unable to make it to the baths. She was angry and expressed to me that we wasted time sitting at cafes waiting rather than getting to a major city.

My mom and I decided to not have this be a bust, so we booked simultaneous Thai massages at the hotel. They had placed matts on the ground next to one another. I could tell my massage person was just a couple steps ahead of my mom's massage. The woman pushed my leg up in a position that was not the most comfortable feeling. I thought to myself how my mom would not be able to do that move. Moments later I heard my mom say, "My leg does not move like that." All four of us were laughing now. While my mom was happy to have received the massage, it wasn't quite the experience she had anticipated.

We did a boat tour on the Danube River. During our ride, it

started pouring, but my mom found us a place to sit in an enclosed area. I enjoyed being on the Danube River to take in all the lights on both sides of Buda and Pest.

By the time we got to Vienna, I was sick and tired of all the museums that we had been exploring. I looked at my mom and said, "Hey mom, guess what? After we look at this room, the next room will have different shit on the walls for us to look at." Typically, I never swore in front of my mom, but I had officially hit my breaking point of looking at museums full of things that I was never going to remember. Luckily, she laughed at what I had to say.

Prague was my absolute favorite city on the tour. I hadn't known anything about Prague before we went there. When we arrived, some of us headed out for dinner. There was a staircase that we needed to descend to get to the public transportation. My mom was struggling as she could not see well enough to perceive the depth of the stairs. She got frustrated with being unable to see clearly and decided to go back to the hotel. She told me to go ahead without her. I felt bad, but I was happy to check out the city. I tried some of the local beer and was surprised that I enjoyed the dark beer.

When I had returned to the room, I heard her crying in the shower. It was not just a soft cry, but rather a hard sob. When I asked her about it, she shared that she was missing my dad. Life was hard for her without him. We got into a disagreement at this moment when I selfishly told her she was ruining the trip for me. I overreacted since we were spending so much time together. To this day, I feel awful I had not been more understanding of her grieving my dad.

My favorite spot was the iconic Charles Bridge. My mom and I got our pictures taken by guards who were protecting the Prague Castle. Overall, I loved the atmosphere of the city of Prague.

The final stop of the Eastern capitals was Berlin. We went to all the popular locations of the Berlin Wall, Checkpoint Charlie, Brandenburg Gate, Holocaust Memorial and the Olympic Stadium. Afterwards, some people in the group were headed home while few of us were continuing onto seeing the footsteps of Luther.

The cities we explored following in Martin Luther's footsteps were Wittenberg, Eisleben, Leipzig, Erfurt, and Eisenach. We saw the place where he nailed the Ninety-Five Theses on the Castle Church, which sparked the Reformation movement. This also included seeing where he was born, baptized, and died. We saw where he had been struck by lightning which made him decide to go into ministry, where he studied to become a monk, and the place where he translated the New Testament.

There was an area along the Kraemer Bridge with little shops. Here I saw a rose necklace. With my mom's name being Rose, I knew that it was a perfect gift to buy her as a small token to thank her for taking me on this trip.

This trip and this time with my mom was such a gift. Upon our return, my mom noticed that she was gaining weight at a faster speed than necessary. Within a month, she gained over 35 pounds. Upon getting her test results, they discovered that her kidneys were shutting down. She would need to start dialysis to keep from retaining the fluids. Having this opportunity with my mom was a special trip, as it would be the last time we were able to freely travel together before all her health issues.

18

I was incredibly reckless after my dad's death. I had an arrogance about myself that believed God would not let me die too. He would never let my mom lose that many people. I am not proud of this moment, but it is true to my story. I am incredibly grateful that no one was hurt in the process of me drinking and driving during this time.

When I finished my classes for my Master of Business Administration, my mom flew in for the ceremony. Afterwards, we went to dinner with all of the girls and the woman who was my Stephen Minister to celebrate.

Shortly after I graduated, Julia recommended a job that was available from the recruiting company she worked for. I landed an interview and then the position. For the first time in my career, I would have a day job where I was able to work normal hours. It was a step in the right direction by making the transition into accounting. I was no longer in management, but I was ready to be responsible for myself versus having to manage others.

Putting in my notice at my old job made me reflect on my experience with this company. It had been my bridge from being let go to starting over in a new career. It supported me through a lot in my personal life such as my divorce, the death of my dad, and getting my masters. It introduced me to a network of women that I needed.

When I started at the new company, it was a way different pace than I had been used to. I was used to the hospitality environment of go-go-go. In the office, it was a much slower pace. Sitting at your desk all day long was now my new norm. It was worth it to have a set schedule of Monday through Friday. Most of the employees were significantly older than me, which was an adjustment.

I was getting to a place of wanting to meet people and possibly have a boyfriend. I had my first date with Mr. Handsome, who I had met online. He had a great personality and was finally someone that I wanted to get to know better. We started dating exclusively. He lived farther away than I would have liked, but the travel time was worth it to me to spend time with him.

When our lease came up for renewal, Julia and I decided that we go our separate ways. While the time we spent together was healing for me, we both wanted to be closer to our new men in our lives.

Wanting to be closer to Mr. Handsome, I knew that I was going to have a longer commute for work, but it was worth it to me. I found a townhome apartment in the suburb of Naperville. Besides the rent being the lowest I had seen in the area, I loved that the setup of the apartment was different from a typical apartment. It felt more like a home with a staircase and its own entryway.

Three months after I moved in, my relationship with Mr. Handsome ended. I took it harder than I needed to. The relationship had only lasted for six months, but I went on to grieve for over a year and a half. I am sure I was grieving more than that relationship but was unable to realize it at the time.

Being in a new town, I needed to rebuild relationships again. The first place I started was with a church that was closer to me. I wanted a church I could be active in outside of the Sunday service. There was a church that had the same name as my childhood church, Trinity Lutheran Church. The very first sermon I heard, I knew that I had found my new home church. Not only was the name of the church the same, but also the sermon had the same dynamic style I was used to hearing as a child. It was powerful and thought provoking. They had several services throughout the weekend, which was an important quality I was looking for. Small groups were encouraged for members to become active in. They had a 20's and 30's group that I decided to check out to meet others my age. I also decided to take classes to become a Stephen Minister.

Here I was, in a new town, starting yet another new chapter.

19

I wanted to meet more people besides those who were connected to church. An old work acquaintance suggested a young professional organization. It ended up not being what I was looking for, but it did lead me to another young person's organization called the Jaycees. The organization provides the opportunity to develop personal and leadership skills through service to others.

The very first meeting I went to, I met Courtney who had introduced herself to me. After a little bit of small talk, she connected me with another girl, Angela. It happened to be Angela's first time too. I was happy that I got out of my comfort zone to go to the meeting.

The Jaycees seemed like a great organization to get involved with. They had various events they hosted throughout the year. Some were just for fun for the members, some were fundraisers and others were volunteering. With it being a non-profit, the money raised went back into the community. The people were incredibly friendly and in my age range. I became a member after I attended my first two meetings. I felt like I had found my people who were passionate about people and volunteering their time.

I started to become involved in all the different events the Jaycees were hosting. One of the very first events I remember attending was a trolley ride to look at Christmas lights around town. I started to hang out with Angela on a regular basis. Angela's cousin Lisa, Courtney, Angela, and I started to hang out often. The weekend before St. Patrick's Day, the four of us along with a couple guys hung out in downtown Naperville. There were several people out to watch the parade that went throughout the town. I was starting to realize that I had made a wise decision moving to Naperville even though I had initially done it for a guy. I was enjoying the connections I was making in various areas of my life.

Angela had been living at home with her parents but wanted to get a place of her own again. She ended up getting a two-bedroom apartment in my apartment complex. I loved that she was a quick walk away. There were many nights where we would drink way too much wine and talk about life. She was the first person in a long while that felt like a best friend to me. While I still talked to Renee often on the phone, we lived so far apart that we never hung out in person. It was refreshing to have a good girlfriend that I could talk to about anything and everything. We would stay up all hours of the night talking about where we had been and what we wanted for our futures.

I became one of the board of directors for the organization. It was a great way to make an impact on the organization by becoming involved. Also, it was a great way to meet more of the people that had been involved in the organization for several years. The largest event that the Naperville Jaycees hosted was an event called the Last Fling, which would take place over Labor Day weekend in downtown Naperville. I was asked if I wanted to chair the parade portion of the event. Not knowing what this entailed, I thought it would be a great way to play a part in the event. Florence Henderson, who played Carol Brady on the hit show The Brady Bunch, ended up being the grand marshal of the parade.. I was thrilled to get to meet her and have my picture taken with her.

Angela and I put in our names to be the chairs of the food basket event. Food baskets were created to help the community to give food out for both Thanksgiving and Christmas to families in need. This was an awesome event to give to those in need. In years past, they had a space to house all the donated food. However, the year we took it over there was a major issue with having a space to house it. We ended up having multiple locations where we would organize it and then move the finished product to another location. This ended up being a lot more work than either Angela or I had anticipated. Even with all the obstacles, I was happy to contribute to all the families who received much needed food for the holidays.

It felt great to be doing something to give to others and building new friendships at the same time. Things were definitely looking up.

20

Mom had so many health issues after our trip to Europe. She had started dialysis – the process of getting this done several times a week was not easy. Typically, most people were exhausted from dialysis, but she soldiered on since she was not in a place to not work. To keep it lighthearted, she joked that she could manage her weight by asking her nurse to take an extra couple pounds. Having her kidney flushed out on a regular basis helped her feel better than she had in years without the excess fluids. While it was not the best situation, she made the most of it.

My mom needed to get a hip replacement. Her decision to deal with her health in the future was now facing her on a consistent basis. Without the emotional and physical support of my dad, her health was slowly deteriorating.

Unable to take care of herself after her hip surgery, my mom stayed with my grandparents for a couple weeks as she healed. It ended up getting cut short since my mom and my grandmother had a couple disagreements while she stayed there. My grandparents were farmers and went to bed early. My mom was talking on the phone one evening which sparked the disagreement. When my grandmother yelled at my mom, this is when my mom decided that she needed to go home.

My mom was so distraught over the experience that she promised me she would never treat me the way she was treated. When she got home, she called me to vent about what had happened. She expressed her hurt over them not having any understanding or compassion for her experience. My mom felt trapped because she was unable to care for herself and had no spouse to rely on. Her mom had no idea what it was like to be on her own. My mom had not only lost her son, but also her spouse too. Being out of her normal routine, she really wanted to talk to a friend, and it backfired on her.

It was the one and only time she ever talked poorly of her mother to me. I knew that my mom was a private person who did not want to ask anyone for support. She had asked her mother for help, and it was turned on her while she was recovering. I listened to my mom and gave her compassion for her experience. She had been frustrated with how she was being treated as a child when she was a grown adult. The last thing she wanted to be was a burden on anyone. My mom repeatedly wanted me to know that she would never want to do this to me.

When she returned to a sense of normal life, she used a walker to get around. When we were out shopping, she saw someone she perceived as being old. She asked me if she looked old. Without skipping a beat, I said yes. "Trudi!" she yelled. I looked at her and said, "Well, you are using a walker – what else am I supposed to say?" She laughed and understood what I was saying.

A year later when I was leaving my boss' office, I heard my cell phone ringing. I tried to answer it since I recognized the school's number and knew it was my mom, but it went to voicemail before I could answer. As soon as the voicemail showed up, I listened to it. In the message, my mom said she had gotten a call from her former student Steve Gould. I had known Steve for years since he was a year behind me in grade school. His brother Eric was in my homeroom class when we had my mother for 8th grade. My mom favored Eric since he seemed to have struggled more than other students. He had died a couple years prior. Steve told my mom that his father, Bob, had had a massive stroke and he was not going to recover. His body had been placed on machines to keep his organs alive until they could be donated. The family knew a couple people they wanted to give the first option to donate his organs to. They knew my mom needed a kidney. He needed her to head to the hospital right away to see if she could be a match. She told me she would be in contact with me as soon as she could.

Tears immediately welled up in my eyes. I never dreamed of hearing this type of news. I had known that my mom had been going through the process to be put on the donor list but was in shock that she was possibly getting a kidney so soon. This was what we'd been praying for! I was upset that I had no way to get a hold of my mom and anxiously waited to hear any update. I went back into my boss's office to share the good news. We both teared up with the excitement of this opportunity. I was not focused on work for the remainder of the day.

She eventually called me and informed me she was enough of a match to go ahead with the surgery. I was so excited for her to no longer need to be on dialysis all the time. I told her that I was going to come see her. However, she resisted me coming to see her, knowing that I had a date. After I got off the phone, I told my boss I needed the day off since I wanted to surprise her. This was too big of a moment to not be there to support her.

She was surprised when I showed up in her hospital room and happy to have me there. I let her know that I did reschedule the date, but that she was always more important to me so I would not have missed this for anything. Living away from home, I was always comforted that she had an amazing supportive group of friends and colleagues to keep her company. She asked me to go to Bob Gould's funeral on her behalf. I really did not want to go, but I knew that I needed to do this for her.

I headed to the funeral. I was anxious about going but didn't realize how much until I got to the church. I saw Steve as I was walking into the church. I didn't talk to him but witnessed him taking care of his mother. It reminded me of taking care of my mom for my dad's funeral. This was why I was hesitant to go. I knew that Steve had lost a brother and now his father. It mirrored what I had been through. I was so grateful to them for my mom getting her kidney, but I knew that came at the cost of their grief. The service was at Trinity. As the pastor talked about Bob, he acknowledged that even in his death, he gave life to others. After the service, I tried to say something to Steve, but all I could get out was my condolences before I started crying. I wasn't sure if he even recognized me since we hadn't seen each other in over ten years.

I had grabbed a few things from the house my mom had

requested. When I brought the mail into the house, I noticed that there was a letter from the hospital where she was staying, so I decided to bring it to her. When she opened the envelope, she discovered that she was approved to be on the donor list. I laughed since I thought it was the bill for her stay. What a funny coincidence that she was already in the hospital with a successful transplant when the letter was received at her home for being on the donor list!

She also had foot problems and had one of her middle toes amputated. Unfortunately, t's not uncommon for people with diabetes to have body parts amputated. She was nervous that this could lead to more getting amputated on her leg. Her foot turned out looking good after the surgery, so she knew it was the right decision.

A sore developed on the bottom of her other foot. When I was in town visiting her, she would ask me to help her out by putting an ointment on it to help it heal. However, it never went away. Every time it would start to close a little, it would get reopened since she put pressure on it to walk. She started to use a wheelchair to allow her foot to hopefully heal. Being a diabetic who did not eat well, her body struggled with being able to take care of itself. She then used the wheelchair full time at school and around home.

Overall, my mom's health was a serious issue. To try to lighten up the seriousness of it, I joked that she was in the hospital at least once a quarter. Every time I would think she was doing okay she would end up in the hospital for something else. It was hard worrying about her all the time. Between struggling with her health and missing my dad, she did not properly take care of herself.

21

While I was home visiting my mom, we went shopping at Macy's. As we were making our way through the shop, there was a counter in the middle of the store that I did not realize was at the time was another company. All I saw were these large blocks of soap that had a strong fragrance. I started picking them up to smell each one. My mom and I liked the same one, so she bought a couple of pieces for us. The woman who was helping us threw in a sample of shampoo she told us to try out. The next time I took a shower, I used the shampoo and instantly fell in love with it.

I needed to learn more about this hippy soap company called Lush Fresh Cosmetics. The following week, I did an internet search to find a store near me in the Chicago suburbs. I needed more of this shampoo. It dawned on me that it would be fun to see about working there for the Christmas holiday season. It was the end of October when I called to see if the shop was hiring for the holidays. My timing was perfect as they were hosting a group interview that weekend.

I ended up getting hired to be a part of the seasonal team. They told us we would only be on staff until the beginning of January at the latest. This was perfect since I had no intentions of having two jobs. However, after working there for a couple shifts, I loved everything about the company, the products, and the team. I started to take it upon myself to study up on the different benefits of the ingredients in the products. The manager noticed my drive to learn everything I could. At the end of the holiday season, I was brought onto the permanent staff. I was so excited to be a part of this wonderful team.

Working at Lush was something I never realized how much I needed in my life until I was working there. Initially, I wanted to work for the company for the discount but ended up meeting some of the best people that I know to this day. Learning all the benefits one can receive through all the various essential oils in the products opened my eyes to a whole new way of being intentional with my choices. The manager led by example, which was inspiring to witness. While I knew that some of my co-workers did not care for the manager, I also saw the business side of why she did what she did. The dynamics of working as a team were key too. Since everyone benefited together based on the sales we did, it helped create unity rather than competition.

Turnover was not as high as I would imagine most retail positions to be. The manager did a great job at selecting people to put on the team. The manager brought in an assistant manager from another store. The assistant manager, Emily, would end up becoming the new manager, leading us through the next several years.

Working with a diverse group of people opened me up to new things. There were crystals around the shop and some of the employees wore different crystals. This was too woo-woo for me. One of our coworkers started chanting "I'm sorry. Please forgive me. Thank you. I love you." She kept repeating it over and over. It was strange. She probably told me that it was a Ho'oponopono prayer, but I did not recall this other than her repeating it over and over. While it was different from what I was used to hearing, I still was respectful that we all had different beliefs that filled our souls.

22

When I went home to see my mom for Christmas and we were catching up, she asked me what size my pants were. I told her, which happened to be the largest size I had been in my life. This conversation became the catalyst to start getting back into shape.

My mom encouraged me to see how much a personal trainer would be. Knowing that my mom did not want me to have a similar story to her, she financially supported me in getting a trainer.

I was committed to being in the best shape of my life. After a year of going to the gym, I lost 32 pounds and even more inches. The endorphins were the best part about working out. I eventually stopped working out with a trainer, but I continued a healthy lifestyle. I found different ways to push myself to stay in shape. I participated in a leg of a triathlon, and I ran a couple different races, the longest one being a 10-mile run that I barely trained for. As my personal life continued to get busier, I managed to still get to the gym. I would either go after a shift at Lush or before I went out drinking.

I felt fantastic, and I think I looked pretty damn good too! Life was getting sweet.

23

One of my closest girlfriends from the church's young adults group told me she had a guy friend, a firefighter, who she wanted to connect me to. Facebook was starting to become more popular, so we connected through on there and would occasionally chat with one another. He seemed like a nice guy, but he lived in Ohio. I knew that nothing would ever become of this, but I really enjoyed talking to a guy.

I posted on Facebook to see if anyone would be interested in a spontaneous trip to Cedar Point. Cedar Point is an amusement park with several roller coasters. The firefighter commented that he was interested and willing to go. Since he lived close to the park, we agreed that we would meet there. We got a hotel room with two beds to make the trip worth my time to drive out there. When I told my mother, I lied and told her we were each getting our own hotel room. I knew that it was easiest for me to tell her what she wanted to hear.

By the time I was on my way to the amusement park, the firefighter still had not left yet. I was irritated that he was cutting into my time at the park. Eventually he got there. When we met in person, I was instantly attracted to him. We spent the day going from ride to ride and got to know one another a lot better while waiting in line. The more we talked the more I started to develop an interest in this guy.

After a fun, long day at the park, we grabbed dinner at a sports bar. We were learning that we had a lot in common. We both enjoyed watching sports, specifically the Detroit Red Wings, drinking good beer, and we were born and raised Lutheran – he was a youth minister for several years. We even enjoyed the same Christian bands!

The second day we decided to go to the water park for the first half of the day. In all the times I had been to Cedar Point, I never had gone to the water park. It was pure joy to be able to be surprised at what the water park had to offer. It ended up being an incredibly fun couple of days being a kid in the amusement park.

We ended up kissing and fooling around a little bit the second night in the hotel room. However, he left early to head back to work. I was saddened when he left because I had started falling for this guy. I never meant for it to happen because I knew that the chances of anything long-term happening between us was not realistic. However, a few weeks after our trip to Cedar Point, I noticed that he was in a relationship with someone. I was disappointed, but it was what it was.

24

Every time that I went home to visit my mom, I would make sure that I took the time to see my grandpa. I could tell that he was lonely. The television would have Detroit sports games on while I was there.

Grandpa deeply missed my grandma and my dad. My dad visited him more often after my grandma died. After my dad died, my mom started to spend more time with him, and they started getting dinner together. They understood one another since they had both lost a child and their spouse.

My grandpa knew he was getting to the end of his life, so he started getting his affairs in order. My mom kept me informed on how he was doing. When he died, he was with my uncle Bob. My grandpa knew that he needed to go to the hospital and died on the way there. It was not shocking that he passed away since he was 94. He'd led a long life and he'd been ready for years, so I was happy for him to be reunited with his wife, son, and grandson.

I traveled back to Michigan for the funeral. All the brothers and sisters were able to get to town for the funeral. Once again, the viewing was in the same damn funeral room that my brother, Grandma Remer, my dad, and now Grandpa Remer were. I hated this room. This was the place where all my family were last seen.

I knew a lot of the people who came to offer condolences. Remer had been a well-known name at Trinity, between my mom working at the school and my grandpa being a lifelong member. The Remers had always sat in one of the front rows of the left side of the church for the 8am service. When my dad and siblings were growing up, they sometimes took up two pews. With my grandpa dying, this was the end of an era.

Right before the funeral my mom asked me if I was ready to go see my grandpa's body one last time. I said, "No, I am not." She scolded me that we needed to do it since people were watching. I shared with her that I was uncomfortable around dead bodies. Even if it were her body, I would feel the exact same way. I don't think my mom ever understood how seeing a dead body was very traumatic for me. She had no problem touching dead bodies, but I wanted no part of that. For me, it was a weird tradition to look at a body that no longer carried the soul of the person we loved. The only time I had gone near a body in a coffin was when she forced me to go with her.

After the funeral, all the siblings went over to my grandparent's house to sit around and tell stories. While this was a sweet moment, I knew this would be the very last time they all would be together alive. It was a beautiful summer day, and I was sad my dad was not alive to have this moment with all his siblings.

25

My friend Theresa, who I knew from the Jaycees, had a generous spirit filled with love and laughter. She had been married for almost seven years, but I'd never met her husband, since he lived in Egypt. She met him while traveling and they had fallen in love. They were working on getting all the proper documentation so he could move here.

His visa was finally approved to move over to the US. Shortly after her husband arrived, I met up for dinner and drinks to finally meet him. She wanted to connect us so we could work out together. Every so often, we would meet at the gym and choose either upper body or lower body as our focus. He never worked out his lower body whereas this was my focus. I convinced him to do legs which led him to not be able to walk normally for a few days.

We had planned to work out one night when they arrived late to the gym. I was angry that they did not have respect for my time. When they finally arrived, I was short with both. Theresa cornered me in the locker room after the workout to question if I was upset at her. This was one of the qualities that I loved about her. She was comfortable confronting the elephant in the room by directly asking me what was up. She apologized. She shared it had been a rough week for them. Her best friend's husband had died unexpectedly. They had been spending a lot of time helping her with the funeral details. I immediately softened my anger towards them and realized that I was being dramatic in how I was acting. I am grateful that Theresa was so direct with me to clear any awkwardness I had.

A day and a half later, I woke up to a text message from her husband asking for prayers since Theresa was at the hospital in a coma. I laid in my bed in utter shock. She'd had an aneurysm extremely late at night. He'd found her breathing funny, so he found her mom to see what they needed to do. An ambulance was called to take her to the hospital. Several of us went to the hospital to sit in the waiting room to offer the family support. Theresa was the glue in her family. She was incredibly close to her mom. It was heartbreaking to witness the pain in her mother's eyes. They allowed some of us to go into the room to let her know that we were there. Seeing her on the machines, I did not think that she was going to come out of the coma, but I was hoping for a miracle.

After five days of Theresa being in a coma, the family decided they would take her off life support. The doctors had said that if she were to ever come out of it, she would not have a good quality of life. It was a gut-wrenching decision, but the right one for her. I was so sad for her husband since he only just moved here to start this next chapter of their lives together. I was heartbroken for her parents because even though she was 45 years old, they still lost their child.

Weeks after the funeral, a friend told me she was worried about me and questioned if I might benefit from counseling. I had no idea why she was saying this to me. A few days later I happened to drive by a golf course where Theresa and I had golfed together, and I started to cry hysterically. I had not realized the effect Theresa's death was having on me until these pieces of the puzzles were put together.

I found a counselor close to my apartment, so close to me that I would be able to walk to her office. I knew that Theresa's death stirred up a lot of unresolved feelings about both my brother and my father's death. When I met my counselor, I immediately liked her. She was around my mother's age. She had lost her father years prior, so she had a background in grief. This was important to me, having a counselor who could understand loss. As the sessions continued, I learned that some of the things that I had assumed were normal were not. After my brother died, I told myself to forget everything prior to his death, as a way to keep myself from missing him. My memories start after Todd's death. My counselor asked me if I realized that this was not normal. I was a little taken aback. However, when able to see it outside of my own viewpoint, it made sense that I had done this to cope the best way I knew how. Counseling helped give me a new way to listen to all the meaning I had created around Todd's death.

Most of the work we did was around the loss of my brother. We explored how I handled it as a child. How I coped in a household where the norm was constant sadness. As I was getting closer to the end of our counseling sessions, I reached out to my mom to ask her what life was like back then. This meant facing my fear of mentioning Todd's name. I had spent years never bringing his name up since I did not want to invoke sadness in my mom. My mom told me that all they ever wanted for me was to be happy and have a good life. She expressed how proud she was of me. When I asked her if she had ever seen a counselor, she shared this was not something she was interested in pursuing. It was at this moment where instead of my mom being the strongest woman I knew, I was now the strongest woman I knew. I was willing to be vulnerable to work on the hard things for the betterment of myself. Working through my grief with a professional took courage.

26

My mom informed me she had a lot of air miles saved up to fly somewhere and asked if there was anywhere I wanted to go. I mentioned there were a few places that would interest me, like Florida to visit Renee while she was on a work assignment. She countered this suggestion with, "What about Cyprus to see Rosey?" Rosey had been a dear friend of mine since grade school. We even went to the same college, but I was focused on starting my own path, so we rarely hung out. She met her husband in college, and he was from Cyprus. When they got married, she moved there since he knew he would run the family business. My mom wanted to watch me enjoy these moments rather than me taking them after she died. It was important for her to witness me enjoying life to its fullest.

Rosey and I connected in Athens, then took a cab to our hotel. We were talking in English and the driver was talking in Greek. Rosey said something in Greek to let him know that she understood him. After she started a conversation with him, he became friendlier and occasionally spoke English. He let us know that there was something going on around our hotel. This meant he would not be able to take us right to the front door of the hotel but would drop us off as close as he could.

As we were walking, we noticed the area was crowded. We got all the way to the end of the street and could tell we missed the street to turn onto. A gentleman came up to us to see if he could help us find our hotel. He used Rosey's map to point us to the road we'd missed. Then a man with a gas mask ran past us. I started to wonder what in the world all these people were doing here!

When we checked into the hotel, the agent let us know that there was a protest that was going on in the area. Our hotel was close to the Greek Parliament which is where people had gathered to protest. We asked about public transportation, but he let us know it was shut down due to the protests. When we got to our room, I placed a call to my mom. I let my mom know I was with Rosey at the hotel in Athens. After I hung up the phone, Rosey jokingly asked why I did not tell my mom about the protest. I laughed and said I would wait until I was back in the US to let her know rather than to have her worry about me.

We headed away from the protest to check out some of the sights in the city. We ended up not staying out too long as I could tell the jet lag was catching up to me. The next day, as we were heading to check out Athens, we stopped by the front desk to ask which would be the best way to get to the Acropolis. He told us to take public transportation. We asked about the protestors, but he let us know that it was only a one-day thing, which made us laugh. We checked out the Acropolis Museum, Acropolis Amphitheater, Parthenon, and the Temple of Athena Nike. We were able to see The Temple of Olympian Zeus in the distance along with the whole city of Athens. While we were walking around the Acropolis, my flip flop broke. There was no way I was going to walk down a rocky bath barefoot, so I dug in my purse for something to fix it. After a bit of persistence and the use of a paperclip, I managed to fix it. I never thought a paperclip could save the day!

We did make our way over to check out the Parliament and the Tomb of the Unknown Soldier. There were so many dogs throughout the city! They would hang out around the outdoor cafes, hoping that food would fall off the table. We had a couple authentic Greek meals – it wasn't until this trip that I realized how fresh Greek food is.

We left Athens to fly to Cyprus. I knew Rosey's husband but was excited to meet her children, a son and a daughter. The five of us headed out to Protaras for a holiday. The water at the beach was so crystal blue that I stared at it for hours. The beach had yellow chairs that you could sit in on the sand or take out into the sea to float. I'd forgotten that in Europe people go topless at the beach without a second thought! Rosey brought snorkeling gear, so we explored the coral and looked for fish. It was a stunning way to see the island.

Throughout the week, Rosey and I went on adventures checking out the country. While in Limassol, we stopped at a Lush Cosmetics, which was my first time seeing the shop in another country. We took a day trip to the mountains, only an hour away from her home. On a day out towards Paphos, we saw Aphrodite's Rock where legend says Aphrodite, the goddess of beauty and love, was born. Between visiting Greece and Cyprus, I loved getting to know more Greek mythology, which was all new to me. We stopped by Paphos Archaeological Park where we saw the Houses of Theseus and Aion. It was cool to see such rich history.

In Paphos, we decided to do a glass bottom boat ride. Now, never seeing clear water, I was skeptical if we would really be able to see the shipwreck they said we were going to go over. Thankfully, I was wrong. Once again, I was mesmerized by how the water was a stunning shade of cobalt. Those who were interested in swimming were allowed to jump out of the boat. While I was in the water, I could see clearly around me into the Mediterranean Sea.

The last night of my trip, Rosey, her husband and I went out for a nice authentic Cypriot dinner. I tried several new foods: souvlakia, sheftalia, and halloumi. I even was brave and ate a snail! It was the perfect way to end my time with Rosey. Her husband told me that I was welcome anytime I wanted to visit. I felt blessed that my mom had given me such an amazing gift.

27

I started 2011 by deciding to run a half marathon.

I had quit smoking in the summer of 2010. Quitting was such a proud accomplishment for me that I wondered, "What's next?" I decided the best way to top becoming a non-smoker was to become a marathoner.

When I got back from Cyprus, marathon training officially started for me. I read a book that helped me learn how to finish a marathon. I signed up with the local running store to be a part of their Saturday morning training runs. The first week was an eight-mile run. Very quickly, I knew running in intervals for a run/walk was going to be the best method for me to survive, but this made it harder for me to find a running partner since most people wanted to run.

The first several Saturdays, I found my pace group. Initially, I thought I was an 11-minute run, but it ended up being more like a 12-minute group. I was still on my own when it came to running since I was doing intervals with the run and walk, but on parts of the run or walk I would be able to talk to others in my group. I quickly discovered that the first portion of the run was always the hardest. It seemed that once I passed the 5k point, my body would open to a flow that made the run more enjoyable. I was so proud of myself for getting up at 6am every Saturday to go running with the group.

As the weeks went on, the runs got longer. After we did a fourteen-mile run, I realized that it was officially the longest run I had ever done. The book I had read had a whole schedule which included smaller runs during the week. I was only committed to keeping up with the long Saturday runs. With my two jobs and my social circles, I was not interested in running during the week. I would do cardio at the gym but choose to use the elliptical since it kept my body from the impact of running.

A girl started the training who was willing to interval runs with me. It was a lot more fun to have a running partner on the long runs. Her husband was in a faster paced group so he would wait for her when she was done. With a running partner, we had several hours to get to know one another. She shared her struggles with diabetes. It was helpful for me to hear her viewpoint so I could understand what my mom was going through. She was not going to be doing the Chicago marathon. Instead, her marathon was scheduled on the day of our longest run of twenty miles.

While working at Lush, I discovered a coworker, Tricia, was also going to be running the Chicago marathon in October, so we planned to do a couple training runs together. One time we took a run that was a lot hillier than I had anticipated. She kept telling me to look down towards the ground as I was running up the hill so my brain would not visually see that I was running up the hill. I didn't believe this would work, but it did help me with running up the steep hill. Thankfully, in Illinois there weren't that many hills for most of my runs. However, it seemed I would always find them when I was running with Tricia!

The running community is like no other community I've come across. They were so supportive of one another. Even though I was at a slower pace, I would see many of the same faces before the run would start, and we would greet one another along the path. While some of the runs were challenging, the benefits were worth it: a clear mind, decreased anxiety, and weight loss. My confidence increased with the strength I developed from running, and it felt really good. While I was physically working out my body, I was also working with my counselor for my mind. I had not planned to do them at the same time; in retrospect it was a perfect way to start moving myself into my best self.

While I met Tricia through Lush, we were developing a deep friendship through training for the marathon. We decided that we would share a hotel room together the night before the marathon. It was her birthday the day before the marathon, so we grabbed dinner together to load up on carbs before the big run. Everyone was either calling or texting to wish me luck. I turned off all the sound on my phone so I could go to sleep without being interrupted.

In the morning, Tricia and I went our separate ways to meet those we planned on running with. My group from the Naperville Running Company met at a hotel before we walked over to the starting line together. There was a woman who held a "run happy" sign. Around mile six, a man ran past me who was smoking a cigarette. This deflated me. Here I had set out to run a marathon since I quit smoking, and someone passed me while doing it. It was the worst. I did the one thing you never should do, which is compare yourself to someone else. When I shared this with the woman holding the sign, she encouraged me to keep going with my own race.

Renee and her husband, as well as my friend Will from church had come out to cheer me on in the marathon, so I knew I could not give up. I had hit a wall earlier than I anticipated – my intervals had become more of a walk with an occasional run. When I saw Renee, I was overcome with emotions. Having her there to support me meant the world to me. She had seen me go through so much throughout the years that it was exactly the push I needed to move forward.

As I got to the final 0.2 miles, it was so close to the finish, but it felt as if I would never get there. I started to run at mile 26, but I started too early to maintain a pace to the finish line. Plus, there was a bridge that we needed to go over right before we crossed the finish line. Knowing that I was not a fan of running up hills, I decided that once I made it to the top, I would run to the finish line. When I completed it, I was so proud to call myself a marathoner.

When Will and I made it to the El train to get to his car, I called my mom to let her know I finished the marathon. She sang her praises of how proud of me she was. Will dropped me off at home so I could take a shower before I headed over to the bar to celebrate. I did a quick ice bath for my legs to recover from what they had just endured. I knew the next couple days I would be walking funny since I had pushed my body to its limit. When I got to the bar, one of my girlfriends gave me a 26.2 sticker that I was looking forward to putting on my car.

While I was training for the marathon, the best benefit was that I was able to eat and drink whatever I wanted without gaining any weight. After I finished the marathon, I continued eating the same way without running nearly as much. Later, as my pants got a little bit tighter, I realized that I needed to adjust my intake of food!

The following day I was incredibly sore. I had known that I was going to be, but it was a little bit worse than expected. I was able to see my timed results for the marathon, and I was crushed that my time was over six hours. For your time to qualify for the marathon, you need to run it within six and a half hours. I barely made it and was really disappointed in my performance. One of my coworkers pointed out that I had done way better than those who never even showed up to try. I had gotten off my couch and managed to complete it within the time required.

28

I got a new car at the end of 2010. It was the very first time in my life that I had a brand-new vehicle. A couple weeks after I bought it, my mom came to celebrate Christmas with me in Chicago. She had taken the train, so I picked her up in the new car. She loved it just as much as I did. A perk of getting the new vehicle was having a free trial subscription to XM/Sirius radio. I started listening to country music again for the first time in years. I had grown up listening to country since it was what my parents listened to. Since I knew none of the new country music, I started paying attention to the artists names to see who I enjoyed listening to the best.

One day in the summer I was cleaning my car out while listening to The Highway. There was a special studio concert that they were airing by an artist called Eric Church. I had not yet heard many of his songs, but I was enjoying the acoustic performance. In between each song he would give a little backstory about the lyrics of the song. When he played a song called "Drink in my Hand," I had officially become obsessed with this Eric Church guy. During the song he had a moment where he let out a little giggle. This added to my new-found love of the man.

Four of us planned a girl's trip down to Nashville to listen to live country music. On the drive down, my friend Michelle told me that Eric Church was going to be in concert at a place called Joe's on Weed Street. I tried to get a ticket, but unfortunately, I was unable to purchase one. I was disappointed, but I knew somehow, someway

I would be at that show.

On a random evening home from work, I had a feeling that I would be able to secure a ticket to the show. I turned on my computer to look and immediately found out my intuition was right. I bought the ticket with no hesitation.

The acoustic show featured songs off his new album, *Chief*. Not only was he singing, but the person who wrote or co-wrote the song would be singing the first verse before Eric would sing the remaining part of the song. To experience the creative process of the songwriters as my first show was a true treat. My only regret from that concert was that I never got my boot signed. As I was walking out of the building, they were handing out copies of his new music. I couldn't believe that not only did I witness the best concert I have ever seen, but also received his cd. All of this for only $25 was unbelievable.

The marketing was brilliant, since it made me a fan for life. I was ready to purchase multiple tickets to see him wherever I could. Immediately, I bought a ticket to see him in May of 2012.

29

Life was going well for me. I was proud that I had accomplished the marathon. Mentally, I was releasing the grief that I had been holding over the last twenty-three years. My counselor asked me after the marathon if I felt if there was anything else I wanted to work on. She had believed that our work together was complete. She informed me it was her job to help people to the point that they no longer needed her help. The point of counseling was to work through things for a period, rather than forever. I loved that I'd experienced so much growth over these last six months and I was grateful for my happiness that came as a result.

While the beginning of the year had started out a little rocky, it was the hard work I had done on my physical and mental health that helped turn it all around. I was back in the dating world again. I even met a nice guy, a dairy farmer who lived in Wisconsin. I was not sure why I always seemed to meet men who didn't live close to me, but I was open to seeing how it played out. The dairy farmer and I met halfway between our homes in a town close to the Illinois/Wisconsin border. Our conversations were incredibly stimulating. He was well read, and I had a respect for him that I had not found in a long time. However, after our first meeting, he shared that he was not interested in dating me but wanted to remain friends.

Life was full between my full-time job, my part time job at Lush, training for the marathon, and volunteering for the Jaycee events. I had various groups of people that I made time to hang out with such as my church friends, my Jaycee friends, and other miscellaneous friends I had connected through the years. Dating was fun at this point too, but I hadn't found anyone that I wanted to be exclusive with yet.

One morning, I woke up from a nightmare and I had to comfort myself. In the dream, my dad was alive, and my mother was dead. It was so strange to have to wake up and tell myself, "No, Dad is dead, and Mom is still alive." While I was obviously happy my mom still was alive, it was an awful sensation to have to remind myself that dad had died. These types of dreams would always leave me shaken for days.

My mom traveled to Naperville to spend Thanksgiving with me. Having her out to spend a holiday was a big deal. This had been the second time in my life she came to me to celebrate the holidays. While she was there, she brought up a conversation that caught me off guard. She was insistent that if she were ever in a coma, I would not keep her alive. My mom and I had always had these types of discussions, but honestly it was too much for me to think of the possibility of her dying, and I didn't want to talk about it.

Afterwards when I talked to Renee about the heaviness of this, I could feel the anxiousness I'd felt when she had cornered me to have the conversation. I knew that I was still way too young to have these kinds of discussions but knew that my mom really needed to express her wishes to me.

I traveled to Michigan for Christmas. As we were heading up to spend the day with my mom's parents, I believed that I came home to spend the holidays with my grandparents. I had no idea how much longer I would be blessed to have them around. Christmas was hard for both my mom and me. While it was great to get to spend time with my grandparents, Aunt Karen and Uncle John, and Jenni and her family, it was hard to see them still have every one of their family members. My mom and I were all we each had.

The family tradition had been getting a dollar store item to give as a gift. That way, if you didn't have a lot of money, you wouldn't need to worry that the gifts weren't lavish. Then whatever money you wanted to spend, you could spend it on yourself. My mom asked me if we wanted to do our gift from the two of us, since each member of the family was getting it with their spouse, so it made sense if we went in on ours together. It was when she asked me that I realized why I struggled every year to attend the Christmas gathering. Christmas had always sucked for me being the odd person out. The rest of the family had been unscathed. This was never spoken, but more so what went on inside my mind. I appreciated having my mom who understood how holidays were always a challenging time for me.

It was great to get to spend time with my mom for Christmas. She would order our favorite pizza for my arrival. We would then sit at the kitchen table catching up. She could see how happy I was with life, and I told her I was the happiest I'd ever been. There'd always been this belief that the moment we were happy with how everything was going in our lives then something bad would be on the horizon. However, I was not willing to buy into this narrative again and vowed that 2012 would be my year.

30

I saw that Eric Church was going to be in Madison, Wisconsin, in late January. I asked the dairy farmer if he would be interested in going to the concert with me. He did not want to go, but he asked if I wanted to head to his place after the concert. This made sense since it would be easier to drive an hour to his house rather than make the trip back home to my apartment which was two and a half hours. I asked my boss if I could take a vacation day on Friday which she approved.

As I was driving up to the concert, I decided that I didn't want to call my mom since I was afraid she'd say something about me staying with the dairy farmer. Also, I didn't want her to worry about me driving so far on my own. I'd call her on Sunday when I was home. We hadn't talked on the phone in over a week and a half, but I knew waiting two more days wouldn't be a big deal.

The concert was everything I'd hoped it would be. There were pyrotechnics whose heat I could feel from my seat that started out the concert. It was beyond worth making the solo trip to see him.

On my drive to the dairy farmer's place, my ears buzzed from having been so close to the speakers. When I got close, I noticed that my cellphone reception was spotty. I had to call him since I couldn't find his house in the dark. I wasn't used to being in the country. He found me in my car and led me to his house.

When I woke up from sleeping in, he gave me a tour of his place and the farm. He asked me if I had ever milked a cow. It made me laugh since my grandparents raised cattle, but it was never something I had done. My mom had loved living in the suburbs, so we were never pressured to live a life that dealt with a farm. I thought it would be fun to try it out to see if I had been missing anything throughout the years. However, when I tried it, milk got sprayed on my shirt which ended my trial period.

We spent the day watching old television shows. Throughout the day, I looked at my phone to see if there were any notifications, and I noticed that my reception was still spotty. Occasionally, my phone would have service, but most of the time my phone did not have any reception, and it needed to be charged since the battery was running low.

My phone rang at 6:24 p.m. The moment I saw that it was Aunt Karen's name on the screen, my heart sunk, and my stomach plummeted. It was out of character for her to call me randomly. Immediately, I knew that this was the moment I had been dreading for years.

"Hello?" I said as I answered the phone.

My aunt responded, "Hi Trudi. I'm sorry to tell you, but the police just left Grandpa and Grandma's house to let them know that your mom died."

"What!?"

"Your mom had called in sick. One of her coworkers was trying to call her to check how she was feeling in the afternoon. When she didn't answer the phone, the coworker went over to the house. When she got there, she found your mom in her bed. It looks like she died peacefully in her sleep."

Shocked and at a loss for words I only responded with, "Okay."

"Are you with anyone or are you alone?"

"I'm at a friend's house now." I responded.

"Good, I don't want you to be alone. Where are you?" my aunt questioned.

"I'm out of town. I went to a concert last night and went to a friend's place after it. I'll need to drive back to my apartment in the morning. Then obviously head to Michigan."

"We can meet at the funeral home on Sunday. That way you can get into town whenever you can tomorrow."

"Okay. Sounds good." I spoke. I was in utter shock and wanted to get off the phone as fast as I could. Also, I knew that my phone was going to lose reception at any point. I did not want my aunt to worry more if the call were to drop.

"Okay, I'll talk to you soon. Please lean on your friend for support. I love you, Trudi." my aunt said with concern.

"I love you too. Bye," I said.

There I sat for what felt like minutes in silence. I was stunned and in absolute shock. What was I supposed to say? When I worked up the nerve to voice it out loud, I told the dairy farmer, "Well, this is awkward. My aunt called to inform me my mom died." The pain started to sink in a little bit as I voiced it out loud.

"I am so sorry to hear," he said.

"I can't believe this is happening." Then I just started sobbing.

He gave me time to cry. A bit later, he said, "You know Trudi, you don't need to stay here tonight. It might help you if you were able to be on your own. It would give you the opportunity to gather your thoughts."

As I weighed out the idea of being alone, driving in the dark, I knew that I couldn't get myself to go. My world had just collapsed, and I wasn't ready to leave the couch I was sitting on. Emotionally, I wasn't in a place to drive. I didn't want to navigate in the dark as I could tell I was not stable. Also, I didn't want to be alone and make the three-hour drive to an empty apartment. Even though it was strange and awkward for both of us, I could only hear my aunt's voice about making sure that I was surrounded by others.

Defeated, I asked him, "Is it okay if I stay? I'll leave first thing in the morning."

He confirmed that it was okay that I stayed, but defended his thought process again, "Yes, I just assumed you would want some time on your own."

I asked if he could hold me for a moment. I am not one who needs to be held, but I was just beside myself and needed to lean on him. After being held for a while, I moved so I could sob.

My mind was racing. Thoughts about the next several days were invading my mind. Since it was not my first funeral, I knew my days would be long and overwhelming. Both my brother's and father's funerals had so many people in attendance, but this time I would oversee greeting all the people walking through the door. My mom would not be there. Her body would, but this was who they would be all coming to see. This was all going to be on me. Ugh. I never wanted to face this day.

The other thoughts that played over and over were, "Why?" "Why me?" "Not again," and "I am all alone." I could not wrap my head around the fact that here I was only 34 years old, and every single member of my immediate family was now dead. How the fuck does this happen? Why was it my entire family? It was not fair that I had to lose my mom, too. I was not ready to face this world on my own.

The dairy farmer headed to bed early, and I joined him since I knew I needed to get on the road as soon as the sun rose. It was going to be a long day. First driving back to Chicago. Then packing for the upcoming week. Finally, the drive to Detroit. Sleep was necessary, but how in the world was I going to get my mind to shut off. I initiated sex with him but he told me that we didn't need to have sex. However, I was desperate to think of something other than the dread that was now my life.

I'd hoped I could fall asleep, but I just laid there watching the clock. Time stood still. There were a couple times throughout the night where I was able to sleep for 20 minutes at a time. Once it was 4:30 a.m., I started getting ready for the journey to Michigan to bury my last family member, my mom.

As the dairy farmer and I were parting ways, I thanked him for being so kind to me the night before. Being true to his nature, he gave me encouragement for the upcoming days without being sappy. He then gave me verbal directions to get to the highway where I knew the reception would work.

Before I got on the highway, I stopped at the gas station to fill up my tank. My phone finally had service, so I posted, "Asks/needs/wants prayers. Thanks." on Facebook. I chose to be vague at this moment out of respect for people who were not yet informed. The last thing I wanted was for people to learn of my mom's passing through a post on social media. My mom's sister would reach out to my mom's side. My dad's oldest brother, Bob, would be contacting everyone on my dad's side. It was important for me for people to hear the news directly from someone rather than reading it online. However, I knew that I needed immediate prayers.

After I made my post, I decided that I would start texting everyone to let them know personally from me. It was rather early in the morning, but I decided that I would send the text anyway. I did not have the energy to call and talk to everyone. It reminded me of calling to cancel my 11th birthday party. I was grateful that I was able to send text messages to help me spread the word to those I cared to let know. It was easy to copy and paste the message, "My mom died. Please pray for me." After I sent all the messages, I started the drive back to Naperville.

Since it was early in the morning, my phone was quiet for the first half hour of the drive. Then I started to get responses of condolences from people through text. Others called me to talk to me or offer to help in whatever way I needed. I answered the phone when I was up for talking. It was a distraction for me to not be alone in my thoughts or to have a break from crying. One friend offered to meet me when I got home to help me pack since I could not think clearly. Jenni told me that I was staying with her and her family. I never even thought about staying anywhere else but my mom's house, so I was thankful she offered for me to stay.

Shortly after I arrived home, a couple of my friends showed up. One friend was helping me organize what would be necessary to take with me. She has helped numerous friends in their time of grief. As we were getting everything together, Courtney and Rachel came over. As they listened to me express how I was already overwhelmed knowing what I was walking into, I shared the hardest part for me was that my support system was going to be back here in Illinois. While I knew that there would be so many people who loved my mom coming to visit, these would not be people helping me. It would be my job to comfort them when I was the one in anguish. I had an idea of how many people would be coming to her wake since I had seen how many people showed up for my brother's and father's funerals. Also, I knew that her students would want to pay their respects too. I felt the pressure. My mom had enjoyed people coming to offer their condolences, but for me this seemed overwhelming. As they listened, their faces showed their love and concern for me. It is not every day that a 34-year-old must bury her last immediate family member.

After I got all my things together for my trip, I headed over to my friend Will's house. I had called him on the way home from the dairy farmer's. Initially, I called to cancel our plans to see the production of *Joseph and the Amazing Technicolor Dreamcoat* the following day. The play had been my mom's favorite, so it was weird to have to miss it for her funeral. Then when I had him on the phone I asked if he would be willing to drive me to Michigan. I was not in an emotional state to drive five hours on my own. Will had been a huge support for me in the hard moments of my life. The drive to Michigan was rather quiet between the two of us. I was overwhelmed with the devastation of losing my mom. He was going through his own thing, so he did not interject much. Every so often people would call and if I were up for talking, I would answer the phone. Other moments when the gravity of what I was feeling became too much for me to bear, I broke down in sobs.

When we arrived at my cousin's house, she welcomed me with huge hugs. She was so gracious and loving to me, which was exactly what I needed. She had rearranged her children to sleep in her bedroom which allowed me to stay in her daughter's room. Will slept in her son's room. I was exhausted so after we had dinner, I decided to head to bed. When I went to get my pajamas on, I realized that I never packed any. I asked Jenni to borrow a pair. We had a laugh about me forgetting, which was needed to break up the heaviness. As I laid down to try to fall asleep, I checked my messages via text or Facebook. All the messages were kind, loving words which I needed at that moment.

31

We went to the funeral home to start planning the funeral arrangements. This time I would be making the decisions. When I arrived with Jenni, the others who had already arrived were waiting for us in the boardroom. My mom's parents, Aunt Karen, Uncle John, and my mom's best friend, Donna, were all there and embraced me with a warm hug. The atmosphere in the meeting room was very somber.

We had decided that two days for the viewing was necessary based on the history of my brother's and father's funerals. Also knowing my mom was a teacher for 40 years at Trinity and having a large extended family, it made sense to have the extended viewing availability.

When questions were being asked, I was being given the opportunity to answer. Both of my grandparents and Aunt Karen and Uncle John didn't say much. They were clear that they came to support me, but they didn't want to make any of the decisions. The only thing I knew was that my mom wanted a bowl of M&M's by her casket so people could have some. She had talked about that for years, wanting that present at her funeral.

I was asked about who I had in mind for pallbearers. I knew that I wanted to have some of her favorite former students that made a huge impact on her life. My other idea was to ask a couple of her coworkers who played a big part of her life offering her support in her teaching career. Also, I asked my Uncle John. Not only was he family, but he also had been so incredibly helpful around the house after my dad had passed away.

We were invited to pick out the casket. Remembering how strange the room was when I went to pick my father's casket, I asked Jenni if she would come with me as no one else was getting up to help assist. She accompanied me into the room. Searching through the room I asked Jenni if this was not the strangest room she had even been to in her life. I was on a mission to find the one we had chosen for my father, but I was not finding it. I asked the funeral director if the Lord's Supper casket was available. He found that he could order it for me. I liked the idea of my parents having the same casket with the detailed woodwork. My mom had liked it for my father, so it was only fitting for her to have one of her own.

We headed back into the meeting room where everyone was waiting for us patiently. We crafted up her obituary sharing the details that she was known for at the school. She had a M&M collection, organized the 8th grade trip to Washington DC, made brownies for the students, and gave herself the self-proclaimed title of the "Queen." Once we completed gathering all the details for the funeral, Jenni drove me over to my parent's house. She had given me the heads up that grandma and her mom had been to the house to clean up my mom's bedroom, so I did not need to see it the way it was left.

When we arrived, we were once again met by my grandparents and Aunt Karen and Uncle John. My grandmother had given me a file that had all the important information I would need in the days to come. My mom had gathered the documents from the purchase of the vault and land for the cemetery. Also, she had her will inside the folder which clearly stated that I was the sole beneficiary. Thankfully for me, my mom had organized everything, so I did not have to worry about the extra details. We went into her bedroom closet to pick out an outfit for them to place on her body. I chose one of her purple suits since she loved purple. While I have no idea what my grandmother had cleaned, I was grateful that it was not something I would need to worry about.

After we left my mom's house, Jenni and I went to a bar called the Hill Top to meet Donna. Donna wanted us to have a toast of Hot Damn in honor of my mom. Since Donna and my mom were Christian school teachers, they named it Hot Darn instead of the real name, Hot Damn. The bartender had told us that they only had 100 proof and neither Donna nor Jenni understood what he meant. In addition to the shot, I ordered a Captain and Coke while they ordered water. When he delivered the three shots, we toasted my mom and chugged them. I was talking about how I was holding up. Suddenly both Donna and Jenni admitted that they were drunk off the shot. I shared that I felt nothing and was ready for another drink. I am not sure if it was due to having a high tolerance or if it was because I needed the alcohol to numb the intense pain I was in.

It was a long day, and I was emotionally drained and exhausted. We headed back to Jenni's house. I felt the grief throughout my entire body. I knew that I was only at the beginning of an exceptionally long week. I did my best to get as much sleep as I could once we had gotten home. Once again, I took time to read the messages friends had sent to me. I reached out to the dairy farmer to let him know that I was okay but that I was worn out emotionally. Overall, I felt completely alone. My mom had been my other person for years and now I was in a place where I needed to do my best to remain as strong as possible to give her the proper tribute. The emotions were all encompassing and downright exhausting.

When I woke up Monday, I knew that I was heading towards yet another gut-wrenching day. I needed to head over to the cemetery to prepare for the arrival of her body on Thursday. As I made my way over there, my stomach was nauseous from recalling all the times we would go visit my brother's gravesite. I pulled into the main entrance and headed to the main office. When I entered the office, all the people who worked there were busy with someone else. Eventually they had me sit in a conference room by myself until one of the assistants could help me. I sat in this moment, angry that I was here at the cemetery by myself. I did not understand how everyone could think it was okay for me to do this by myself. Granted, I never asked any of them to come with me, but I really did not know how difficult it would be until I was sitting alone in this office of the place that I had dreaded for most of my life.

I nervously reviewed the documents as I recalled the conversation my mom had with me after my father's death. She inquired if she should buy her vault, so I did not need to worry about it when she died. I never realized she ended up buying her vault until my grandmother gave me the paperwork the day before. This meant there was not too much I needed to do in this meeting other than to let them know of the upcoming funeral I was having for her. Since my mom and I hadn't gone to the cemetery after my dad's service, I decided I would do the same for her too. Also, since it was the wintertime, it made it easier to not have everyone drive to the cemetery after the service.

Finally, the assistant came into the room to help go over the details. I showed him the documentation for both the land and the vault that had already been purchased. He checked the records, and we headed out to find the location so I could verify it was correct. At the cemetery, we walked to see my brother and father's headstones and stood there for a brief moment of silence. Then I looked up at him and said, "In three days' time, you will have all of my entire family here." He politely said yes. In total silence, we walked back to our respective vehicles.

The level of shock that was happening internally was higher than I ever have known. Coming to the cemetery and telling the guy that he would have my family really started to solidify that this was real. How in the world was I only 34 years old and my entire family was dead? We had been that family full of love, and then one by one, they all died. The grief was overwhelming.

Next, I made my way to Trinity Lutheran Church to meet with the pastor to set up the service. I had done this before with my mom. It would just be me meeting with the pastor. This was slightly different from my dad's situation since my mom had been a current staff member. She had worked closely with everyone in both the church and the school. Pastor Koy shared his condolences with me. We sat in his office and talked about my mom. He gave me some of the bible verses I could choose for the funeral. I asked for the brass ensemble to accompany the organist for the service. I had until Tuesday midday to let the church know what I wanted in the service so the bulletins could be printed in time. My mom had been interviewed in a contemporary service where she spoke of her faith months prior. The pastor asked if I would be okay if these were available to anyone who might want a copy. I was honored it would be available on cd for people.

As I was leaving my meeting with the pastor, Donna asked me to come with her to see something the students had done at the school. She had me peek out into the hallway of the 7th and 8th grade floor. All I saw was a sea of purple. The students were all wearing purple in honor of my mom since they knew she loved purple. It was touching and overwhelming to see the students paying tribute to their teacher in this way. I was touched by getting the opportunity to witness it.

I headed back to Jenni's home. My focus was to plan my mom's funeral to be an uplifting experience for those who attended. My mom's favorite song was "What a Friend We Have in Jesus," so I wanted that song included in the service. I also wanted the song "I Can Only Imagine" to be in the funeral since it had meant so much to me for my dad's funeral. Overall, I really loved the service that I planned for her since it was a celebration of her life. My mom's faith was a huge part of who she was.

Exhausted after heading to the cemetery and planning my mom's funeral, I decided it was time for sleep. Tomorrow would be the first day of viewing her body. Ever since my father died, I had worried about having to go through the process of burying my mom too. Now these next three days were all about facing my biggest fear head on. What I was feeling was heavy and draining my entire body. Rest was much needed.

32

Tuesday was the first day of the viewing. My cousin had taken off from work and we headed over to the funeral home together. The rest of Jenni's family would be coming later in the day. Jenni was going to be my support system to help me through the day and it was greatly appreciated. The family was invited to come an hour early to be able to have privacy to view the body before others came to pay their respects. My grandparents along with my aunt and uncle were waiting outside for me to enter the funeral home. When we walked in, we were greeted by the funeral director. He opened the doors for us to go into the room to view her body. The funeral home has a couple of different viewing rooms, however, each one of my family members were laid in state in the exact same room every time.

I was nervous to see her body since it made it real, seeing her lying in a casket. I slowly walked up with my grandma and grandpa to say a prayer and have a moment of silence. However, I quickly realized that it bothered me to see another body lying in the casket. There is something about a staged body that just does not compute for me. It is not them. It is only a body cavity. I stood there questioning what I should be doing and thinking.

My grandmother commented on how she looked good. I agreed with her even though this still bothered me when anyone say this. I really will never understand why anyone comments how good of a job they do making them look as normal as they can. It is still a dead body. We stepped away and allowed Aunt Karen to have the opportunity to view her sister's body. My aunt shared that she looked to see if the sadness she had seen on my mom's face after Todd died was finally gone. She was relieved to see that it was no longer there.

After I stepped away from my mom's body, I made a silent promise to myself. I acknowledged that this was going to suck. Not just the viewing and the funeral, but also the aftermath of dealing with her estate. It was going to be gut-wrenching and painful for me. I vowed to myself that at the end of this journey of grief, I would treat myself to a trip to Europe to get through every minute of the pain. I could go on an adventure after it was complete. Europe was a special place for my mom and me. Not only had we had gone on the trip to see the Eastern capitals, but also she treated me to a trip to see Rosey in Cyprus. In this quick moment I did not worry about the details of how it would happen. I knew that the best way to help me through this next horrific year was to make a promise to myself.

My mom had always prided herself on being strong for those who came to pay their respects at the visitation of my brother and my father. Somehow, I was going to have to step into a similar role. She felt as if it gave her the love and support she needed to get through these first several days. It was only after the funeral that she would give herself the permission to cry and grieve her loss. However, when people came through the funeral home doors, she felt it was her job to show them how she was resilient. I found it to be strange that my world had caved in and now I needed to console those who wanted to pay their respects. I was the one that was devastated that my mom was no longer on this earth.

The steady pace of people started to arrive, so I headed back to the viewing room to greet everyone. My grandparents were by the casket since my uncle John knew they could not stand the entire day, so he took it upon himself to make sure that they had chairs to sit on. I kept moving farther away from her coffin and closer to the entryway as the day progressed. It was not something I had done on purpose, but I also knew it was because I am uncomfortable with corpses. Remembering how my mother had touched both my brother and dad's bodies, I knew I would never touch hers.

A student of my mom's was one of the first students to come to the viewing. She was with her own mother. As we talked to each other, I observed that it was an incredibly awkward situation. I was unsure what to say to her and she did not know me. It was after this first encounter with my mom's student that I realized I needed to change the way I greeted all her students. While this was not my first funeral, this possibly could be the first time many of her 7th and 8th students were seeing a dead body. I wanted to make this not awkward for them or myself.

Quickly, I questioned what my mother would do. I knew my mom loved to hug everyone. Also, I knew that I needed to ask them a question to keep the small talk from being awkward. I decided to ask them what their favorite memory of my mother was. This would allow them to think of a memory of my mom and would give me a wonderful gift of hearing how my mom impacted their lives. When I used this approach with the next student, the encounter felt more natural. Well, maybe natural is not the right word, but the conversation flowed and helped both the student and me feel connected. It made it less weird talking to a complete stranger.

Asking my mom's students to tell me their favorite story was a creative way to learn about my mom's relationship to the kids. I heard several times how my mom had her desk taken outside by her class, the wheelchair races she had with another teacher, how much they enjoyed traveling to Washington DC with their 8th grade class, and her making the students brownies for winning their sporting event. When I asked one boy his favorite memory, he said the many lunches he had with my mom. Jenni was standing by me when he said this. She asked how often he had lunch with my mom. His response was every time he got in trouble. Jenni and I laughed so hard that he was open with how he was a troublemaker in the class. My mother always had a soft spot for the ones who were outcasts.

Within the first hour of the viewing, there was a line to wait to see me and then the body. My grandparents and my aunt stayed nearby for anyone who wanted to pay their respects. With the line being so busy, I was unable to step away to get any of the food that had been brought for the family. Jenni was given permission to bring some food into a side alcove so I could get a quick bite to eat along with a drink to stay hydrated. While I was eating, my Uncle Rick who was my godfather and his wife were standing there with both of their children who happened to be around the same ages as Todd and me. My aunt must have been uncomfortable with this moment since she said to me, "Now you are all alone." Her daughter looked mortified at this. I quickly responded with, "Thank you, I wasn't quite aware of this fact." I finished eating so I could head back to greet those who were coming to visit.

After seven hours at the funeral home, it started to clear out. People were respectful by leaving promptly at 8 p.m. It had been an incredibly long day and I was ready to head back to Jenni's so I could get some rest. Truly a very exhausting day. While it was wonderful to get to see so many people that loved my mother dearly, I was beyond overwhelmed and exhausted. I could feel the prayers that everyone was offering up to support me during this time. Even though it had been hard to sleep these last several days, once my head hit the pillow I was in a deep sleep.

When I awoke Wednesday morning, I still felt exhausted. The nice part was I had the entire morning to get moving before I needed to head to the funeral home. I knew there were going to be some of my girlfriends traveling to Michigan to support me. Courtney, Lisa, and Rachel made the drive from Chicago. Several other groups of my friends were headed to the viewing on Wednesday since they could also attend the funeral on Thursday. I was moved that my various support systems would be there for me when I really had not expected anyone to make the trip during the middle of the week. It meant so much to me for them to take the time off work and make the long-distance drive.

I got to the funeral home a little bit before the crowds would start to show up. I took a couple deep breaths to calm myself before another long day would start. It would be good to get to see so many who loved my mom and family dearly. I knew that my mom would have been touched to have seen how many people came to pay their respects to her.

There was a moment I was off in the alcove grabbing a drink when Mrs. Gould asked if she could ask me something. She had overheard some whispers that were bothering her. I asked her to please share what was troubling her. She'd overheard some people saying that my mom's kidney was the reason that my mom died. She wanted to make sure that I did not blame her for the kidney giving out. I reassured her that both my mom and I were so incredibly grateful for the gift of her husband's kidney. I personally did not believe that her kidney was why she died. I had nothing but love and admiration for her for choosing my mom to receive the kidney for a better quality of life. I told her to no longer listen to the hearsay. We hugged to give each other the comfort we both needed at that moment.

I was rather angry that people were sitting around the funeral home talking about their theories, not realizing that others could be impacted by their gossip. I had always witnessed the odd conversations people have in funeral homes, but I was less than pleased that it hurt someone I deeply cared about. I am not sure if people feel so uncomfortable in this environment that word vomit comes out of their mouths. Thankfully, I had not witnessed too much of the rumblings going on because I was occupied the entire time greeting people. It saddens me that I still had to deal with the thoughtlessness of some who wanted to spread lies so that they could keep from feeling any of their emotions.

The firefighter showed up to offer his support. I had not seen him in person since our trip to Cedar Point. There was some kind of spark between us, but since we lived in different states, nothing ever progressed. He was no longer in a relationship and had been single for a while. He had reached out to me when I had posted that my mother had died. We had been texting more in the last several days than we had in years. I knew that he was coming up to be a part of my support team. When I saw him, I was touched that he made it a priority to come and be here for me. After we visited, he sat in one of the chairs so that he could show his concern for me. He stayed in the room for a couple of hours. When he went to leave, he came to tell me he would see me at the funeral tomorrow. He left me with encouraging words to stay strong. He was going to continue to pray for me.

I was able to catch a glance of Courtney who was standing a little farther back in line. As I was continuing to greet those who were in front of all of them, I was hugging them all. I kept telling everyone, "I am a hugger" to reduce the awkwardness when I leaned in for the hug. When the girls got to me, Courtney gave me a hard time mimicking that I was a hugger. Courtney and I never would hug each other because it was not our thing. However, as soon as she said that to me, I understood why it was so important to have them there. These women got me. They knew me. They got that I was doing the best I could with what I had to do. They ended up staying in the visitation room until almost the end of the night. They wanted to go get food and I let them know that I would meet up with them as soon as the visitation was over.

Once it reached 8 p.m., people once again were respectful of our time and left. Those who were still there joined in a group prayer along with the Lord's Prayer. We headed to the kitchen to grab any of the food that remained since we would not be returning. I let Jenni know that I was going to head over to grab a drink with my friends. I would then head back to her place a little later. I knew that I would not be gone too long since I would need to be up early in the morning. I said goodbye to my grandparents and my aunt and uncle. Tomorrow was the day I was dreading the most.

I headed up the road about a mile to meet them in the restaurant. I thanked them for taking the time to come all the way to support me at this time. I was beyond grateful to have them there as they were my people. They asked me how I was holding up. I did not shy away from telling them how exhausted and emotionally spent I was. We did not stay too long since I knew that the morning would be here soon enough. I did tell them to make sure that they got to the church early, no later than 10:30 a.m.

I made the trip back to Jenni's house. Even though I felt like a zombie throughout this whole process, I was so happy that my friends took the time to travel to Michigan to support me. I immediately went to bed to get as much sleep as I could before we needed to head out in the morning. These last two days had felt like years. The hardest part of all of this was the one who I wanted to talk to the most was the one who I was burying tomorrow.

33

When I woke up, I needed to get moving as there was not a lot of time before we needed to leave for the church. This was officially the day I never wanted to have to face. It did not seem fair that I was only 34 years old, and I was burying my last family member. Before I fell asleep, I noticed the funeral was going to be on 2-2-2012. It reminded me how my mom had wondered at the beginning of 1988 what she would be doing on August 8th. What ended up happening was that she buried her son on 8-8-88. As fate would have it, her funeral would have repetitive numbers too.

Jenni rode along with me to the funeral. She had been unbelievable this week, my rock when it felt like I had no one else. Once I parked at the church, Jenni went to get out of the car, but I paused. I needed to say a prayer before I walked into the church. I prayed that God would be with me as I faced this day that I had been dreading. Jenni put her hands on top of mine to show her love that she was giving to me. After one more deep breath, I knew it was time to head into the church.

My mom's body was in the narthex of the church. By the time I walked into the church it was starting to fill up for the funeral. What I appreciated was that most people did not come to talk to me as they had over the previous two days. A few people greeted me, but most did not. While I was waiting, I reflected on standing in the same spot when my mom asked me to go see my grandfather's body for the last time. What made me smile to myself was no one pressured me to go look at her body when I had arrived in the narthex. I did say my last goodbye to her body as I knew the time was drawing near for a pre-service that was going to be happening.

Before the funeral started, the pastor had the family head to the Chapel of the Good Shepherd which was in the front of the church. Jenni held my hand as we walked to the front of the church. I was amazed that the entire church was full of people in every single row. There had to be over 1,000 people there to honor my mom's life. I knew that having this many people at her funeral would have made my mom so happy to know how loved she was.

The service in the private chapel was something I appreciated since it was a moment to have those who loved my mom the most. This chapel had not been there for either my brother or my father's funeral. It meant a lot to me to be with only my grandparents, my aunt and uncle, and Jenni before we would go sit in the front pew of the church for the funeral. I appreciated being able to have a private moment with the pastor and the family. We headed out to take our seats as the funeral was starting.

Even though I was in a church, it felt as if God had abandoned me. It felt like a cruel joke was being played on me. I had been one in a family of four. Now I was in a family of one. My mom had asked me about the good dying young, and she wondered why she was alive. Now she had gotten her wish, but that meant that she left me too.

As the service began, the tears welled up in my eyes. I tried to sing the first song but was quickly reminded why my mom never sang after Todd and dad died. My former band teacher from high school had some of the students play the brass for the funeral. I had always associated trumpets to be what you would hear when God called you home to heaven. I had hoped that the song "I Can Only Imagine" was going to be like it was at my dad's funeral, but instead there was a soloist that sang it. While in theory it was nice to have a live performance, I sat there angry because it was not what I had wanted. The church wanted to honor the woman by allowing her to sing. I was irritated since I wondered if this was a service for Trinity or if it was a funeral service for the family.

My mom had the nickname of the "Queen" at Trinity. During the sermon Pastor Koy said, "She was a good queen. You know what made her a good queen? Because the queen knew her place. She knew if there was a King by her side, the King received all the glory. The King received all the allegiance, not the queen. Rose knew her place. She knew she was subject to the heavenly King." He also acknowledged how my mom was a private person who was not one to enjoy the limelight. Also, how she was passionate for those who were less fortunate whether they were the underdog or did not fit in. While she was known for loving M&M's, they were like her, hard exterior shell, but soft on the inside.

The final song was the class song from my brother's 8th grade graduation, the perfect song to have at the end of the service. My mom had wanted for years to be reunited with her son and husband. We followed her body out of the church and headed to the entrance of the church to witness it being carried to the hearse.

We headed downstairs after the funeral to the luncheon. Typically, the church would have the luncheon in the Fellowship Hall. However, since they knew there would be a lot of people attending the service, they had decided to host it in the school gymnasium because it would be able to accommodate everyone. The Ladies Guild prepared the food for the luncheon so the family and friends would not have to worry about putting it all together. They did a wonderful job being able to have enough food for everyone that decided to come down to have lunch. My mom would have been so happy to know that not only did they close the school for her funeral, but also there were so many people that they had the luncheon in the gym.

I went through the food line first. Finally, I sat down to eat. A man, Bill, who my mom enjoyed spending time with was looking lost as to where he should go. He was not her boyfriend, but rather he was someone that understood what it was like to lose the love of your life. I knew Bill since he was my brother's best friend's father. My mom found it nice to hang out with him since they both deeply grieved their spouses. Plus, my mom enjoyed being around a man since she had spent a lot of time with women. I invited Bill to sit next to me. He shared how he was deeply saddened by my mom's death. He had gone over to my mom's house to sit in the driveway after hearing she had died. He sobbed at losing his friend after all these years. This deeply touched me to know that she had surrounded herself with a wonderful man her last several years of her life.

After I finished eating, I was able to connect with others that I had not had the chance to talk to yet. I went immediately over to Renee and her husband to talk to them. It meant everything that she had made the trip to be there. I really did not think she was going to be able to have work off to drive over for the funeral. Renee was pregnant with her first child. I had not seen her in person since learning she was pregnant. While I was extremely happy for her, I cannot lie that deep down I was incredibly angry how our lives were vastly different. She represented what normal looked like for friends my age. Not only were her immediate family members alive, but also, she was at a point in her life where she was growing her created family. It was painful for me to see how different our worlds were. I knew it was not her fault in the slightest that our lives were opposite of each other. Her coming to be there for me had meant everything to me. When she went to leave, we hugged one another. This was the first time we had hugged each other, which I pointed out to her.

After the luncheon, my grandparents and I went to the bank to sort out my mom's account. Once we finished, Jenni and I headed over to the bar where my friends were waiting. With being pregnant, Renee was not going to go, so her sister Teresa came in her honor. Renee's family was a second family to me. Robin, my friend from my high school job, was there, and while she had wished that we could see each other more often, I knew that this was not the way she wanted to see me. Angela, my friend from Naperville Jaycees, and her husband were there too. The firefighter also came to drink with me. When I lived in Michigan, I had never been to the Hill Top. Now I was there twice in the past week. I had been looking forward to getting incredibly drunk now that I had buried my mom. I had played by the rules to comfort everyone in their sorrow and now it was my time to drink until I could not feel a thing.

The firefighter kept my drinks coming so that I never had an empty drink in my hand. My cousin was very leery of the firefighter and his presence. At one point in the night, she told him that he better not hurt me. I thought that she was overreacting. I was incredibly grateful to have my friends with me while I got drunk. Angela and her husband left for the night. Jenni was ready to head home so she drove my car home. Teresa, Robin, or the firefighter told Jenni that they would get me back to her home safely. I had been flirting a little bit with the firefighter, but mostly I was just devastated with how my life no longer had my mother in it. The firefighter strong-armed Teresa and Robin that he would be taking me to my cousin's. On the drive to Jenni's house, the firefighter kept telling me that I was a strong woman. He promised he would be there for me in the aftermath.

When I got to my cousin's house, everyone was already sleeping. I got into bed and quickly fell asleep.

PART 2

34

When I woke up on Friday, I needed to get out of the state of Michigan. However, I needed to stop by the house before I headed out of town. Angela met me there to help me clean out the fridge and other things around the house. I wanted to grab a couple things such as money in her hiding spots, the safe, documents for her bills, and other various items. I deeply appreciated that Angela had been there to help me, as it all felt surreal. I could still smell the essence of my mom in the house. I finished up what was necessary for this right now since I would be back to deal with the house as soon as I was ready.

I stopped by the funeral home to collect some of the items before I headed back to Jenni's house for one last night. The funeral director had gathered all the donations that were given in honor of my mom. I kept the family tradition of having them be donated to the Todd Remer scholarship fund which my mom had started. My mom believed that all children needed to have a Lutheran education. She did not want the tuition to be a reason that they did not go. Leaving the funeral home, I said out loud how I never wanted to go there ever again. Five of my family members had gone through that funeral home. There was no reason why I ever needed to be back. Everyone in my family that went to Trinity was dead.

I had been away from home for over a week and was ready to

be home. I missed my cats and looked forward to being around their unconditional love. I needed to sleep in my own bed. The five-hour drive allowed me the time to process a little bit of the whirlwind of a week it had been. I was not ready to go to work on Monday, but I was looking forward to the distraction. This week felt way longer than a week. The emotions that I was experiencing made it feel like years. It was the beginning of a life that I was not ready to face.

It has been said that every loss you experience changes you. It made sense since I felt in this short period of time that I changed. When Todd had died, I had to be with and around adult emotions that I was not necessarily ready to experience. Now with my mom's death I was experiencing what my parents' generation typically dealt with. I knew this was heavier than most people my age go through.

When I got to my apartment, I did not want to be alone. One of my friends who had helped take care of my cats while I was in Michigan came over to keep me company. We ordered pizza from a place that reminded me of my mom. The pizza chain had just opened in the Illinois market, so it seemed fitting to have it in honor of her. After my friend left, I was finally alone. The tears fell from my face at an uncontrollable pace. The cats sat around me to give me the love I had been craving.

I now regretted my decision to not call my mom on the way to the concert. I would never get to speak to her again. Why didn't I call her? Who cares what she would have thought? If I would have known, I would have called her more often. I would never get to have these moments again. I listened to the voicemails I had on my phone. Tears flowed. She ended every call with a "Love you lots!" I missed her. She was who I wanted to talk to when I was grieving. Now it was just me.

I did not want to accept that this was my new normal. Everything hurt. My heart. My head. My eyes. I hated being back in this place. Had I not already experienced it enough in my short years? I needed to trust and believe that everything my parents instilled in me would be enough to help me through these next days. I was scared to see which version of Trudi would show up now that no one was left. When dad died, I drank excessively. I was reckless. I believed God would protect me. Now I wondered where the fuck God was. Hadn't I had more than my share?

I was alone in my grief. No one else was experiencing the gut-wrenching pain that I was. They were able to move on like nothing happened. Everything stopped in my world. It was a very dark place. Friends reached out. However, I knew that they could not relate. I was angry that I did not have a single person. No husband, not kids, not even a boyfriend. Nothing. Not a distraction to make me want to move forward.

Super Bowl Sunday was that weekend. Lisa and her husband were having their annual party and she reached out to see if I was going to be there. It made sense to go since I wanted to be around people. A few of my friends would be there. It beat sitting at home alone, but it was strange being there. People were carefree. I guess that is how I was the week before my life collapsed. Things were happening around me, but I felt like a zombie. Part of me that was jealous that they all could have fun and celebrate something so unimportant.

The next morning, I returned to work. It had been a week and a day since I had been there. I dreaded sharing what happened. I was not ready. When I had called my boss on the way to Michigan for the funeral, I had let her know that I did not want my personal life broadcasted throughout the office. I was hoping this would minimize the awkwardness that I would have to walk back into, but in hindsight it made it worse.

Monday typically was my busy day so I knew it would be easy to keep my head down and work. Also, I would need to clean up anything that my boss was unable to do with my unexpected leave of absence. She caught me up on what needed to get done. One of my coworkers, Joe, walked into my office to ask how my vacation was. Taken off guard, I snapped that I was burying my mom. He quickly apologized and gave his condolences. When I returned from my lunch break, there was a handmade card from him. Deeply touched, I started to cry. As a female coworker came into my office at the end of the day, she asked how my time off was. When I shared what happened, she gave me a huge hug.

Being at work was hard, but truthfully, being anywhere was hard. I was a little over a week out of losing my mom. Typically, I was always bored at my job, but it ended up being the perfect place for me to work. Other than Monday and Tuesday, I had a lot of free time to start making calls to manage my mother's affairs. I started canceling her accounts. A blessing my mom had given me was paying all her bills the week prior to her death. I never got any slack from my employer since I always managed to be on top of my workload.

The company I worked for was a private family-owned company run by two sons. Their father had been in charge for years, however, he stepped down years prior. The father was trying to give me his condolences but called me an orphan. This insensitivity shocked me. While, yes, both of my parents were dead, I was an adult which does not qualify me as an orphan. Why would someone ever say that to someone who was in intense grief? If you are unsure what to say, say "I am sorry for your loss."

After work, I made sure that I was occupied somehow. I had spent the last five years building up my network of friends and I utilized that network to stay busy. I would meet people out for drinks, go to dinner, or whatever anyone was up for doing. I did not care what. I was only focused on not being home all night long.

The firefighter drove out to Illinois a week after the funeral. It was touching that he made it a priority to drive five hours to be there for me. In my vulnerable state, I believed that he was sent by God to be my new family. He flat out told me that I was not in a place to be in a relationship. However, I could not hear this at all. We were intimate that night, which complicated it even more. Sleeping with him made me believe that he cared about me more than he did. I thought we were moving to the next level, which was not the case at all. He simply wanted to be there for me. We planned on seeing Eric Church in a couple weeks together.

When I contacted the manager, Emily, at Lush about my position, we discussed how I needed time off for a while. I was relieved to know that I did not need to put on a pretend happy face. Now I did not have an ounce in me to fake it. I was devastated and she recognized that. She needed to manage the sales floor and I needed to manage my life. The bonus was they were not going to let me go. I would be on a leave of absence indefinitely. I was allowed to participate in all the team meetings and any extra events. Having this time off would allow me to travel back and forth to Michigan without having to worry about coordinating it with Lush. I was going to miss the team, but knew it was the right decision.

I started to write thank you notes to anyone who gave in some way to honor my mom. There were various ways people gave such as donating to the Todd Remer scholarship fund, flowers, money for expenses, or supporting me in an extraordinary way. A couple weeks after the funeral, I sent out a batch of 256 thank you cards. It was a lot to write but it let me see how many people were generous in honor of my mom. A second batch of 82 thank you cards were sent out a couple weeks later. The church continued to receive donations after the funeral. They shared who contributed so I could thank them for their generosity.

Whitney Houston died two weeks after my mom. I really felt for her daughter. I overheard a couple friends talking about this where they said, "God doesn't give you more than you can handle." Immediately I responded with, "Oh yes He can." This is one of those platitudes that really bothers me. Platitudes are never helpful but are constantly said without a thought.

Over the first month after losing my mom, my feelings were

intense. None of my peers were able to relate. Several were working on growing their created family versus burying their last of the family they grew up with. My body ached from the heaviness of the loss. Being so damn angry all the time. What did I do wrong to deserve so much anguish? I desperately wanted the pain to ease its

35

grip on me, but it was relentless. I was heartbroken. I was shattered. Every moment felt as if it was an eternity. I felt absolutely no gratitude. The opposite in fact. No one knows how I feel. I felt sorry for myself that this was the shitty ass life that I had received. How was I ever going to move forward from this?

Life was slowly moving forward. I was doing my best to take it day by day, if not moment by moment. My world had crumbled, and I was not certain how I could ever be happy again. I focused on making sure that I was always busy with a friend. By spending time with friends, it gave me a little reprieve from the internal voices. There was something about being distracted that helped me from going farther into a spiral in my mind about how sad, angry, overwhelmed, and alone I was. I rotated between my church friends, volunteer friends, part time job friends, full time job friends, old job friends, and even my cousin Jodi. Jodi had lived in Chicago after college, but we rarely got together prior to my mom's death. It was good to have family in the area.

The dairy farmer reached out to me daily to check in on me. He was someone that I could be my full self with, mostly because I knew that he didn't judge me. He was straightforward. He had a positive attitude without being over the top. He would give me a different perspective without being fluff. What had initially started as someone I wanted to date ended up being the best support I could have asked for.

Anytime I caught myself laughing it felt incredibly foreign to me. I had prided myself on being a positive person right before my mom's death, but this felt like a completely different world I was now living in. It felt good to have a moment of happiness. However, it would be followed up with guilt. How could I laugh when I was in misery? It was a reminder of how overbearing the pain was.

The firefighter I met halfway between our places for the Eric Church concert. While I was thrilled to get to see Eric Church and the firefighter, it was another one of those distractions to keep me from spiraling in my grief. We grabbed dinner and drinks before the show. The firefighter did his best to make me smile even when I really did not feel like it. During the two-hour concert, I was able to let go of the heavy grief I was carrying to enjoy the show. This is when I realized that music helped me in this process.

When the one-month anniversary of my mom's death came, it was unbelievable what I had experienced in a month's time. From closing accounts to thank you notes to staying busy to keep from being depressed 24/7. It had been a month since I had been on my own and I was somehow doing it day by day. Interestingly, the one-month anniversary was also the four-year anniversary of my mom getting a kidney. She had been given three years and eleven months of not being on dialysis.

In her will, my mom said she wanted me to give a monetary gift to all of her and my father's godchildren. It was fun to be able to send them each a check for them to do something nice for themselves. Brian gave a portion of the gift to the Todd Remer scholarship fund which was so incredibly thoughtful. Others shared with me what they purchased as a gift for themselves.

There was a day when I woke up and could not muster the energy to go into work. I called off sick and went back to sleep. When I woke up, I knew that I needed to talk to my boss. I was terrified to call her since I was not actually sick. I really did not want to get yelled at for blowing off work. However, when she answered the phone, she was incredibly compassionate towards me. She knew I was grieving so she asked me if I had gotten out of bed yet. I barely could respond as I was ashamed. She asked if I called off because of grief. Once I stopped crying, I acknowledged that it was the reason I had. She made me promise that I would find a friend to spend time with even if it were only to go for a walk. Instantly, I cried harder since I was struggling with asking people for help.

I reached out to a friend. She invited me to come go for a walk with her and her dog. While we were walking her dog, she shared she had been thinking about me. I asked her why she did not reach out. She did not have a good answer. I asked her if I came to mind to please reach out since I might need to know that she was sending me her love.

36

I was touched that my boss knew what I needed at that moment. Yelling at me at was the farthest thing from her mind. She told me it was okay that I took a needed mental health day. I was so happy that she understood when I really did not understand.

When I was on my way to Michigan to plan my mom's funeral, I texted my former counselor. It was short and sweet and said, "My mom died. I will see you soon." I knew when my mom died that I needed to get back into counseling as soon as possible. What helped me in getting professional support was that we had already established a relationship. It helped knowing that I did not need to give the background story, as I did not have the strength to do so.

I was frustrated since I had been in the best place emotionally right before my mom had died. I graduated from counseling. Now to have to go back to work through emotions made me angry. It was not as if I caused this. It happened to me. It felt as if I was being punished through no fault of my own. However, I was choosing to get the support I needed. I had learned in seeing her in the months prior that I was strong enough to face my grief. As much as I was angry to go back, I knew somehow it would be worth it. I had seen how Todd's death came back years later. I did not want to carry the anger I was experiencing forever. Knowing that my peers did not understand, this would be my safe place to show up raw and vulnerable.

I went to my first session a little over a month after losing my mom. Not too much was said. Mostly tears were shed. It was comforting to have a safe space to openly cry in front of another human. No platitudes were stated. Just love and space to be me. She never told me how I should be feeling. The emotions I experienced on a constant basis were emptiness, despair, and deep loneliness. Every time I cried, I told myself that I was crazy and completely emotionally unstable. In the company of my counselor, I never felt judged for the deep pain I was expressing.

The counselor informed me I was experiencing compound grief. This made sense to me. It was not only the grief of my mom, but also my brother and father. Yes, I had processed my brother's and father's deaths, but it still added to my grief. Every death was a shock to me. When I lost my dad and then my mom, the trauma I experienced as a child was relived each time. My support system of grief was taken from me when my mom died.

The counselor shared at one of my first sessions that months three through six are typically the heaviest grief period. I did not believe her since my grief was currently intense. However, when I hit the three-month mark, I unfortunately realized that she had been right. The intensity spiked to a level I never imagined it would. She had tried to warn me that the moment your brain can no longer deny that your loved one is not coming back is when you experience grief at the top of its peak. I could not comprehend that I had been slightly numb when she warned me. The anguish let me give up the hope that my mom was ever coming back.

My counselor suggested checking out a grief support group. When I looked at the places she recommended, I was surprised that my church was on the list. I was shocked I hadn't thought of checking the church. However, I really was not able to process anything during this time.

When I showed up to my first GriefShare group, I was greeted by a woman that I had known through Stephen Ministry. Most of the people in attendance were widows, one male and the rest females. I was the youngest person in the room as everyone was around my parents age or older. There was a couple in the group who had lost their teenage son.

I'd never been to a support group before. There were several things that I appreciated the group offered. It was Christian based group in a Lutheran church. Weekly meetings started with an introduction to who you were grieving. It was interesting to me that most people were dealing with the loss of one person while I was the youngest person in the room listing off all my family members. A video was shown to showcase a different theme for the week.

What I appreciated most was everyone was going through their own experience of loss, so they did not pity me. They understood the pain in their own way. I did not have to hide what was going on for me. There was comfort in knowing that others felt just as shitty as I did. To be with others who were hurting with intense pain meant that what I was experiencing was normal, which contradicted the belief that I was starting to have that I was crazy. I was not crazy. I was exactly where I needed to be in my journey with grief.

One lesson that has stayed with me to this day is how your grief is like a fingerprint. There are no two that are alike. Hearing this helped me know that while we may have similar pain, each person's journey through grief is unique to them. It was a beautiful illustration that I have carried forward. While I may meet someone who has experienced a similar loss, it does not mean I know what they are feeling. Their relationship was unique to them and their loved one who died. As my relationship to all my loved ones was unique to me. This is helpful in understanding if you have a similar relationship with a loved one – such as a sibling and you both lose a parent. The grief can be quite different for you and your sibling. This is why grief is so hard on families: everyone uniquely experiences it.

I signed up to do another marathon before my mom died. I was committed to running it to improve upon my time. However, the moment my mom died, I had no drive to do anything. Especially training to run a marathon. The guilt lingered. Between not working out and eating poorly, I was starting to gain weight. I had spent several years working on being in my best shape, but now all I wanted was comfort food – pizza, wings, beer, wine, or chocolate, I ate or drank it all. My counselor asked me about taking the marathon off the table for now. This released the guilt I was carrying about not wanting to train. I was grateful that she helped release a small piece of the heaviness.

Someone close to me told me I needed to take an antidepressant. While I know it has helped several people, this is not something I felt comfortable taking. I was not depressed. I was grieving. I am allowed to grieve for my mom. It is a process. I asked my counselor if her professional opinion was for me to go on antidepressants. She did not rule it out completely, but she also understood I was not interested in taking them. She said if I did not make progress over time, she would recommend it, but currently I was in a state of heavy grief.

I was frustrated with being told I needed antidepressants. What I needed the most was for people to listen. I was doing the best I could by seeing my counselor, going to a support group, and reaching out to people.

I was trying, but it was a long hard road – and I was traveling it alone.

37

The first major thing I addressed was the ownership of the house. My mom had been proactive by adding me to the house shortly after my dad died. This would make things easier for me. Two months after my mom's death, I made my first trip back to Michigan to start dealing with cleaning out the house. The thought of going through everything was something I had dreaded for years. My mom had talked about how she wanted to clean out the house so I would not have to do it. However, she never did due to her health.

I asked a couple of people to help me go through the house. My cousin Jenni, Donna, Robin, and Steve came over to help. I asked the firefighter to help, but he was unable to help during the day. It bothered me how he constantly said that he wanted to help, but it only meant he wanted to help in doing fun events together.

Everyone took a different room to clear out. I was unsure how to decide what to keep and what to let go. As we went from room to room, I realized that this was not going to take as long as I had been dreading. Jenni was in the same room as me and when I would hold up an item, she would say yes or no to keep it or not. Her help was vital in helping me let go of many things that were unnecessary to keep.

Donna was in my mom's room going through things when I overheard her laughing hysterically. She came to show me that she found a VHS tape that had my mom's writing on the tag that said "adult movie" on it. Immediately I was grossed out that she found a tape that my mom watched to get her in the mood. Donna giggled as she asked me if I wanted to watch it. I yelled "NO!" While it may be funny to her as a friend, it was disgusting to me as her daughter. Her and Jenni kept laughing. I had known this should be funny, but there was no part of me that wanted to think of my parents having sex.

We had been talking about how I did not remember a lot of the stories behind several of the items we were going through in the house. Donna showed me a vase that she said my mom had received as a wedding gift. I was impressed that she had known this detail about the vase. She replied that she was creating a story to add meaning to the vase. I loved the creativity. It was this simple moment that taught me I could create a memory out of thin air to bring myself joy.

We found all the Star Wars toys that my brother had as a child. I knew my mom kept all his toys, but I never found my Strawberry Shortcake stuff that I believed she kept as well. I joked that you could see who my parents favored. It was hard for my parents to get rid of Todd's stuff. I was excited to find a box of all his WWF wrestling dolls. Todd had loved watching wrestling, so this was one of my favorite finds for the day.

Even though the trip home had been something that I stressed over, it ended up going smoother than I anticipated. I had a great support team to help me get through the house quickly and efficiently. Robin asked if I wanted to move a bed over to her house so that I always had a place to stay when I came into town. This was a perfect suggestion. It put my mind at ease to have options on places to stay while I was in town taking care of business. I had been staying mostly at Jenni's house, but this gave me a backup location if she were out of town.

Midday, the firefighter asked if I was up for seeing a Detroit Red Wing game that night. We agreed to meet at the casino before we headed over to the arena together. I was looking forward to seeing him. While I was annoyed that he was only available for fun events to hang out, it was helpful to take my mind off the heaviness present in my life.

The firefighter and I headed over to the Joe Louis arena for the game. While I was happy to see him, I was still processing what occurred during the day. As he got out of the car to head into the arena, he ripped his pants. It was so funny that it lightened up the mood. Thankfully, he had a jersey on so that he would be able to hide the gigantic hole. The seats we got were in the standing section. I had been spoiled with glass seats, but really thought the standing area was perfect since you had a head start getting to the lines when the period would end. It was a much-needed relaxing end to a long day.

38

Easter was my first holiday being family-less. As an adult, I never drove back to Michigan to spend Easter with my mom. Growing up, this was the holiday that my mom hosted with her family. I was struggling with the fact that it was my first holiday alone. My coworker, Nancy, invited me over to her house to have a few drinks with her and her sister on Good Friday. She had been my support at work. I was hysterical with grief. The anguish I expressed worried them. They hadn't lost anyone in their family, but they allowed me the space to express my suffering. I would have been embarrassed, but all I could do was release my sorrow. On Easter Sunday, I went to Angela's parent's house.

The firefighter's birthday is at the beginning of April. He went to a baseball game with friends and posted about it online. I noticed that he was with a girl that looked to be more than a friend. I asked him about her, but he was rather tight lipped about it. I was hurt. I could tell he was interested in her romantically. I was jealous that he started dating someone.

Trinity held an auction that I decided I wanted to attend. I donated some of my mom's M&M collectables to help raise money. In addition, I made her special brownies that she was known for.

After I had moved away, she started a tradition of bringing in brownies for the students when they won a sporting event. When I visited her once, we went to the grocery store where I saw her buy several boxes of brownie mix. When I questioned the quantity she was purchasing, she told me she would stock up when the brownie mix went on sale. I wondered if it was a certain brand, and it did not matter to her. Her secret was the pan she used and the added oil she put in the mix. It made me laugh that my mom made a big deal out of her brownie recipe and after all it was a box mix.

I stopped by the church and school to grab some of the items that were left in my mom's classroom, including her laptop. They students had put together a special book of letters that they had written me to share their appreciation of my mom. It touched my heart seeing the impact she had made on their lives. Whoever thought of this gave a gift to the students by allowing them a way to process their own grief in losing their schoolteacher. It also gave me a priceless gift to be able to read touching moments of my mom in their lives.

Angela had accompanied me to the auction. Before we left town, we met with the financial advisor that my mom invested with. I appreciated Angela being a second set of ears as he explained all the details. It became overwhelming for me at times. She asked questions when I was not sure what I needed to know.

At the beginning of May, Renee had her son! It was so exciting to get to meet him and see her in her new role of motherhood. When I got to the hospital, her parents were in the room. In celebration of his birth, her mom started singing "Happy Birthday." It was the first time I was able to sing happy birthday on the actual day of birth. It was so fun to see how life can change. When I first met her, she was not interested in having children. Seeing her with her son brought me joy to witness this moment with him.

One evening after I left my grief support group, I saw a picture of the firefighter at the Eric Church concert cozying up with the girl from his birthday celebration. Immediately I saw red. I did not handle it well. Yes, I knew that we were not in a relationship, but seeing him enter one hurt me deeply. In my rage, I sent him several angry texts. I then deleted him from my phone and unfriended him. Sleeping with him after my mom died made me realize it was a mistake. I had wanted more, but it did not mean the same for him.

I had other guy friends who had never violated my trust the way the firefighter had. The dairy farmer and I texted each other daily, but he never led me on. He was straight with me about not wanting anything romantic shortly after we met. The firefighter constantly told me that he adored me, but that I was not ready to be in a relationship. His reasons were valid with the distance, but it felt like a cop out. Seeing him with the girl was the last straw for me. He was toxic to me, and I was officially done subjecting myself to the added pain of him. He was unable to say no directly to me, so it was my turn to say no for myself.

Eric Church was in Chicago the following day. My friend Megan went to the concert with me, her first time seeing him in concert. She was an amazing support for me as I was a mess. However, once the music started, I was able to turn off the internal voices to enjoy the concert with my friend. There was something about his music and seeing him live that really helped me with all my grief. It was a way to escape.

While in the area, I stopped over at my parent's house to load the Ms. Pacman machine into the car. (Yes, we had a Ms. Pacman machine – probably considered an antique now!) I finished gathering all I wanted to keep in April, which worked out as this trip was on Mother's Day. I was already dealing with the heightened emotions of my first Mother's Day without my mom. Jenni was spending time with kids so they could honor her for the day. Aunt Karen and my grandma came to the house so that I did not need to be there by myself, which I appreciated. It had been a long weekend between the concert, as well as going to Donna's daughter's wedding, and then Mother's Day. Over the course of the three days, I felt all the emotions. I was ready to have a quiet night at home before the week ahead.

Some of us gathered in honor of Theresa's birthday at her best friend's house who was an artist. Her home reflected her artistry, with several stunning pieces of artwork throughout the house. There was a pond with lily pads in her backyard which I stared at to embrace much needed serenity. There was a labyrinth of rocks to walk through. This was not your typical Midwestern house. It was a beautiful way for all of us who loved her deeply to gather in celebration of her life.

I started getting massages on a regular basis after my mother's death. One of the girls that I worked with at Lush was a massage therapist. Carey had a massage table in her home. I loved the privacy and the comfort of being in her home. Every time I showed up, she gave me a long strong hug. Initially it annoyed me, as I am not one for hugs, but it was a true representation of who she is as an individual. She gave freely with her hugs versus my belief of wanting to take your energy. This helped with softening me up. She shared that getting massages was good for me. Touch was necessary for me during this grief period in my life.

Several friends from the Jaycees were headed to Mexico for our friend Rachel's 40th birthday. Twelve of us in total went to celebrate. When we arrived, we grabbed drinks to get the party started. I was slightly buzzed when I entered our room. The girl who I shared the room with and I were having a deep conversation about loss and grief. I was unpacking and went to put my toiletries in the shower. I slipped on the tile since it was wet from her rinsing off in the shower. I landed hard on my butt where I fell onto the edge of the shower which had a raised tile. My feet had been swept out and my left foot slammed into the wall. One of my toes was immediately throbbing. I knew that the others would blame it on me being drunk. However, right after I fell, my roommate almost slipped too with the slickness of the water on the tile.

We had been getting ready for a group dinner. When I showed up, they gave me Xanax to help calm me down. Being in pain made me long for my mom and her sympathy. I was completely out of it once they gave me the drugs. After dinner, a few of us were sitting on swings that were on the beach. I was so disappointed that while I had wanted to go on vacation to get away from all the drama, now I was ready to head home. One of my pet peeves is listening to someone complain over and over about something. The last thing I wanted to do was be the one who complained about being in pain, so I kept it to myself. I took a break to the lobby to text a few people and have a cry away from the others. A large black and bruise showed up on my ass and crept down my leg. Once I returned from Mexico, I went to the doctor who confirmed that I had a broken toe.

I guess you could say it was a painful time both emotionally and physically.

39

At the beginning of June when my mom's class graduated, the valedictorian of the 8th grade class did a tribute to my mom in part of her speech. She was going through the alphabet for different memories for the students. She used P, Q, and R in honor of my mom. P was for purple which was my mom's favorite color. Q was for queen which was her nickname. R was for Remer. When those who were in attendance shared with me, I was deeply touched. My mom would have been pleased.

The entire 8th grade class donated a bench in honor of my mom. They had her favorite bible verse put on the bench along with a rose emblem. The verse said, "For I know the plans I have for you, declares the Lord, plans to prosper you and not to harm you, plans to give you hope and a future," Jeremiah 29:11. There was a portrait of my mom on display that would be hung in the library. My mom had always wanted her portrait to hang in the library after she retired. While she never had the opportunity to retire, I was happy they honored her wish. After working at Trinity for 40 years along with being the vice principal for over 20 years, it made sense that she would want to be remembered in the school library.

Mid-June was when the estate sale was scheduled. I had already made plans with my friends to go to an all-weekend long country festival. When I asked if I was needed to be present for the estate sale, she recommended that I not be there. My two girlfriends Beth and Michelle and I headed up way north to Wisconsin. Beth's parents lived close to where the event was. We would have a bed to sleep in rather than needing to camp out with most of the attendees. It was a perfect distraction while the estate sale was happening. During the day, we would hang out at her parent's house. They spoiled us by making home cooked meals before we headed out to the concert. Their house was off a lake where they had hung a hammock in their backyard. I immediately claimed the hammock when I saw it. This would be a perfect location for me to find some peace and serenity.

We would look at the schedule each day to see when it made the most sense to head over to stay for the concert. Our seats were in general admission which allowed us to bring in our lawn chairs to relax and enjoy the show.

The afternoon the estate sale was happening was when it was time to lay in the hammock. There was a light breeze as I listened to the birds chirping. It was the best place I could be at that moment. I needed to allow my body and mind to relax. I had done so much to get to the point of being able to sell off my parents' possessions. Aunt Karen informed me that she and my grandmother stopped by to see if there was any memento they wanted to buy. I apologized that she felt that she had to pay for something. She told me it was her choice to go and not to feel bad. She shared the estate sale was busy.

The weekend in northern Wisconsin was exactly what I

needed. Being with my girlfriends listening to country music was perfect. Music was one way I was able to sit with my pain. It gave me so much comfort. This did not mean that I was not still grieving. However, it helped bring me some solace during this dark time of my life. Beth's parents bestowed so much kindness with providing a place to stay and incredible home cooking.

The following weekend there were other outdoor concerts that I attended. Naperville had a large festival called Rib Fest. The Steve Miller band played there on Friday. The next day I went to see Jimmy Buffet at a large amphitheater for the first time. I had heard that Buffet concerts were incredibly fun. I am glad that I experienced it, but I never need to see another concert of his. His one song about fins I found to be a crowd pleaser, but to me it was strange.

Time was continuing. I was still utilizing what I could to walk through my grief. I knew that I still had a long way to go.

40

I arrived at the GriefShare support group a little bit late one evening. They had already started going around the circle sharing who they were mourning when I got there. I sat in an empty chair between two people that I had never seen there before. This evening it was a packed room. The woman to the left of me explained that she had not lost anyone to death but was there to support her friend who had lost someone. She did acknowledge that her daughter was in jail, so she was grieving this. My internal reaction was immediately anger. It was my turn to share who I had lost. I explained that I had lost my brother, my father, and my mother. The woman to my left then tilted her head. This always signaled sympathy when one tilted their head. My anger flared even more because I had always felt safe in this space to share my grief since I was surrounded with others who understand the pain of grief. However, I was instantly taken aback with her tilting of her head in this sacred space.

The woman to my right was at least in her mid-40's. She had lost her mother. She then went on a tangent about her strained relationship with her mom because they fought about her high school boyfriend when she was younger. While she was sharing this fact for over five minutes, internally I was contemplating if I had walked into a twilight zone this evening instead of the grief support group. If she had issues for over twenty years with her mom, why didn't she go to therapy? Overall, I realized I had been so triggered by the woman without any dead people that my tolerance was low for listening to bullshit I couldn't care less about. When I left the group, I hoped the woman with no dead people knew not to come again.

However, she did show up again. What made it worse was her friend she tagged along with that was grieving did not come. When she spoke, she shared how she was grieving not having her daughter around. I was flabbergasted that the leader did not do something about it. It was insensitive to sit there listen to her talk about how she was struggle with her daughter being locked up. She was still capable of seeing her. I was not capable of seeing my mom. I understood that she was grieving, but it was not the same type of grief.

How were we supposed to support her when none of us knew what it was like to have a loved one in jail? She was not able to relate to us either since she could not comprehend what it was like to have the loss in the finality of never speaking to our loved ones ever again. The videos we watched had to do with grief through the loss to death, not jail. I was fuming with anger that this was being tolerated by the leader.

After the meeting, I waited for everyone to leave the room except for the leader. I expressed that I was struggling with the woman with no dead people being allowed to participate in our meeting. The leader responded that the woman was grieving. Because she was grieving, she was welcome to any of the meetings.

I disagreed and stated it was not the same type of grief. What shocked me is the leader told me I could not compare my grief and say that it was more than hers. I was dumbfounded as to how this leader was not listening to anything that I was saying. I politely acknowledged again that I understood that the woman was experiencing her own grief, but it would serve her better to be with others who understood what it was like to have someone in jail or prison. I even brought up how the videos did not relate to the grief that she was experiencing. It did not matter what I said since I continued to be shut down for expressing my disappointment. I told her I did not know if this was the right place for me to be anymore. The leader hoped that I would not make that decision.

After this encounter, I had my counseling appointment. I wanted my counselor's opinion since I was made to feel as if I was completely wrong with the leader. When I witnessed my counselor mirror the same reaction I had, I felt validated in my anger. My counselor went on a longer tangent than I had anticipated. She kept saying how wrong it was for them to allow her to participate. She encouraged me to go and politely say that I was troubled that she was there. The key word being politely. I was not to go off with spiteful angry words. She helped me prepare what to say in a respectful manner.

For the third week in a row the woman was there for the grief support group. Once again, she was there without her friend. I was getting nervous to speak up and start the conversation. There was only about ten minutes left of the meeting when she shared with the group. She said, "I hope that no one is offended by me being here." She had revealed that not only was her daughter in jail, but her son was gay. I fucking lost it. An anger I never knew existed shot through my whole body. We were in the walls of a Christian organization. Saying she had a gay child felt as if she was justifying those with a closed mind to agree to the sinful nature they believed it to be. It disgusted me to my core. She went on to say that her children were not who she had raised them to be. She felt as if she had "lost" them. I could not believe the bullshit that came out of her mouth. I was beyond livid she would use that as her reasoning to be justified in her grief. It showed me she was a bigot. Her son's sexual orientation had nothing to do with anything other than her refusal to love him for being himself.

What shocked me even more than the words that came out of her mouth was that every single person in that room acknowledged her, saying, "We know you are grieving," and "You are welcome here." Most of the people were a minimum of twenty years older than me in this room. I spoke up, saying I had a problem with her being there. And that bitch said back to me, "Is it because my family is alive and yours is dead?" My quick response was, "Pretty much." The cowardly leader said, "Thank you for sharing." I was in absolute shock.

I immediately walked out of that room as quickly as I could. I never returned to that grief group. I had lost three family members to death and was in need of a grief group to support me. However, the leader thought someone who had a loved one in jail needed support in the same space. There is a belief in the Christian community to help everyone who is in need. While I understand this, it is not loving to those who are being violated. They did not consider the damage that could happen to someone who is too afraid to speak up. The fact that I was the only one to stand up alone was despicable. It pushed me back to the feeling of loss that I had come to find solace for. It mimicked the feelings I had when I found out my mom died.

I sent an email to the church, explaining the situation in detail. Here's an excerpt:

> The website says "Are you struggling with the death of someone close to you? GriefShare is here to help." Those are the first two sentences on the website. Nowhere in that sentence or the paragraph explaining what GriefShare is does it say for all types of grief situations. For me – THEY ARE DIFFERENT! I do not get a choice

ever to have a relationship with my loved ones again. She has opportunities that I simply do not: the chance to spend holidays with family, send a birthday card, or talk on the phone. She has the hope of getting them back in a restored relationship, and while my family's relationships were not strained, I can do none of those things. This was NOT a choice my loved ones made. It is difficult to sit in a room where it is supposed to be a safe place where others can empathize with me rather than sympathize with me. The woman with no dead people can only sympathize. Period. She does not know how I feel. She will not, until she has lost someone, anyone to death. Nor do I understand how she feels since she can talk to her loved ones (even though it might be difficult or strained). We are not in the same place. I feel/felt violated. And to be flat out honest I am still angry to this day that the needs of this group were hijacked by the leadership condoning this woman's "grief" to be on the same page as the grief of death. Just since the word grief is used in the title, does not imply all types of grief should come to GriefShare. If someone lost their job or went through a divorce and came to GriefShare since they were grieving a loss, I believe they would be encouraged to go to a more appropriate support system where they are able to get practical and insightful ways to deal with their life struggles.

I am deeply saddened that I had to leave a place that was meant for me to go. I have lost a loved one to death. Actually, I have lost three immediate family members to be exact. Here is the thing...I am outspoken so I will say how I feel. I spoke up to the leader and to the group and was made to feel I am the only one who felt this way. So, I left. I cannot be in an unsafe place. I cannot be angry at a woman when I need to be angry at my situation and continue to walk through my process. I have waited over a month to calm down and be rational in what I had to say. However, everything I am expressing has been my exact same view since day one. I realize that more than likely nothing will benefit me from speaking out about what is going on within this group, but I feel I need to stand up for the individual who cannot stand up for themselves and say that this is just wrong. It truly is apples and oranges. I feel the need to say I believe that the leadership has lost sight of the purpose of this group. I believe that in a church environment people feel we need to help everyone even if the outreach program is not meant for them. All churches cannot do all outreaches for all their members. However, I feel they can direct them to an appropriate environment that will suit them best.

I am struggling with my decision to leave a Christian based support group because I wonder why God has let my whole family be taken at such a young age. I wanted to go to a God-fearing group so I could be surrounded by God's Word when my biggest struggle is my faith through this devastating loss(es). I had hoped that could be my own church. However, I cannot tolerate having to listen to someone's life's complications of feeling they have lost their expectations of someone when I am trying to cope with the loss of a loved one (or three) to death. I am hoping that God does help me on this journey because I truly need it. I am hoping He can lead me to the right environment where I can have my needs met. My faith has been a struggle because while I know in my head that God is there for me, it is very hard to trust and feel His love through this. Which is why I had liked going to my church for this support.

I will be honest, I don't think I'm wrong, and I don't think there is anything you can or will be able to do. I had to voice my opinion. Even if that means I do not get a response, I had to speak up for those who can't speak up themselves.

What ended up coming out of the situation was that they ended up changing the name of the group from GriefShare to GriefCare. Since GriefShare is a ministry that follows a certain program, they would not approve of having people at their meetings who did not have a loved one who passed away. It was a small victory, but I was proud of myself that I possibly helped someone who needed true healing to avoid this group. They also changed the verbiage on the website to acknowledge they were allowing anyone with any grief to participate.

Being honest, this was my own turning point with organized religion. I had seen enough throughout my childhood and now as an adult. It was not about supporting your neighbor as yourself.

41

After no longer being in a grief support group, I wanted to try out a couple other ones to see the one that would be the right fit. One was at the local hospital. It was a quite different style since it was not faith based. People had various views on grief. The room held a different energy. I had been used to everyone believing their loved one was in heaven, but for those who had no faith, it felt so final. With limited places to go I went for a couple of months. The couple who had lost their son ended up being there once. We talked for a few minutes after class, but I was uncomfortable that they were there. I ended up taking a break from this one too. There were a couple groups that were starting in September.

July was the six-month mark of being completely on my own. A friend of my mom had befriended me. When I reached the six-month mark, she said, "You seem stuck in a place between the logic of knowing the 'right answers' but feeling all the raw pain of so much loss." It was perfectly stated. I was taking care of myself by seeing my counselor and utilizing a support group. Yet it did not take away the anguish I was experiencing. I desperately wanted to feel good, but the grief had its hold on me. There were moments where I was to come out of the morass, but it was still currently where I resided.

I went to Michigan over the summer. When I went to Trinity

for a service, it was strange to be the only Remer there. My grandfather had been a lifelong member. After the church service, Donna took me to see the portrait of my mom hanging in the library. I teared up when I saw it. My mother would have been so proud. We also went to see the bench her 8th grade class donated in her honor. It was a little overwhelming to have two family members who had memorials at the church.

For my birthday, I listened to my mom's voicemail of her singing "Happy Birthday" to me. The year before, I had a jammed packed day, so she left a message of her singing to me. To this day, it is my favorite birthday tradition. Hearing it made me cry, but I am so grateful that I will forever have my mom singing me happy birthday.

At the beginning of September there were a few other Grief-Share groups located at other churches. Since they went by a scheduled curriculum, there was a start and end date. I had called two different locations to ask if they allow people who are not grieving a loss through death. Both were rather shocked I would ask this question. One even commented that even if it were the death of a pet, they would not be allowed unless they lost a human too. Knowing this boundary was in place brought me comfort. The first one I checked had a good vibe to it, but there were so many people present that it made me a little uncomfortable. The second place I checked out was perfect for me. There were fewer people which made me appreciate the intimacy of the group. I decided to attend the second group for the course of the next several months.

One woman in the group had lost multiple people. I am sure that having her there was why I wanted to stay with this group. It was easier for me to relate to her. She was raw and honest with how hard it was to lose multiple people. There were a mix of people who had lost parents and spouses. Even though they were older than me, the age gap was not as great as it had been at the previous one. I fit right in. Over the months, I was grateful that I was able to deeply connect with everyone. I never had the connection with the people at the Trinity GriefShare as I had with this group of people. In the end, it worked out that I changed locations.

During the fall I kept myself busy with different events. One was the second annual girl's weekend in South Haven, Michigan. We changed Lisa's bachelorette party into an annual trip with the usual women that hung out. While I focused on being involved in a lot of fun events, I did this to help increase the moments of happiness in my life so that I could keep walking through this process.

42

I went back to work at Lush in June. However, that was short lived as both Emily and I became quickly aware that I was not ready to be back. I was immediately sent back on a leave. In September, I reached out to Emily letting her know that I was ready to get back to work. I had noticed that I was able to see outside of myself and care about others' needs. Since I had jumped back in too soon the first go around, she put in more boundaries before she would let me on the sales floor.

If I wanted to work there again, I needed to write up a plan of action on the three areas of customer service, maintaining a positive attitude, and a safety plan. Including how I was going to handle myself, so I did not negatively impact the sales floor. Once I completed my action plan, we scheduled a meeting with Emily and the soon-to-be new manager. They prefaced the meeting with by expressing caring about my well-being along with needing to be mindful of the team. I do not really recall the meeting other than I am sure I practiced not rolling my eyes. Being business minded, I understood they had to meet certain expectations. However, this seemed to be a little much. I wanted to work there so I was willing to jump through this hoop. The Christmas season was quickly approaching which was my favorite time of the year to work.

I was given a strict warning that they were not going to be compassionate towards what was going on in my personal life. They had been willing to give me more time off if it was needed, but if I chose to return that I would be treated as if I was good to go. By the end of the conversation, I was added back to the schedule on Thursday evenings only. Once they had regained confidence in me, they would reassess about giving me the opportunity to work more shifts. How perfect was this? I was able to work one shift a week and still have the weekends to myself. This meant that I could be back without being invested in the drama the leadership was creating.

I was slowly making my way back to "normal," or at least as normal as my life could be now.

43

I headed back to Michigan in November since it was my mom's parents 65th wedding anniversary. It was a huge accomplishment to celebrate 65 years together. They were a beautiful representation of love lasting throughout the years.

Afterwards, we headed to the fellowship hall for some desserts in honor of them. I had a moment where I was overwhelmed by the fact that both my mom's parents were alive celebrating this momentous occasion, but my mom was not there to celebrate too. I was standing off to the side when my grandfather came up to speak to me. My grandpa was a man who did not talk too often, but when he spoke you would listen to the wisdom he was bestowing upon you. It meant everything to me that he came over to keep me company. My family consists of strong women who were supported by their husbands. The men observe what is going on to be of assistance in the down times.

I had received a voicemail from a neighbor of my mom's that told me something needed to be winterized to the house. I had no clue what he was talking about, so I called Steve to see if he would be able to meet me at the house before I left town. When we both arrived, I let Steve know that I was told I needed to blow out something. Steve laughed a little bit and then explained that it was something that needed to be done to the sprinklers so that the pipes do not freeze. He showed me where in the house it was and told me that he could take care of it for me. I was so grateful that he could help me with it.

While we were catching up in the kitchen, he asked me if I had any plans for the house. Did I want to sell it or something else? I let him know that I was currently unable to sell it as I was emotionally attached to the house. My dad built the house and did the addition to the kitchen. However, I had no idea what I wanted to do. I did not want to make any major decision until after the year anniversary.

He asked if I would be open to him possibly renting the house for him and his family. This was the best-case scenario for me. However, he shared he would not be able to move until his mom was ready to sell her home. His family had moved in with his mom after his dad passed away. He was hoping his mom would be ready by mid to late 2013. If it would be something I could wait for, he wanted to be considered to rent the house. I didn't hide my excitement and told him it was a perfect scenario for me, and I would happily wait. It felt great knowing that somehow everything would fall into place.

Three days after that conversation, I received a text from Steve that said, "You're never going to believe this, but my mom wants to put her house on the market." He was right, I could not believe it. Instantly I was tearing up because I knew this was a God thing. We talked on the phone and he told me that he could possibly move in by early spring. This was a perfect situation since I did not want to sell the house and I trusted Steve to take good care of it.

As it unfolded, he ended up moving in February which was right after the year mark. It all worked out for everyone's greatest good. When we figured out what the rent was going to be, we happened to have the same dollar amount in mind. It gave me such a sense of peace to know that we were on the exact same page. It gave me even more confidence that this was the right decision for us. We have had an incredibly commutative relationship where we both feel blessed by the other. It absolutely was a God thing.

Thanksgiving rolled around and I was less than excited to celebrate a holiday that was all about being thankful. This had been by far the worst year of my life. How was I to be thankful about needing to live in a world without a family? I started the day at Lisa's house. Our friend group went to her house to watch the turkey trot race that passed by her house. Her husband made Bloody Mary's to get the day started. As everyone started to go to their families for the holiday, I headed over to my cousin Patric's house. Patric had lived in a suburb close to me years prior but left for a couple years. He had recently moved back, and I was thrilled. His wife was so nurturing to me.

Michelle and I went to Nashville to see a hockey game and a football game in December. Since Michelle's work gets busy at the beginning of the year, she wanted to do a trip before the craziness began. I wanted a distraction so I would not wallow in knowing that it was about to be Christmas. We were unable to see a hockey game since the NHL was on a strike. Instead, we went to the Ryman Auditorium.

The season was thick with everyone posting their happy shit on Facebook, which was getting on my last nerve. I asked my coworker if he could organize some pictures for me. He agreed before he knew what I was asking him to do. I sent him pictures of Todd's and my parent's gravestones. Then I asked him to put a holly border around the pictures. I wanted it to say "From my family to yours."

He created it for me, and I posted it. It was inappropriate, but for a moment it made me happy to share my truth.

Knowing my situation, many people had invited me over to celebrate the holiday with them and their family. I chose to spend the day at Lisa's house with her family. We did a gift exchange with her brother and sister-in-law and played games late into the evening. I had always thought that I would go to Michigan to spend Christmas with my grandparents, but this year I realized I always did it for my mom. I no longer felt the pressure to make the drive home. Throughout the year, I had driven back to Michigan more than I ever had in the past. It was nice to have a break from making the drive in the winter.

The last two things I needed to get through were the anniversary of my dad's death and finally New Year's Eve. As I approached the New Year, I was elated to no longer be in the worst year of my life. Even though it was not going to magically get better as soon as it turned to 2013, I knew that none of my family members could die. Therefore, I was thrilled to get into the new year.

44

In preparation for the year anniversary, I wanted to make sure that I was with people for the day. In meeting with my counselor, I shared my struggle with it being a year since I had talked to my mom. I felt guilty it had been a couple weeks before she died. She asked me if there was anything I wished I had said that I didn't say. I thought about it and honestly replied that there was not a thing I didn't tell her. Her response gave me the closure I needed by saying what a blessing that we left nothing unsaid. After we lost my dad and brother, we understood that there is no guarantee of tomorrow and never hid behind the fluff. There is power in always saying what needs to be said so that if your loved one dies, you don't have any regrets over things not said.

Throughout the year, the dairy farmer had been a constant support. He would text me daily checking up on me. His no bullshit attitude was something that I had enjoyed having in my life. He was positive without being sugary sweet. I felt blessed that I was with him when I found out my mom died. He was exactly what I needed because he did not get weird when it was awkward. He also did not tell me that everything was going to be alright. He was quiet with a loving supportive presence.

The first-year anniversary was on a Sunday. My mom had passed on a Friday. When I showed up to work on Friday a year later, we were informed that a female coworker had died. It messed me mentally. It might not have been the same day, but it was similar timing. When I realized that she was the same age as my mom when she died, I was triggered and lost it. My workplace was concerned with how all the employees were handling losing our coworker. They held conferences for us to be able to openly discuss the emotions we were experiencing.

My boss knew the year anniversary was coming up, so she checked on me to see how I was doing. I tried to play it off, but when two different bouquets of flowers were delivered, I was done for the day. Steve and Angela wanted me to know they were thinking of me, so they sent me flowers. They meant well, but I was getting trigger upon trigger that day. A coworker had seen the flowers and asked what the special occasion was. Responding with the anniversary of my mom's death meant I was going to receive the dreaded head tilt. At this point, I'd had enough. I asked my boss if I could go home since I was mentally fucked for the day. She allowed me to go home to take care of my mental health.

My friend Amy wanted to do something to support me on the anniversary death date and asked what she could do. I asked her if she would attend church with me since I did not want to go alone.

She had been raised as a Jehovah's Witness, so going to a church was the last thing she wanted to do. However, she went with me, and I let her know that this would have meant a lot to my mom, having a non-believer go to church with me.

The church service was good. I realized when I was there it was the first time I had been back since my confrontation at the GriefShare group. In the afternoon, I headed over to Rachel's house where all my girls would be. We all brought a bottle of wine and played games. We laughed so hard it helped me forget the reason everyone was there. I felt a sense of relief and joy that I'd made it past all these firsts without my family.

A week later, I was talking to a friend saying how my cat Abby was not cuddling with me anymore and that I would find her in strange corners. My friend told me rather abruptly that Abby was going off to the corner so she didn't need to die in front of me. Shocked by what he said, I yelled no way. He said that this is what animals do. They're strong until they can't mask it any longer. When I got home, I realized that she felt colder than normal which let me know that he was possibly right about the situation.

Monday is my busiest day at work, so I waited until Tuesday to take her to the veterinarian. I dropped her off at a veterinarian on my way to work. They were going to run some tests and would call me as soon as they had results. I cried having to leave her, but knew she was in the best care. Two hours later they called me to share she was riddled with cancer. They let me decide what I wanted to do, but they told me that the most humane thing to do was to put her down. I didn't want to have to do this but knew I would never be ready to put her down.

I left work a little early for the appointment and to say goodbye. I cried hysterically from the time they told me until I got to see her. I told a couple of friends what was happening later in the day. Rachel offered to be there with me when they were putting her down. I said it wasn't necessary, but she told me I shouldn't do this alone. I was thankful that she knew better than I did.

Abby was my first pet. She had been with me through so much and I was absolutely heartbroken to have to let her go. She was there for me through my divorce, my dad's death, and my mom's death. She taught me all about unconditional love. Losing Abby felt even more painful than my mother's death. I think it hurt so bad because I was responsible for her care. It had been a rough year and I was starting to wonder if it would ever get better. I was exhausted from being in constant pain with grief. I wanted 2013 to be a better year, but it was not headed that way quite yet.

45

As time progressed, I started to think about that promise I made to myself about a European trip. I had taken care of all the details with the house and even had renters in the home. I was past the year mark, so it made sense to daydream about my month-long vacation. As I shared with friends, they put a new idea in my mind. Why not go for two months, or better yet, three months? I loved this idea. I was never going to be able to take a month off so why not maximize my time by going for three months? I realized if I waited another year, I would have earned another week of vacation that I would be paid out for. Knowing I had put in my time at this company, I was willing to wait one more year before I quit the job. In the meantime, I would start to travel on shorter stints until the timing was right. This would give me a little bit more time to make sure I was emotionally ready to be away for so long.

I befriended a friend of Renee's brother, Sherry, who was in his master's program years earlier. She had moved to Calgary after she had graduated and posted beautiful pictures of Banff National Park. The more I saw them, the more I needed to see it for myself. Calgary seemed to be the perfect place to travel to. I would know someone, and I would be able to do a portion of the trip solo. I wanted to spend time in the city so I could see a hockey game and I wanted to head out to the mountains to see the beauty for myself. With the completion of the NHL strike, they extended the season into April. This meant I would be able to visit when it was not freezing cold.

The day of my flight, the airline I was flying had a company-wide computer issue. All the planes had been grounded when the malfunction happened. This delayed my flight indefinitely as they were doing everything through paper tickets.

After several hours, I was given an option to switch to another airline or wait until the following day to leave. I chose to switch airlines, knowing there was a possibility that my luggage would not make it there.

I arrived in Calgary after midnight. Since the day did not go as I had anticipated, I met Sherry on her lunch break the next day before I headed out to the mountains. She wasn't interested in going to the hockey game in the evening, so this was our only time to see one another before I left for the park. After lunch, I headed to the store to get essentials I would need that were in my luggage.

The hockey game was at the Saddledome. I set out to see a game in every arena, but I was still incredibly early in my quest to accomplish it. This was the first arena I was able to see in Canada. Canada is passionate about hockey and their ticket prices reflect that. I purchased a ticket close to the ice by the visitor's bench. I was thrilled to be so close to my favorite team, the Detroit Red Wings.

While I was planning my trip to Calgary and Banff, I knew there were some winter activities I had to try: going on a helicopter ride and dog sledding. The helicopter pad was on my way out to the park. My first experience on a helicopter was magical! Seeing the majestic beauty of the view from the sky was invigorating.

After the helicopter ride, I continued on to Banff National Park. I passed the city of Canmore where I would go the following day for my dog mushing (sledding) experience. The view of the mountains kept me mesmerized as I made my way into town. The city of Banff, where I was going to be staying for the next couple of nights, was a couple of miles into the park.

I checked into the hotel and dropped off what few items I had in my room. I found out before heading out to Banff that there was a Lush, so I headed over to get all my toiletries I was missing. When I walked out, I was shocked to see a mountain in the town. It was funny since I knew I was in the mountains but was still taken aback by it being right there.

I went up a gondola to see the views and go to the hot springs. As I headed to the hot springs, I saw a sign about spa services. I checked to see if there was availability for a massage, which there was. After the massage, I sat in the hot springs to unwind even more. The sun set and I was able to see the moon in the sky while I was relaxing.

I headed back to Canmore for my mushing adventure. They had snow pants we could use to stay warm on the ride. I bought gloves and a hat the day prior, but I needed something warmer for my legs. I was partnered up with another solo traveler who was from the Netherlands.

The mushing company drove us out to the middle of the mountains where we would start our tour. As the crew was setting everything up, the leader explained what we would be doing for the tour. He told us about the dogs, the sport of mushing, their company, and how to operate the sleds. We were able to greet the dogs.

As soon as the dogs were lined up and ready to go, we made our way to our appointed sled. The dogs were barking with excitement since they knew it was almost time to go. My partner and I took turns either sitting or steering in the sled. When I was assisting steering the sled, we went over a frozen lake in between the mountains. It was fantastic!

I was having a beer in the hotel bar when the bartender told me that I needed to hike in Johnston Canyon, so I did. As you make your way into the canyon, there is a catwalk that leads you through the canyon on one of the sides. There was still ice and snow on the pathway, but it was worn out from people who had already been hiking through the canyon. The water flowing through was clear with a slight tint of aqua to it. Johnston's Canyon has two different paths, the upper and lower, to hike to see the waterfall from different angles. When I made it to the waterfall, the water that was pooled up was the prettiest blue I have ever seen in my life. I am glad I took the recommendation to do this hike.

Since the following day was Saturday, I drove back to Calgary to pick up Sherry so we could spend the day together. The drive back to Calgary was nice out, but as we headed back out to Banff, it started to snow. Eventually we made it to Lake Louise. We went to the Fairmont Chateau Lake Louise to have lunch before we hiked around the lake. I'd seen this hotel featured on an episode of the Bachelor so thought it was a cool opportunity to check it out.

Before we started our hike, I walked out on the ice for her to take a picture of me. There were people ice skating in designated areas on the lake. We decided to walk out on the pathway to see a frozen waterfall. There was a slight hint of blue in the icicles which made me appreciate the beauty of this natural area.

Sherry had lost her mom recently. We were able to be candid about how excruciating the pain of losing your mother was. I was grateful to have this time together and to be with someone in my age range who was struggling with the loss of their mother too. It gave me a sense of comfort.

My first semi-solo trip was a success. I was able to experience what it was like to be on my own. What I learned was I loved being able to do whatever made my heart happy every single minute of the day. It got me excited to start planning the trip to Europe. While my grief was still present, going on adventures was helping me heal. It let me see that there is so much to life, and I was not willing to miss a moment of it.

46

Shortly after I got back from Canada, I went on another vacation with a couple of girlfriends to Nashville. This was the third time that I had gone with my friend Michelle. I was utilizing my allotted vacation time by taking long weekends to stretch out the two weeks I had in my PTO bank to use. We crashed the start of a bachelor party at one of the bars we went to. We got their phone numbers so we could hang out again later during the weekend. However, we needed to leave to make our reservations at the Bluebird Cafe. I was elated that we had gotten tickets to see this iconic music writer's establishment. This was the place I had always wanted to see when I was visiting Nashville and it most certainly did not disappoint me.

Eric Church was an opener for the Kenny Chesney stadium tour. I had never seen Kenny in concert before. I organized a trip to Milwaukee with five of my girlfriends including Michelle, Beth, and Megan. Besides Milwaukee, I was going to see him in Denver and Detroit, with Brian and then Jenni.

I signed up for the meet and greet for every concert I attended. I had only received rejection emails until the Tuesday before the Milwaukee concert. I was beyond elated to get to meet Eric Church himself. His music had been instrumental to me in going through my grief journey. As soon as I found out, I called the dairy farmer, screaming with excitement. We usually only texted each other, so it was abnormal for me to call him.

I anxiously waited in line for the meet and greet at the designated time. We were brought to a room to meet him where we would have our picture taken. People were discussing what they were going to say when they saw him. I was not completely sure, but I knew that I did not want it to be generic. The way the room was set up, you couldn't see him until it was your turn. As soon as it was my turn to go, I jumped out and screamed with excitement. The look on his face was one of happiness and a little bit scared. I thanked him for his music as it had brought me peace while grieving the loss of my mom. He leaned in to hug me, they snapped the picture, and the moment was over. I ran back to the seats, over the moon that I finally had met my obsession.

At some point the firefighter and I started talking again. I am not sure how this happened, but he no longer had a girlfriend. Talking about the upcoming hockey playoffs was a safe subject for us, and we bought tickets to see game 4 of the matchup. On the way, the firefighter posted on Facebook that he was with me. I was annoyed that he did not ask me if it was okay to tag me in the post. Instantly my cousin Jenni texted me questioning why I was with him. She was not a fan of his and thought we were no longer speaking. I think maybe life's too short to hold grudges.

47

The people from my grief group decided to stop going, but we kept in contact with one another. Five of us would meet up every so often for dinner to touch base with each other. I was so blessed to have connected with all these wonderful people. Meeting for dinner was lovely since we were able to support and love one another even if we no longer met weekly.

The firefighter had planned on coming to Chicago for a vacation. The weekend he was coming to visit, a country concert was going to be in town. When he expressed interest, I asked my coworker, Joe, about his connection for two tickets for the show.

Friday, we went downtown Chicago to explore. We were

hanging out in an area I never had explored before. As we were walking through the city, the firefighter saw a Chicago city fire truck. His eyes twinkled when he saw it. He talked to the guys at the firehouse and asked if he could have his picture taken in one.

Something had felt off with him. I was not sure what it was until I saw him in the firetruck. He did not light up when he looked at me. However, I could not really break free from my own hope of wanting more with him. I kept making sure his needs were being met but doing everything he wanted to do, rather than speaking up for what I wanted. The insecure girl in me was transfixed on making him happy. I wanted to be loved and this meant sacrificing my own needs.

Joe's contact ended up getting us better tickets than Joe – third row seats. Before the concert, we grabbed drinks with Joe and his wife. The concert was amazing and made me realize that I was at an age where having good seats was important to me. The firefighter left to drive home after the concert. I was sad to have to say goodbye to him since I didn't know when I'd see him again.

The following weekend was the country festival that I had gone to the previous year. I'd planned to meet the dairy farmer on my way up there. I was nervous to see him, but once we got together, I realized why I love him so much. He'd made such an impact in my life by being a constant support system. I admired his wit and honesty. In the hard times, he was the only one who told me that I really was not that strong and in fact he had met stronger individuals. He saw my struggles and flaws and still was a supportive friend.

It was hard for me to not compare the presence of the firefighter and the dairy farmer in my life. The dairy farmer was a solid presence who didn't feel the need to promise to be there for me. He just showed up. The opposite could be said about the firefighter. He vowed over and over that he would be there, which I took to heart, but it always showed up as less than. Then he said I was expecting too much. While it is true that I had unrealistic expectations, it felt as if I was something else he needed to rescue. Oftentimes when I would express my feelings, he would twist my words to his benefit.

I was incredibly angry during this time in my life. Yes, I had started to let go of the deep grief, but the anger was transparent to everyone. The firefighter was an emotional punching bag. Since he tolerated my bullshit, I would say mean spiteful things to him. Somehow, he would forgive me, and we would move forward. I was not right in what I was doing, but he lacked the strength to tell me to stop. While he thought he was doing the best thing by forgiving me, we should have walked away from one another for the betterment of both of us.

As 2013 continued, I was finding a lot of solace in country concerts, hockey games, hanging with friends, and traveling to new locations. I even tried skydiving! Emotionally, the grief was still very present for me, but the heaviness was coming and going a little bit more. While it was never going to be my best year ever, I did focus on making it a decent year. Wanting to get back into shape, I decided that I would sign up for three different half marathons. Being a numbers person, I loved how it was 13.1 miles in a half marathon for 2013. I was focused on continuing my journey to get back to being in a better place, and slowly, it was looking like this was a possibility.

48

Early on the 5th of July, I caught a flight so I could make the hike to see the place where my brother died. It was going to be the 25-year anniversary the following month. My dad's goddaughter, my cousin, was getting married the next day within driving distance of the Smoky Mountains. I needed to see the place that had changed my entire life. I had wanted to make this trip five years earlier on the

20-year anniversary, but I knew I would have to hide the trip from my mom, and my plans had fallen apart. Now was my opportunity to go without having to be secretive. Being on my own, I no longer needed anyone's approval but my own.

I flew into Greenville, South Carolina. As I was making the three hour drive up to the Smoky Mountain National Park, I realized my timing was already behind schedule. However, the determination for me to see Charlies Bunion with my own eyes kept me moving forward. Being from the Midwest where it is mostly flat, driving through the mountains kept me from going as fast as I thought I could with the curvy roads. I was anxious to get there so I could complete the journey before nightfall.

Finally, I arrived at the parking lot, grabbed all my gear and headed out. I had estimated that the hike would take me an hour since it was 4.4 miles to Charlies Bunion. As I started hiking, I realized that this, too, was something I had underestimated. My thought process was that I could walk a 15-minute mile. What did not make my equation was the elevation of the terrain. The tree roots protruded out in several spots along the path. Hiking up the elevation and then hiking down meant that it was not the standard mile I was used to walking.

There were a few people that I crossed on the path who were returning from somewhere farther out. As I continued to make my way, I needed to take several breaks to catch my breath. I was pushing myself to pick up the pace since I did not want to be hiking in the dark with all these tree roots coming out of the ground. I was doing my best to calm my mind from thinking about what I was walking towards. It was easy to focus on how I felt out of shape rather than I was heading towards the place that had haunted me all my life.

When I arrived close to the overlook, I observed a sign that said, "Charlies Bunion – Closely Control Children." I let out a bitter laugh and wondered if it was there when Todd and his friends walked by or if it had been added afterwards.

The path I was walking on became dramatically smaller and there was a steep drop to the left of me. While it was nice to finally be out of the covered wooded area with sunlight, I was a nervous wreck because of the steep edge. This caught my breath. I said a small prayer to keep me safe. THIS was the location I had been fearful of since I was eleven.

Finally, I got to the overlook of Charlies Bunion. I had expected to be overwhelmed with grief, but I was shocked how uneventful of a moment it was. I paused and took a selfie. Then I started to take pictures of the beautiful scenery: the greenery of the trees lining the mountains, which went on for miles, and the vibrant sun shining down. The temperature was warm with a slight breeze, and there were birds chirping in the background. While I was taking these photos, my mind struggled to comprehend how the vision I had for this place was one of darkness, yet it was a peaceful view.

I had thought about bringing some roses to leave in memory of him. However, a dear friend had suggested throwing a baseball since it was my brother's favorite sport. I knew this was what I needed to do. I would throw it off the cliff where he fell. I retrieved the baseball from my bag. On the baseball I wrote, "In loving memory of Todd J Remer," and left personalized messages on each side of the ball. After getting a picture of this view with the ball, I threw it off where I envisioned he had fallen.

I was not quite ready to leave so I decided to sit on the rock that led out to the cliffside where my brother and his friends had gone to look out. However, it was nerve-racking for me to be in the exact location I was fearful of. I stayed as close as I could to where I could easily be on solid ground. I was mesmerized by the scenery. After a few moments, my mind wandered, and I checked my phone to see if it had service. I was shocked that I had a signal, so I reached out to a friend of my brother's to let her know I was there. I wasn't sure what else to do so I played five games of Candy Crush. I laughed out loud that here I was in the most dreaded place, and I was playing a game on my phone.

After about thirty minutes, I knew I needed to head back. I'd been disappointed that I did not have an "aha" moment as I thought I would. The sunlight was starting to drop, and I wanted to get back to the car before it was pitch black. When I was on the narrow path, it started to sprinkle. When the path widened out, I decided to put on my rain gear. Shortly after I put the gear on, it started to downpour. Within minutes my shoes were completely soaked and I could hear them squish with each step.

As I was walking back in the rain, I started to think about my journey to see Charlies Bunion. I had spent my whole life envious of Todd. He was always athletic, adventurous, and fearless. I never felt as if I measured up. My parents' sadness after the loss of him had made me feel like the consolation prize. I was always in his shadow. However, I was in a dead boy's shadow. Using my way of coping, I do not remember him. But in this quiet moment I felt connected to him. I saw myself as adventurous. I did possess the drive to see the world. I needed to see this location to let me move forward and stop living in the shadows of a dead person. I was courageous to face my fears. On my own! At this moment, I was proud to be following in his footsteps and to now be creating my own. It felt powerful to be me at this exact second.

Then a new fear emerged as I was making my way back to the car. The forest was getting darker and darker. I used my phone as a flashlight to avoid falling. However, I still fell. My first fall wasn't too bad. I was able to get up and wipe off the mud to keep going. Those branches were turning out to be a bigger obstacle than I originally gave them credit for. I was desperate to know how much further I had to go. It was pitch black out, and my feet were cold and wet since my shoes were soggy. I was getting frustrated having to manage the phone flashlight and using the trees as a balance to step down a stair's length. I would conserve the battery every so often.

When I was not using the flashlight, I mis-stepped going around tree branches and fell incredibly hard. My right shin took the most direct hit and was throbbing. I was concerned that I did more damage than a scrape and was now limping in pain. My frustration and fear were skyrocketing and I was ready to be back to safety. I cried out loud to God wanting to be done. I was contemplating if I'd made a huge mistake making this trip. I was all alone in the middle of the forest and wondered if I would ever make it back. I had no clue how badly my leg was injured. Shortly after I cried out loud, I realized I was back to the beginning of the path which was flat and free of tree roots. I was thankful knowing I'd almost made it. Once I was sitting in the car, I thanked God for hearing my cry and getting me through the darkness. I could see that my leg was bleeding but wanted to get to the hotel to see how bad it was.

Once I dropped my stuff off in my room, I had to get some food as soon as possible. I chose the first restaurant I saw which was Bubba Gump Shrimp. I sat in the booth and put my leg up to keep it elevated. I stared at the menu, but it was as if it was a foreign language. I was so exhausted, and nothing jumped out at me. I was mentally, physically, and emotionally exhausted. The server helped me by telling me her favorite items and I picked one of those.

While I waited for my food to be cooked, I went through the photos I had taken. They were stunning photos, but everything stopped when I saw the selfie I took at Charlies Bunion. I had thought I smiled, but what I saw was my mother looking right back at me. My mom had this look after Todd died that I would not be able to properly explain it other than to say it was a sadness that came from her core. I'd forgotten this look until I saw my face. It had the exact same expression. It was my mom's look I remember seeing as a child. What I had been feeling about this location was captured on film. It made me see what Charlies Bunion had meant to my family. Not the beauty I saw today, but rather the anguish of losing Todd.

I texted the firefighter for comfort. I shared with him how I hurt myself, but I was finally sitting down to have some dinner. He tried to be empathetic, but I knew he could never understand the gravity of the day I'd had. What I had done was huge. I faced my second biggest fear and faced my trauma head-on by seeing the place that had haunted me for almost 25 years. I texted my girlfriends, who asked me to keep them in the loop. As soon as I finished eating, I headed back to the hotel to get a good night of sleep. I was gone as soon as my head hit the pillow.

49

I got up later than I wanted, but I'd needed the rest. I headed south in the direction of my cousin's wedding. I'd been so angry at the Remer family for their insensitive comments at my mom's funeral. I'd told myself at the funeral that I never needed to see any of them ever again. However, I chose to go to this wedding and make peace. Since it was my father's goddaughter, I wanted to be his representation.

I sat by myself towards the back of the church to watch the ceremony. I was able to see most of my aunts and uncles at the reception – all but two of siblings were there. It was nice to be at a celebration rather than one of my own family members' funerals. I was able to be myself rather than needing to put on a show.

My cousin's father had cancer, but fortunately his health was good enough to be able to walk her down the aisle. When they danced the daddy daughter, I started to get choked up and left the room to collect myself. It was too much for me to witness. It brought up the moment I'd felt fortunate to have with my dad at my wedding. One of my aunt's came out to check on me to see if I was doing okay.

After the reception was over, we all headed back to the hotel and gathered in a hotel room, looking at old photos of the family. One of my aunts ended up giving me a couple of pictures of my parents. This was my favorite moment of the weekend. It was a raw and real opportunity to see them just as they were, in our comfy clothes. I stayed for a couple hours laughing at all the stories they had to share about growing in a house with nine siblings.

The day after, a few of them wanted to go for brunch, but I wanted to see the ocean – it was only a two-hour drive to get there. I needed to hear the waves and see the water. It was a slightly longer drive than I would have liked, however, my soul craved it.

Overall, it was a quick weekend, but it was wonderful for my heart to experience all the elements. I was able to see the place that single-handedly changed the trajectory of my life. I was able to take something that haunted me for my entire childhood and see that it was a stunning location. I celebrated the union of my cousin and her husband. I learned that hanging out with the Remer family was a fun time when it had nothing to do with burying a family member.

I flew to Denver for the Eric Church concert with my cousin Brian. When I got there, I realized I could live there. We tailgated in the stadium parking lot before the concert. Brian had warned me about not drinking too much with the altitude. I heard him but did not proceed with caution. After I puked, he had me sit in his van so I could pass out. I have no clue how long I was out, but he sat in the van as everyone was heading into the show. He told me we could skip the concert. Then I heard the first couple chords of Eric's set and I sprang up out of a drunken stupor. I told him we needed to go into the show. He repeated himself, saying that it was okay that we missed it. Angry that he thought such a stupid thing, I told him to get his ass out of the car and we were going in now. Never in my life have I rallied the way I did that night. Brian was impressed, too.

The following day, Brian and I went to a baseball game. We were getting overheated since our seats were getting blasted with the sun, so we moved to an air conditioned place where we could still watch the game. I'd never spent so much time with my cousin as an adult. It was great to have quality time with him. I was starting to realize that we had more in common than I had previously thought. He was the oldest grandchild, and I was the youngest grandchild, so as children, the age difference was huge and we were going through different life experiences,. Now, as adults, we had evened out and had both experienced a divorce. We had a lot of fun together.

In August, I headed to Detroit to spend time with Jenni at the Eric Church concert. I was thrilled I was able to watch him perform with both of my cousins. She got a kick out of how excited I got when Eric came on the stage. As I did with every concert I went to that year, we left after the song Eric sang with Kenny. It was perfect so we would be able to beat the traffic home.

In honor of what would have been my brother's fortieth birthday, I raised money for the Todd Remer scholarship fund. I was going to match any donations that came in by his birthday. The total donated was around $3,800. I decided to round it up to an even $4,000 to honor him for his fortieth birthday. It felt wonderful to be able to give in honor of my brother.

50

Aunt Karen called me towards the beginning of October. Anytime I saw her name pop up and it wasn't my birthday, I held my breath. Historically, she did not have the best news to share with me. She was calling to inform me that my grandpa had not been feeling well, so he went to the doctor. They found cancer on his kidney. Surgery was scheduled for October 17th. Immediately, I started crying. I couldn't explain it, but my intuition said that he might not even be alive by then. My aunt told me not to cry since he would be fine, but the voices in my head would not stop telling me that something was seriously wrong.

The following week, my aunt called to share that the surgery for my grandpa was cancelled. His entire body was riddled with cancer. It explained why he had been in such intense pain for the last several months. My grandparents were incredibly stubborn and never talked about problems. I believe that my grandpa knew something was going on but did not want to address it. When the pain got unbearable, they finally went to the doctor to see what it was.

My parents' birthdays were three days apart – my dad's on October 17th and my mom's on October 20th. As I cried finding out the news of his surgery, I'd thought, "Please do not die on my parents' birthdays." My grandpa ended up dying the day before my mom's birthday. From that first call, my intuition was spot on.

My grandma decided to have the funeral on the weekend so it would give my cousin Brian the opportunity to make it there. This was the first funeral that would be held at a different funeral home and church. I was grateful that I was able to be in the background, but I felt for my grandma. My grandparents would have celebrated their 66th wedding anniversary in a couple weeks, had he survived.

I was there to support my grandma if she needed anything at all. I didn't know most of the people coming for the visitation unless they were family. A few of my dad's extended family members came to show support for my grandma and me too. It touched me that they came.

After spending the day at the funeral home, my cousins, Brian, Jenni and I went to the small-town bar to toast my grandpa. Our second cousins joined us as they were close to my grandparents too. He was one of the best men I had ever known. My grandpa was not one to speak up too often, but when he did, I always took note of what he was saying. He had a strong work ethic for his entire life. Before I was born, he had been a mason. They moved to a small town a year after I was born so he could spend his retirement working on the farm. We were all going to miss him deeply.

After the funeral and the luncheon, I headed down to spend the evening with the firefighter. I'd already made plans to see him before the funeral was arranged. We were going to Cedar Point for the fright fest. We changed our plans since it was cold outside and neither of us wanted to ride the roller coasters in the cold. Also, the funeral changed our plans since we only would be seeing each other for the evening, so we went to see a mid-level professional hockey game. We had gotten tickets to see the Winter Classic in Detroit, so this was preparing us for the upcoming game. Again, it was a much-needed distraction after a sad day.

51

I declared I would run three half marathons in 2013. Knowing that I had backed out on the marathon in 2012, I felt it would be easier to run a half marathon. The city of Naperville had an inaugural race and I wanted to be a part of it. The second one I signed up for was the Fox Valley race that my cousin Patric decided to run in as well. The third and final one I signed up for was in Atlanta, Georgia. I was going to be running with a friend's sister.

I had committed to running the race, but mentally I had not committed to training. This meant that I was not prepared for any of the races. The first one was with my cousin Patric. What I loved about this race is that he was there with me to celebrate after we finished. Also, the view was stunning since it was along the Fox River. The race itself was a horrible run for me even though I was able to finish it. After the race, we sat and had a great conversation about life now and my family. Patric was my brother's age, and his sister Jodi was my age. They were my favorite cousins on the Remer side.

Next, I traveled to Atlanta for the final half marathon. I fell over a speed bump not even a whole mile into the race – I wasn't picking up my feet enough and stumbled over it. I received medical attention, but by the time they were finished patching me up, my friend and I were at the tail end of the race. We needed to keep a pace so we wouldn't get disqualified. My friend did a great job encouraging me to keep going. There were many times I wanted to quit since my leg was throbbing. Finishing this race meant a lot to me as I did not give up.

After the race, I flew home. While waiting for my flight, I kept my leg iced and elevated. Whenever I participate in a race, I wear my medal all day, so I wore my medal on the plane ride home. I could feel my leg swelling up during the flight. I was doing my best to walk off the plane, but I had to pause every couple of aisles. A flight attendant asked me if I wanted a wheelchair. Initially, I said no. However, I realized that I was never going to make it to the baggage claim if I didn't have help.

The last and final half marathon was in Naperville. This was my favorite race of the three since it was the last one I had committed to doing. The last mile, I smiled knowing that I would stop running half marathons for years to come. I spoke to my running coach who told me that if I was not enjoying it, I should stop running long races and find something I do enjoy. I started playing soccer again.

After the run in Naperville, I went to see David Nail at Joe's on Weed Street. I had fallen in love with his music sitting in a bar in Greece. It was my first opportunity to see him live. I wore my medal for the concert, proud of what I'd accomplished.

52

The holiday season was coming up and I was dreading year number two of being family-less. While the first year after losing someone is hard, it feels as if year two is worse since this is the new normal. Most people have forgotten how hard it is for you to be going through the holidays. It is not as if you move on – rather, you move forward. I can move through but will never move on from missing my loved ones.

Tricia and I had been getting together to splurge on sushi dinners. We had been talking about the holidays and decided to go to Nashville on Thanksgiving for the long weekend. I wanted to be spared from being awkwardly invited to someone's family dinner. She was okay to skip so she did not have to hang out with brother's fiancé.

Instead of shopping on Black Friday, we bar hopped to listen to live music. I finally got to check the Nashville arena off my list since we saw the Nashville Predators. We also went for sushi while we were there.

Overall, it was a great weekend spending time with Tricia. I was curious how we would do as travel partners, but I learned that we traveled well together right away. It was a needed getaway with a friend for the holidays.

For Christmas, I once again spent the entire day with Lisa and her husband's family. It was a rather relaxed environment. Lisa's husband had a brother and sister I knew since I had seen them at many different functions over the years. They treated me as extended family. That evening, we spent the night laughing as we played games. Courtney came over after she was done with her family's celebration. While the second year was hard, I was happy to spend it with my created family.

53

I was excited to be going to see the Detroit Red Wings play in their second Winter Classic. I went to the one at Wrigley Field in Chicago in 2009. I had been planning on going by myself, but I ended up going to the game with Erik, Jenni's volleyball coach.

The game was in Detroit at the University of Michigan's Big House. Erik, his girlfriend Laurie, the firefighter, and I were going to go together. The Detroit Red Wings and the Toronto Maple Leaf's were going to be playing against one another. Besides both being original six teams, it was the first time the Winter Classic had a Canadian and American team play against one another. Typically, the games were held in the city's professional baseball field, but this one was held at a university football stadium. This meant it could be the largest attended NHL game ever.

The Winter Classic hosted an alumni game the day before so that fans could see retired players play again. Knowing that most of my favorite players had already retired made me excited to have the opportunity to watch them play again. Since Toronto and Detroit had so many retired players, they had two alumni games. There were almost 100 retired players between the two teams.

After they introduced all the players, the announcer said, "Tonight's starting lineup is the Russian Five." The Russian five from Detroit made a huge impact on getting them to be a Stanley Cup contender. Six days after they won the Stanley Cup in 1997, a couple of the players were in a limousine accident. The accident caused Vladmir Konstantiov to suffer head injuries and paralysis. This ended his hockey career with the Red Wings. After the announcement was made, the camera showed Konstantinov hitting his stick on the ice. Chills went through my body and there was not a dry eye in that stadium witnessing this epic moment.

After the day at the alumni games, the firefighter and I went to ring in the New Year watching the Zac Brown Band. During the concert I was drinking faster than I should have been. I knew I was drunk before the countdown to 2014 happened. In my drunken stupor, I was emotional and jealous. After the concert, I tried to have a conversation about being hurt that I was an occasional hookup for him. We had all these things in common, but it was never good enough for us to be in a relationship. He kept telling me that he adored me, but we lived way too far apart for us to be anything more than friends. I really don't remember too much of the conversation since I was highly intoxicated. We ended up getting kicked out of the arena because they needed to clean.

The next day, we met Erik and Laurie so we could take one car into the tailgate. I was hungover and moving slow. When we started tailgating, I struggled to drink my beer which kept freezing. The fans seemed to be split 50/50 for Toronto and Detroit. There had been a little bit of trash talking, but overall, everyone was respectful to each other. I wasn't used to this, since Chicago fans tend to chant "Detroit sucks," so it was refreshing experience.

Making our way into the stadium, we had split up into couples. The firefighter was pulling my arm to try to keep up with him as he led the way through the arena. Our seats were right by the sky boxes. I'd thought this was too far away from ice rink, but with the weather it ended up being the perfect location. The seats were just outside the glass window. We had easy access to the bathrooms, and we could go inside to get warmed up in between the periods.

It had been snowing all morning and kept snowing hard throughout the game leading, to them needing to shovel the snow off the ice at any stoppages. Not only were the temperatures freezing, but with the wind chill it was even colder. I was happy to be at the game, but I was cold and hungover.

The regulation game ended in a tie. Therefore, it went into

overtime. After five minutes of overtime, there was a shootout, which Toronto won. It was a great day to watch some outdoor hockey. The game did make the record books since it was the largest NHL attendance record ever at 105,491 people.

The traffic after the game was a nightmare. Between the snowstorm and the number of attendees, traffic did not move. It took us over an hour to the shopping mall parking lot where the firefighter and I had left his car. We said our goodbyes to Erik and Laurie and headed into the mall to use the restrooms. We decided to walk around the mall rather than sit in the car getting annoyed. It took close to five hours to get to the firefighter's house.

54

Now that I was in 2014, the end of my job was just around the corner. I had decided back in August when my actual termination date would be. Being obsessed with repetitive numbers, I realized that April 4th was a Friday. This seemed to be a perfect day to quit. Most people close to me knew that I was quitting my job and heading to Europe.

I was making the most of my time before I was going to leave. I was Tricia's date to her sister's wedding. I was planning with my friend Kayla for the Italy portion of our travels together. I still was enjoying various country concerts and flew to Nashville for less than 36 hours to see Eric Church at the Ryman. I hung out with my cousin Jodi and her children by going sledding after a snowstorm. I won a free ticket to a special show that Eric Church was doing to promote his new album. I was still working at Lush. When I had time, I got together with my various friends for either dinner or drinks. My time was full.

I was overjoyed that I was finally cashing in on my promise I had made to myself two years earlier. I had taken care of all the logistics of my mom's estate. I had renters in the house. Steve and I had an agreement that I could keep some items I wanted from my childhood in a secure location. I handled all the hard stuff and now it was time for me to go explore. I worked closely with my counselor over the last two years facing my grief.

I gave a one month's notice to my full-time job. It was the end of the day on March 7th when I popped into my boss' office to let her know that I needed to talk to her. Jokingly, she asked if I was quitting. When I did not respond, it was her first clue that I was going to be leaving. I handed her my resignation letter. She was shocked. When she asked what I was going to be doing next, I let her know I was headed to Europe. As my boss, she was sad I was leaving. As my friend, she was incredibly happy for me to be able to follow my passion of seeing the world. I never anticipated staying at the company, but it was the best place for me to be while I processed my grief, and it was finally time to move on.

I had a theme song for my resignation. It was a song from Sugarland that I posted on my Facebook page as my announcement: "Five (eight) years and there's no doubt that I'm burnt out, I've had enough. So now boss man (woman), here's my two weeks (month). I'll make it short and sweet, so listen up. I could work my life away, but why? I got things to do before I die. There's gotta be something more, gotta be more than this. I need a little less hard time; I need a little more bliss. I'm gonna take my chances, taking a chance I might. Find what I'm looking for. There's gotta be something more. Some believe in destiny, and some believe in fate. I believe that happiness is something we create. You best believe that I'm not gonna wait 'cause there's gotta be something more! – Sugarland (Trudi)."

Freedom has always been important to me. I now had complete freedom! It had been hard to be transparent in what I was up to, so telling my boss meant I did not need to be careful about what I said anymore. When I planned on leaving the job, I never realized how much joy I would feel in this moment, saying, "Fuck it" to the social norm we are all told to buy into. I was leaving my job to go see what else is out there in the world.

My last session with my counselor was the day after I quit the job. My counselor was retiring within a month of me heading to Europe. We were both making life transitions that perfectly lined up to have congruent closure. I valued her presence in my life over the last two and a half years. She helped me heal my grief over the loss of my brother and my father. By having worked with her earlier, it allowed me to get immediate mental care when my mom died. I needed her support since my world had been rocked without any consistent support. Being able to be completely raw helped me move through the process of how I needed to feel the grief to move forward.

As I was completing my last days, a coworker asked me if I was quitting to go travel the world. I smiled to myself and said yes. He said, "That's so cool." My coworkers had a going away party for me. My last day, they gave me a cardboard Bon Voyage sign that everyone signed. It was lovely to close this chapter in my life. I was grateful for this opportunity, but it was time for me to find my passion.

I had two going away/bon voyage parties to say goodbye to those who had been there for me over the previous two years. I would be back but wanted to see everyone one more time before I left. My former running coach said, "I see. You're just scheduling two parties so that people will buy you drinks. Then you get two nights of free liquor. Don't get me wrong. I'm not complaining. Just sorry I didn't think of it first." It was great to see everyone. People from church, Jaycees, Lush, soccer, running, cousins (Remer side), work, extended friends, and even my grief group showed up to give me their love and well wishes on my travels.

The last thing I needed to take care of before I left was to drop my cat off at a friend's grandmother's house. I had inquired if someone would take my cat while I was traveling. I had no idea what I was going to do, but when my friend told me her grandmother would love to have her in her home, I was elated. With her grandma being home all the time, Circe was going to love having someone there all the time. She was skittish, but I knew that she would eventually come out of her shell.

I finally arrived at this beautiful moment that I had created for my future. When my mom had passed away, I was devastated with the heaviness of all the emotions and thought about treating myself to a trip. Now it had transformed into something grand for me. I never rushed anything. It took time to get everything aligned for this adventure. One of the greatest things that happened was the money I invested earned enough that essentially the trip was paid for off the interest I had earned in the market. Not only did I need to be responsible, but it paid off that I was able to do this with earned income. It felt as if this was my mom's way of approving of me taking this journey.

55

It was the night before my three-month trip to Europe and I could not find my passport anywhere. The full-blown panic was activated within me. I needed to find it, or I would not be able to go. I had a moment where I told myself that I wasn't going to be able to go. When I was sitting in the recliner, I started to backtrack my steps. I recalled that I had dropped it by the chair. I got up and found it hidden underneath the chair. Being 2 a.m., I would not be getting much sleep as my ride was coming at 6 a.m. to get me, but that was perfectly okay since I could sleep on the plane.

My first leg of my flight was into Boston. I had a six-hour layover. One of my friends whose father had taught at Trinity with my mom happened to live in Boston. I'd reached out to her about possibly connecting while I was there. She would be working during the day but was able to meet me for dinner. I took a pedicab tour around downtown Boston then waited in the bar at the restaurant for her to arrive. Once she got there, we caught up over a lobster dinner. She dropped me at the airport for the second leg of my flight to Iceland.

Iceland had been a bucket list location of mine for several years. I had heard of the country's beauty and, more importantly, I wanted to see the northern lights. With the time difference, I landed in Reykjavik early in the morning. Between jet lag and minimal sleep, I was functioning at an awfully slow pace. I knew that I needed to take a bus to get to the downtown area, and I eventually found it. It was my first taste of getting used to not having signs in my native language.

Since it was still rather early in the morning, I was unable to check in. I dropped off my bag and headed out to find a place to eat. I chose to have an Icelandic breakfast to get into the culture of the country. The dish had several things on it, but the thing that was the most interesting was the cod oil. While I knew that fish oil was good for you, it was strange to see it served in a little cup for me to drink.

I desperately needed a nap before I could sightsee. When I got into my hostel room, I slept for a couple of hours. I forgot that I'd booked a co-ed room, so when a man opened the door, I gasped in shock. I'd just gotten out of the shower, so he respectfully went to the community space to give me a moment. I found him to thank him for giving me the space. I apologized that it was my error for thinking I had booked an all-female room.

The very first museum I went to was the Icelandic Phallological Museum. It was the very first place that I had tagged myself in online and it most certainly got a reaction. The museum itself was rather boring, but the gift shop was hysterical. There were postcards, shirts, and other items to purchase to show people you had been to the Phallological Museum.

The tallest building downtown is Hallgrímskirkja, which is a

Lutheran church in the shape of a rocket ship. I wanted to see what tours I could book for the next couple of days. There was a northern light tour that I could take the following night since it was overcast and raining all day long and I wouldn't be able to see anything tonight. So, I chose to go on a beer tour. The beer was not the best beer I'd ever had, but I got a nice buzz off the tour.

I went on the Golden Circle tour, which seemed to be the most popular tour. The first place they took us was to Thingvellir National Park. Inside the park lies a rift valley that separates the North American and Eurasian tectonic plates. They then took us to see Gullfoss Waterfall which was stunning. After we spent some quality time at the waterfall, they took us over to see the geysers. Strokkur geyser was a magical moment for me to witness. I had always wanted to see a geyser in action, and I finally witnessed one. You could smell sulfur in the air. I wanted to pinch myself that this was my life, but it was just the beginning of the three-month adventure.

I had taken another tour to go through the lava caves. As we were making our way out, I fell asleep, so I never heard what the announcer was saying. However, the bus stopped for us to get out. The foulest smell of fish permeated that air – there were several thousand's fish heads hanging to be dried out, a strange thing to wake up to see. I really had no desire to understand what in the world I was seeing, as it was gross.

We made our way to the cave. They provided us with a hard hat with a headlamp to protect our heads inside the cave. The ground leading to the caves was covered with moss. The different shapes of the magma within the cave were beautiful. There were areas where it looked like icicles. It was a unique experience to check out how majestic our earth is. There was a moment where we needed to crawl through a tight spot to get to another larger pocket in the tunnel. I was worried about getting stuck but was able to make it through without too many bruises on my body.

I went to see the Blue Lagoon, which was magical. As I walked up to the geothermal baths, I admired the blue milky water which was a pretty contrast next to the dark volcanic rock. You could smell the sulfur, but it was not nearly as strong as it had been by the geysers. After rinsing off in the locker room, I made my way into the geothermal baths. The water was a beautiful, milky blue, hot bath. I observed people drinking and putting mud on their faces. I got a beer from the same brewery I had been to two days prior. I was curious about the mud on everyone's faces so I found a sign explaining why everyone was putting it on their skin. It was silica which was said to be rich in minerals. I tried it, and it felt luxurious. I checked out the steam rooms just outside of the pool. It was a relaxing day at the Blue Lagoon. Even though I did not get a massage, it still felt as if I spent the day at a spa. I left very relaxed.

When I had been creating my journey through Europe, I'd chosen Iceland because I found an inexpensive flight from Iceland to Norway. I was able to get from the US to Europe via Iceland cheaper than it would have been if I went directly to Europe. I had wanted to see the northern lights, but unfortunately, they weren't visible the night we went. However, because of this, the tour I was on told us that we would be able to take it again within the next three years. This had me planning on coming back to Iceland before I even left. Next time, I would need to go all around the island to explore as it was a beautiful country. This was a great start to my three-month journey.

56

As much as I wanted to see Iceland, I had always wanted to see the fjords in Norway even more. I flew into Bergen where I could start the "Norway in a nutshell" tour. When researching traveling in

Europe, I learned a lot from Rick Steves. On his webpage, he jokingly stated that if you go to Norway and do not go on this tour, your passport should be revoked.

I took the train at Floibanen to head up the mountain to take in the overlook of the city of Bergen. It was a steep train ride up the mountainside, so the cars were slanted. I walked along the pathway to take in the breathtaking views of the harbor below. I went into a couple shops to see if there was anything I might want to buy. I saw that you could buy a can of air, which made me laugh out loud. After walking around for a bit, I found a bench to catch up on my journaling. As I made my way back to the hostel, I started talking to a couple who were from Wisconsin. He happened to be a Lutheran pastor – it shocked me, how small of a world it was. I had not realized that the Scandinavia countries had a large Lutheran population.

I started the "Norway in a nutshell" tour in Bergen. It started with a train ride. When we got to Voss, we moved to a bus to take us to see the fjords. We explored Sognefjord, Norway's longest fjord, and took in the sights of the stunning cliffs surrounded by water.

When we arrived in Flam, we got onto another train that would eventually take us all the way to Oslo. The train stopped at Myrdal for us to take photos of Kjosfossen Waterfall. Since it was winter, it was frozen. As the train continued to make its way to Oslo, we went through land that had a lot of snow. Some houses must have been summer homes since they were surrounded with snow.

When I was in Oslo, the weather was rather dreary with the rain. Not only was the weather poor, but it was Holy Week. Several places were closed due to it being Easter weekend, which I had not anticipated as places didn't tend to close on Easter weekend in the States. From what I had learned, most people are not religious but are willing to use it as a reason not to work.

Now that I had activated my train pass for the tour, I was going to utilize it as often as I could, so I headed over to Copenhagen. While I was on the train, there was a full double rainbow that I admired. It made me think of my mom since she loved witnessing rainbows.

I learned in Copenhagen that the best way to see a city was to do one of the walking tours offered. We walked by the typical canals with the picturesque houses in the background. We saw the statue, the Little Mermaid. The guide told us that Denmark is one of the happiest places on earth.

A group of us from the hostel were having a couple of beers in the hostel bar. We decided to go together to see Christiania. I had no idea what this meant, but I was open to seeing anything, especially with a group of people. It was a hippy commune area that lived under their own laws. Marijuana was free trade in this area. The buildings were painted bright, and you could see creatives lived here. It had a different vibe compared with what I had seen all day on the tour of Copenhagen. I laughed that as you exit there is a sign that says, "You are now entering the EU."

As I was having breakfast in a cafe, "Islands in the Stream" by Kenny Rogers and Dolly Parton played. This song made me think of both of my parents. They had listened to country music for all my childhood. My mom really did not love the music, but she enjoyed both singers. I felt their presence with me at this moment.

I took the train to Stockholm. When I arrived, I felt the vibe of the city was different from Norway cities. It was a spacious city, and with it being spread out, I got a day pass to sightsee by riding a hop on hop off bus. On the tour, I learned this was where the book The Girl with the Dragon Tattoo had taken place.

It was recommended to go to the Vasa Museum. I am not a museum person, so I had to ask what it was about. It was a shipwreck that had sunk but was now on display at the museum. This sounded intriguing so I decided to check it out. It was impressive to see the ship, as huge as it was. As someone who does not care for museums, this held my interest.

I was making my way to check out a Lush store when I came

across an Ice Bar. I thought this sounded like fun. I had on flip flops but knew this would not be a big deal for me. They give you a special coat to wear so that you can stay warm while inside the bar. The drinks were even served in ice glasses! I took several selfies in the place. There was a sign that said Ice Bar Stockholm so I asked someone to take a photo of me in front of it. After I saw the photo, I remembered why I never asked people to take photos of me.

I flew from Stockholm, Sweden to Helsinki, Finland. The only agenda I had in Helsinki was to sit in a sauna. When I got to the hostel, I felt uncomfortable. It wasn't that I didn't feel safe, but it had more to do with the vibe – most people seemed as if they lived there. An Irish man arrived right after me and wanted to grab a drink. I joined him for a couple of drinks. I realized on our way back to the hostel that I could relax since I was walking the streets with a man.

Finally, I arrived at the sauna. Since it was my only priority in the country, I wanted to spend my day there. There were two saunas, one for men and one for women. Knowing that it would only be women here, I went into the sauna naked. There was a lounge where you could rehydrate and relax in between times in the sauna. It was like a spa experience. My mission here was complete.

57

When I planned the trip, I knew I wanted to go to Russia to see the beautiful buildings with my own two eyes. I had to get a special visa on my passport which included sending my passport to Washington DC to be expedited. I was a nervous wreck sending it out and hoping I would get it back in time. I breathed a sigh of relief when I got my passport with the Russian visa on one of the pages. To be allowed into the country, I needed someone to sponsor me. A hotel could be your sponsor so prior to leaving, I had to figure out exactly when I would be in Russia.

There is a ferry that leaves from Helsinki, Finland to Tallinn, Estonia. Tallinn had never been on my radar, but I was excited to add a place to my travels. As a bonus, I got to watch the sunset over the Baltic Sea from the ferry.

My time in Tallinn was short since I had to catch my flight to Saint Petersburg. With the limited time, I focused on the Old Town of Tallinn. In some of the higher elevated areas, I was able to see the landscape of the entire city. In the shops, there was a lot of amber for sale. I also found a can of air. This was the second time I was seeing a can of air for sale. It said for best results to open it outside of the country. Before I left, I grabbed some local cuisine in the center square.

Once I arrived in St. Petersburg, culture shock instantly happened. I knew it was going to be challenging, but I had underestimated how hard it would be. I'd read how you needed to always have your passport on you, since the police officers could ask you to verify your citizenship. While I was in the subway, I sat down to see if I could calm my nerves to try to understand which way I needed to go. While I was sitting there, I witnessed someone being asked to show their passport. I could not understand what was being said due to the language barrier, but I could tell based on the body language that they were frustrated. It is one thing to hear that this is something that happens, but it was another thing to see it play out before my eyes.

After the police were no longer talking to the gentlemen, I walked up to them to see if they could help me. I started every conversation the last few weeks by asking "English?" They were able to point me in the right direction. However, this was the first time that the energy in the exchange was vastly different. It was not as friendly as I had been used to. It was stern and direct. It was one thing to not understand the spoken language, but the letters in their alphabet did not compute in my mind. When looking at a sign, I could not understand it since I was unable to have cognitive recognition with it. In other countries I was unable to speak it or read it, but I could make it make sense. In Russian, I was completely lost. I would see signs from famous chains and could only tell what it was based on the logo, not by reading it.

I had downloaded an app to help me with my adventures – a map that would work even if I wasn't on Wi-Fi. If I had downloaded the map ahead of time, I could use it to navigate. I relied heavily on this trying to find the hotel. I would look at the map on my phone and look up at the street sign – I was so confused. It was all foreign to me and I wondered how I was ever going to make it to the hotel. I passed by the Kazan Cathedral, which I felt I had seen it before, but I wasn't sure what exactly it was. I could see the Church of the Savior on Spilled Blood in the background. Even though I was frustrated, I was happy I was here to see this in person. I finally found the hotel to drop off my bag. I wanted to go see the sights.

I went immediately to the Church of the Savior on Spilled Blood first. Its beauty was majestic to witness. The imagery inside the building was overwhelming to say the least. Everywhere you looked, there were bright mosaics with gold features throughout. It was stunning and gaudy. I walked around the building but chose not to invest in the audio tour as you looked around. I would never retain the information as it would be information overload.

As I was exiting the building, I saw a machine that imprinted coins which would make an excellent souvenir. Since I was unable to read the instructions, I ended up with two coins. A woman must have observed me having an extra coin. We were unable to speak to one another with the language barrier, so we gestured to one another. She showed me some chocolate that she had, and she pointed at my hand that held the coins. We exchanged the items and thanked the other with our new treasure. It was a sweet moment for me to have a connection with someone in the country. I walked out of the Church smiling with my heart warmed.

I walked into a massive open space surrounded by giant buildings. It was the Palace Square where the Winter Palace, Hermitage Museum, National Pushkin Museum, and General Staff Building are located. It was so vast that I was blown away. I had only focused on seeing the church and I had no idea what else I would see in Saint Petersburg's stunning architecture.

Dinner was the most isolating experience I had on my trip to date. Typically, I would speak to someone, but there was a different vibe. The way it came across to me was that the Russians didn't give a shit about communicating randomly. It was a way more reserved atmosphere than I had anticipated. I knew that conversation would be challenging since I didn't speak the native language. It was a different culture than I was used to. I decided to head back to the hotel room after I finished eating.

When I walked back into the hotel, I accidentally saw into a room that I believe had cameras. This caught me off guard, but at the same time made sense with the environment that I had been experiencing here. It really did feel as if you were being watched all the time. I was curious as to where the cameras saw. I called one of my friends for comfort. It was nice to have a conversation with someone. As we talked, we joked about being spied on, so we pretended to be secretive.

There was a Lush store in Saint Petersburg. I wanted to see all the products since I knew the names and wanted to see if they were in English or what it looked like in Russian. Upon entering the shop, I asked the sales associate if she spoke English. She told me a little. As I looked around, a security guard followed me around the shop. I didn't stay long since it was uncomfortable being watched.

The canals added to the ambience of the city. I took a tour on a boat through the canals. When I was talking to the tour guide, he was speaking to me in English. However, once the tour started, it was done all in Russian. Therefore, I learned absolutely nothing about Saint Petersburg. I was so upset that I took an expensive boat tour for no reason other than to be on a boat. I had been trying my best to keep my composure, but this was starting to defeat me. The isolation I was experiencing was getting to me mentally.

I continued to the Hermitage Museum to check out some art before heading back to the hotel. Shortly after I started walking through, I realized I was uninspired by the art I was seeing. Once I acknowledged that no one cared if I wanted to leave, I left. It had been one of my first art museums and it just was not my thing. Plus, I was ready to just go back to my room and relax.

When I got back to the room, I noticed that I was feeling a little under the weather. I watched the last playoff game Detroit played in by skyping Megan's television. It was a creative way for me to watch. I appreciated having the downtime so that I could start feeling better. The hard part about traveling on the road was I felt guilty for needing a moment to myself. It had been needed for my soul to rejuvenate. Feeling a little sick along with the cold reception received from those who lived there, I needed to have this time to cry. There were parts of the isolation that triggered the feelings I had experienced after my mom passed away.

My flight to Moscow the following morning was rather early. To ensure I did not miss my flight, I decided to take a cab to the airport. A personal rule I had made for myself was to rely on public transportation rather than cabs. However, it made no sense to miss a flight because of a made-up rule. It was a challenging environment for me to know how to get around. The hotel had breakfast to go to take with me and the cab was waiting for me when I got to the lobby. It had been an excellent decision to get to the airport with ease.

In Moscow, I stayed at a hostel again since I had already gotten approved to be in the country from the hotel I had just stayed at. Once I locked up all my stuff, I headed out to see the city. One of the perks of hostels was they always seemed to be in the heart of the city. Walking around seemed to flow a little bit easier since I was close to the Red Square.

I wanted to see the Cathedral in Moscow. The Saint Basil's Cathedral was stunning to behold as I walked across the square. I headed inside to look around and see the mosaics. I ended up enjoying how this was one was decorated more in comparison to the one in Saint Petersburg. There were separate churches within the building. The four larger churches were viewed as the four compass points. Each one had its own color scheme that distinguished it from the other.

The best way for me to see the city was to utilize the hop on hop off buses. You would get an audio description of the city on the headset in your own language. At one point, I was sitting next to a woman from New York City. Her experience in Russia was vastly different than mine had been. She was an opera singer and touring the city on her day off. It was lovely to have a moment to talk to someone.

Turkey was my next destination. Being at the hostel with other travelers, I learned that to go to Turkey you needed to have a special visa. This was why I loved staying at hostels – other travelers would share details to help you have a great experience in the countries you were going to. Plus, in the conversations you would learn about other great countries or cities that you needed to add to your bucket list. I learned that the visa was not as extensive as the one for Russia, so I was able to complete it immediately.

I walked around the Kremlin to see what was there. As I walked back towards the Red Square, I found their Tomb of the Unknown Soldier. Even though this was a different country, I loved how this was another place where they honored their military in this fashion. This made me think of my mom since her favorite place to take the students on the Washington DC trip was the Tomb of the Unknown Soldier.

Even with the difficulty I experienced here, I was grateful that I was able to have the courage to jump through all the hoops to see the beautiful architecture this country has to offer. It was hands down the hardest place I traveled on my own.

When I boarded the plane to head to Istanbul, Turkey, my phone rang. I did not answer it since I did not recognize the country code that was calling my phone. I was shocked that my phone even rang since I typically did not get phone calls while I was in Europe. I ignored the call and got on the plane to the next leg of my adventure.

58

When I booked the hostel, I chose it because the listing said it said that it had a stunning view of the city from the rooftop. However, when I got there, I had to climb up several flights of stairs on a circular staircase. Carrying the luggage up made me rethink my decision. Once I dropped my stuff off in a room, I headed to the rooftop for the view. As soon as I saw it, I was happy with my choice to stay. There was a clear shot of the city, the mosque, and the Sea of Marmara. There were cats all over and even on the rooftops walking around. The mosque then had its call to prayer, which initially took me off guard, but the manager of the hostel explained what I was hearing.

I connected to the Wi-Fi and had received an email from the previous hostel I had stayed at in Moscow. It turned out I accidentally left extra credit cards and other documents in my locker at the hostel. I had put secondary cards that were my backup in another wallet that I must have missed seeing when I was grabbing everything. That's who'd been trying to call me! I immediately panicked. If something were to happen where a credit card was compromised, I had no back up anymore. I asked the woman to send my stuff to Cyprus. It was then that I learned she was unable to send the credit cards to another country. There were restrictions in Russia that considered sending credit cards to be an illegal activity. I was angry that I had been so careless to forget something so important. I was nervous that I was just at the beginning of my trip. I was grateful they contacted me, but I had a meltdown at being so careless.

But, there was no point in beating myself up about it, so I headed over to see the Blue Mosque. Before I could go inside the building, I needed to buy a scarf to cover my head in respect to their beliefs. The woman whom I purchased it from helped put it on me securely. While I was trying to get into the building a man helped me by showing me where to go. I took my shoes off to go inside the beautiful building. This was not the first time I had been in a mosque since I had gone into one with Theresa and her husband. Even though I knew that there would be a separate area for women to worship, it was strange to see the signs posted for where women needed to go.

Afterwards, I headed over to see the Hagia Sophia. Truthfully, I had no idea what this was, but I knew that it was a place I needed to see. I was waiting in an incredibly long line to buy a ticket to enter when the man who helped me get into the Blue Mosque found me again. He grabbed someone so I could buy a ticket to get inside.

The way I understood the Hagia Sophia is that it has housed multiple religions over its existence. The mosaics were stunning, and some fit the various religious symbols that were for the different religions. It has now become a museum where people can admire the beauty inside. There were renovations going on while I was there. It was a stunning place to experience all the different changes the Hagia Sophia has gone through.

Afterwards, my new friend met me again when I walked out. He took me to get some Turkish coffee. For as odd as it was, he was a gentleman and I never felt worried about my safety. Coming from Russia where they are very standoffish, I was now in a culture that was overly friendly where they complement you about everything.

I knew there had to be a catch, but it was nice to talk to someone after having experienced the isolation.

He took me to his uncle's store to show me all the custom carpentry that he had available. I told him that I was traveling so it made no sense to purchase, to which he replied that I would be able to have it shipped. I told him that I was moving and had no place to send it to. After he realized I was not an ideal customer, he took me to another relative's shop where the merchandise was jewelry and scarves. Knowing I would be having to buy something before he would let me go on with my day, I decided to just buy a scarf. The manager at the hostel later informed me that it was common for men to approach tourists to sell to them.

I had dinner with a new girl who just arrived at the hostel and the manager. She was from Michigan. Dinner was a whole fish that had been cooked with its head and fin still intact. It was a little different than I am used to seeing fish served, but I understood that I was in a different culture. The Michigan girl and I chose to check out the city together to keep the Turkish men from approaching us since there would be two of us.

We went to Topkapi Palace. I would not have gone there on my own, but I ended up really being taken with the whole place. The views of the Sea of Marmara were breathtaking. It overlooks the Asian side of Istanbul. There were rare jewels on display which were securely placed behind glass panels. There even was a section where it showed sacred relics in one of the privy chambers. As you walked through, there was someone reading the Quran over the speaker.

As I was checking out the things on display, it occurred that those who held the same beliefs would find these items way more interesting than I did. However, it made me think about my beliefs. What we were raised with gave certain items more value to us. I was fascinated that many people in the bible were also in the Quran. They had a staff rod from Moses and a tooth from Muhammed. The tooth was very sacred to them, although I didn't fully understand why. Visiting Istanbul gave me an appreciation of the Muslim religion. Hearing the multiple calls to prayer throughout the day reminded me how devout they are and how sacred prayer is to them.

We walked over to another location in the city to see another mosque. There were fewer tourists, which made it a more enjoyable experience. We went to the Grand Bazaar to check out spices and other goods available at the market. There was a handsome guy working at one of the shops that pulled me into his shop. He had me try on various scarves and was flirting hardcore with me, telling me how beautiful I was. My friend took our picture together and called him my Turkish boyfriend. He invited us to meet him and his friends at a hookah bar later that evening.

We had dinner as we made our way back to the hostel. During dinner, I noticed how many smokers there were here in Europe. It was bothering me as I was trying to eat and all I could do was smell cigarette smoke. I noticed that Turkey had more smokers than the other cities I had been to.

We invited another one of our roommates to come out with us to meet these guys. It ended up being a fun evening out with my new Turkish boyfriend, his friends, and my new friends. He even kissed me goodnight as we went our separate ways.

On my way to the airport, I freaked out about how they drive. From the front seat, I watched how cars somehow maneuvered themselves to merge without any lines directing them. The driver told me that this was normal, but I was terrified of getting into an accident. I'd wanted to get to the Asian side of Turkey and achieved that, since the airport was technically in Asia.

Since I didn't have my priority pass, I was unable to use the lounge in the airport and there was no complimentary Wi-Fi. I flew to Budapest and by the time I got to the hostel I was tired and cranky. The hostel ended up providing dinner for all their guests, which helped shift my mood.

The only reason I came back to Budapest was to go to the baths in honor of my mom. Before I headed over to the baths, I went on a walking tour of the city. I learned so much on this tour and found a new appreciation for the city and culture, starting with how to properly pronounce Budapest. I started talking to a girl from New Orleans on the tour, and we ended up getting lunch together. We shared our stories of why we were traveling. She was taken with my story, and I was honored to share with someone who listened. It was an incredibly therapeutic moment to own that I was taking this trip to heal. Being here was symbolic in my healing process.

Afterwards, I headed over to the thermal baths, which were incredible. My mom would have loved soaking in the water. Some areas were warmer than others. I decided to spoil myself by getting a deep tissue massage. Being on the road for over two weeks, my body was ready for a massage (even if it turned out to be just okay). I was happy to complete this part of my journey.

Rosey met me in Prague so we could explore the city before I headed back to spend the week with her family. Since she had never been to Prague and I absolutely adored it, this was the perfect city to tour together. We used the hop on hop off bus, as it was the best way to get around to see all the top locations. I wanted to climb up the miniature Eiffel tower which was the Petrin lookout tower located on Petrin Hill. Rosey was not as excited as I was to climb up. There were two observation decks where you could take in the panoramic views of the city.

I knew there was a location in the city where my mom and I had taken a picture with soldiers, but I was unsure where this was. Once I saw the outside of the Prague Castle, I knew that this was it.

We talked about going to see either a ballet or an opera performance. We ended up going to see *Carmen*, which is an opera and ballet all in one. After the show, we saw a man who had a table set up with cups filled with water. He was creating stunning music as a water harpist. His ability to play songs only using water cups was impressive and mesmerizing to watch. He even played a song from *Carmen*, which we had just watched.

59

When we arrived at Rosey's house, her daughter welcomed me in and showed me all her toys. It was adorable. She had grown so much over the last three years. I assumed that she did not remember me as she was so young back in 2011. She was very talkative. Rosey eventually asked her daughter to let me settle in for a moment. Being in her home was going to be a fantastic break from being on the constant go. I was on a mission to see everything on my trip to Europe, but it was nice to schedule downtime with her family. Rosey always had felt like a sister to me since we knew each other's families as we were growing up.

The entire family took a day trip to Ayia Napa. We went to Cape Greco to take some photographs. The cliffs along with the water make this magical sight perfect for photos. I used my phone, but Rosey's husband used his professional camera to get some stunning shots. Rosey brought kites for the kids to play with. After we took our photos, we headed to get some food at a cafe. I was learning that Rosey's daughter loved to take selfies just like me.

That night I got to experience an event called Eurovision. I had seen advertisements in Copenhagen when I was there but did not really understand what this was. The event was being held in Copenhagen and broadcasted throughout Europe. I'd decided to liven up my hair with a henna conditioner I'd purchased at Lush in Prague. Rosey helped me by applying it to my hair, and while the henna worked its magic, we watched the show. It was uneventful until Conchita Wurst, a bearded drag queen from Austria, took the stage. She sang "Rise like a Phoenix." Twitter blew up while she was performing. In the end, she ended up winning Eurovision 2014.

We headed out to Zygi for lunch after we went to the home

church. The views were absolutely stunning with the bright blue water of the Mediterranean Sea. I had not thought about this when I planned the trip, but I was with Rosey over Mother's Day.

I was excited to go see a professional soccer game. I had not been to one in the US, but truthfully, it made sense to see my first game in Europe. Rosey's husband was a huge fan of Nicosia's Apoel team. He warned me that they had not been winning, but I must have brought them good luck by wearing one of the team's scarves to the game. The final score was 8-1 which Apoel won. I loved playing soccer so seeing a professional team play was exciting.

Rosey and I took a day trip out to Kourion to soak up some history. It was always cool to see the archaeological sites, as they were rare in the US. It was remarkable to witness what they were finding. I loved seeing the Greco-Roman theater. The mosaics they unearthed were stunning. One of the best things about being here was to get to see true history.

When we arrived back at the house, the package from the Moscow hostel arrived with all my stuff. I opened it up, and Rosey's son said, "That's it?" It made me laugh because here I had gotten myself all worked up over something so small. A child can show you how much you overreacted. They'd destroyed my credit cards, so the package only contained the case and a few other non-cash associated cards.

The rest of the time was quality time with Rosey. We visited the beach, went on a girl's night out, and took a trip to the mountains. It was refreshing to have my trip broken up by spending this time with Rosey and her family. Her husband told me I was welcome back any time I wanted to come. I warned him to only say it if he meant it as I do keep coming back. He told me that he knew how much it meant to Rosey to have her people visit so it was an open invitation.

60

My friend Kayla flew into Rome from the US to meet me. I timed my flight to arrive close to when she landed. We were going to be traveling together for the next two weeks and had planned where we wanted to go. First up was traveling all around Italy. I was a little nervous about how the trip would go but was hoping for the best.

"When in Rome" was our motto. We wanted to see all the major sights and consume all the food and wine we could. We went to see the Colosseum, which was massive. I had no expectations of most of the sights I went to – I wanted to be surprised. Inside the Colosseum was a gladiator's dream. I imagined what it must have been like for people to go during its heyday.

Kayla had requested that we tour the Vatican. Thankfully, Kayla had gotten us tickets ahead of time, so we did not need to wait in the huge line we saw on the way over. The first building we went in had an artistic sculpture of a male booty. This is where I discovered she was obsessed with male butts. She took many pictures with her grabbing the behind, which was pretty funny.

We did a tour with a guide through the museum portion. But, as I've said before, I'm not interested in museums so I was glad when the tour was over. We went into the Sistine Chapel, which was beautiful, but honestly it was a little much for my liking. They warned you not to take any photos or they would take your camera. I had expected to really take some time here to enjoy all the paintings, but it was quite busy so I was ready to leave as quickly as I could.

I did prefer the St. Peter's Basilica to the Vatican Museum. I loved that we could climb up to look out into Rome from the dome on St. Peter's Basilica. The stairwells were tight and at moments it felt very claustrophobic, but the view was worth it.

We went to the Trevi Fountain, we ate gelato, and we saw many of the other well-known landmarks. I saw all the places I wanted to see in Rome, but I had not fallen in love with the city the way others did. The history was phenomenal, but I prefer a little more nature in my travels.

We took the train over to Venice. This was a must see on my wish list. We walked around the city and then decided to take a gondola ride when we were approached by a cute Italian man. Kayla jokingly said that she wanted to kiss him under the bridges. She never realized that she was going to get it from the gondola driver himself! He gave us a tutorial on how to steer the gondola. After he showed Kayla how to maneuver the boat, he kissed her under the bridge.

When we got to Florence, I was not in awe. For some reason, I was not enjoying Italy like I thought I would. Tours of museums and cathedrals are not my thing. Kayla wanted to shop the markets, which is another thing I am not a fan of. I wanted to see more nature. I was making the most of it, but this is where it was tricky traveling with someone. If I'd been on my own, I would have moved on quicker to the next location.

We headed up to Piazzale Michelangelo to see the panoramic view of the city of Florence. We wanted to see Michelangelo's David in this area. Kayla loved seeing the butt cheeks, of course. We realized that the sun would be setting soon so we stayed to watch it. There were several people sitting on the stairs. We were sitting next to another traveler who was from Brazil and befriended him. The sunset was a stunning view. It was my favorite moment in Florence. We walked back to the hostel with our newfound friend.

On our way to Cinque Terre, we stopped in Pisa to check out the leaning tower of Pisa. I was happy to check it off the list as a place I have seen, but we didn't climb up the tower. I tried doing the artist photo where it looks like you're holding up the tower, but I couldn't quite manage it.

Cinque Terre was a must see for me. I saw Rick Steves talk about this area and knew that I would love to see it in person. There are five towns along the coast that you can only get to via train. We found a place to stay in the middle town of the five villages. When we arrived in Corniglia, we realized that we were going to have to hike up the stairs, all 33 flights of them or a total of 382 steps, with our luggage on our backs. Neither of us were too happy about this.

After we checked in and put our stuff in our room, we wanted to explore. We hiked to the next town, Vernazza, which only took an hour. This was finally a place in Italy that was exactly what I was looking for. The views were out of this world. You could see the colorful buildings in the next town over. We walked past vineyards and took in the beauty of the Mediterranean Sea along with the plush greenery of the vegetation on the side of the mountain. We saw a bar that overlooked the town, so we stopped to have a couple of drinks before we headed into the village. A full moon was shimmering over the sea.

The first morning, I awoke to a rooster crowing. Initially, I thought this was cool. However, when it did not stop throughout the day, the novelty wore off. Kayla was complaining that it wouldn't stop. While I agreed with her, it wasn't an alarm clock to turn off.

Kayla wanted to have a day at the beach, so we headed to Monterosso al Mare to lay out and enjoy the sun. It was a little bit overcast. However, this was the last full day, so we needed to make do with what we had. Once the rain started, we gave up on our beach day and hung out around the city before heading back to our hotel.

We had gotten into an argument the night prior, so when I woke up the morning we were leaving, I left the hotel to get breakfast at a cafe on my own. Kayla was still getting ready, and I needed a moment on my own. The view from the cafe looked out onto the Mediterranean Sea. I drank my coffee and enjoyed my moment of bliss. After an hour, Kayla found me at the cafe. She confessed that she thought I'd left without her. She had run down to the train station to see if I was there and then returned. I had to laugh that she had an extra roundtrip on those stairs. I told her that I'd never leave her but just needed to step away and have a moment to myself.

61

We arrived in Paris after a long day and night of travel, first from Cinque Terre to Milan, then on a sleeper train from Milan to Paris. Blake, my friend from my high school days, posted that he was going to be in Paris. He was travelling with his mom. I messaged him to see when he was going to be there. Coincidentally, we were going to be there at the same time. We were going to play it by ear but thought it would be fun to meet up. Kayla and I joined him and his mom to see Notre-Dame de Paris. While it was a gorgeous cathedral, I had officially got to the point of my travels where I never needed to see the inside of another museum or cathedral. The French Gothic architecture was beautiful, as were the stained-glass windows. We did a quick walkthrough while Blake and his mom took their time to see it all. We said our goodbyes and went our separate ways.

Kayla and I went to a pub to grab some food. While we were there, it started to rain. The rain provided the opportunity to take a break from being a tourist. By the time the rain stopped we were drunk. We walked around, but I really do not remember too much other than the love locks on the Ports des Art bridge. I had seen the same thing in other cities, but there were so many locks at this location that I wondered how the bridge did not collapse. A year later, they ended up taking the locks off the bridge to keep it from collapsing. I am glad I was able to see it before it was taken down.

Kayla and I headed towards the Eiffel Tower. It was nighttime so the tower was lit up. I contacted Blake to see if he wanted to join us. He got there just in time for us to take the last tour to the top of the Eiffel Tower. Afterwards, Blake walked us back to our hostel. We had a couple more drinks at the bar inside the hostel, then Kayla went to bed. Blake and I stood in the lobby of the hostel talking for another hour or two. He was exactly what I needed at that moment. I was transparent where I was in my grief with him. He had lost his father recently and was able to understand the pain of losing a parent. It felt as if it was a God thing that we were both in Paris at the exact same time. I was grateful for his time and friendship.

We were going to Amsterdam next but hadn't booked a train. When we went to the train station, we were informed that we needed to wait a couple of hours before we could get there. When we finally were able to get on a train, I was standing in a standby area until a seat opened for me. Kayla was in a different part of the car because her train pass was for a student. I was standing next to an Australian guy who was waiting to be seated too. Eventually we were moved to the first-class area in seats facing one another. The Aussie and I talked the entire train ride to Amsterdam. He had been there multiple times and was excited to be going again.

I met up with Kayla after deboarding the train. The Aussie, Kayla and I made our way to the hotel. The Aussie and Kayla wanted to check out a coffeeshop (where you can smoke marijuana, which is legal in Amsterdam), but I told Kayla I wanted to check into our hostel before we got high. It was a rule I had to have my bearings down before I became impaired with alcohol or marijuana. I wanted to know where everything was. Kayla was insistent on going to the coffeeshop with our new friend. Against my better judgement, I got high with my luggage in the coffeeshop. Our Aussie friend helped us find our hostel which was good because I was too high to be able to do anything.

I am not going to lie; Amsterdam was a complete shit show! I was high the entire time I was there. This meant I had no clue where I was at any moment. We checked out the Anne Frank House but quickly walked through. At some point, we went to a sex show with the Aussie. It was an interesting experience, to say the least!

Later, Kayla's phone was stolen. We tried to retrace our steps, but eventually we gave up. Kayla kept insisting that it was taken off the counter where we ate. She was upset that it had been stolen. I tried to be sympathetic, but I was frustrated.

When we were stoned, Kayla insisted that we rent bicycles to ride around Amsterdam. Again, I tried to say this was not a good idea only to be told it would be fine. It was not. I was in a foreign city riding around having no clue where in the world I was. I wondered how we would find where to return the bikes. I took a picture to use later to find the location. Every single street looked the same to me. We were able to drop off the bikes, but since the shop was closed, we couldn't get back Kayla's collateral – her license – until the morning when the office opened. We'd need to come back before we left the country in the morning.

It was incredibly late when I went to sleep. I didn't hear my alarm go off so we overslept and missed our flight. Kayla had stayed up to smoke the rest of the weed we purchased since we couldn't take it with us to Ireland. Kayla no longer had her phone, so she was relying on me. I woke her up in a panic. As we finally got everything together to head out to the airport, we saw a sign that said "Amsterdamaged." This was a perfect representation of what Amsterdam was for us.

By missing the flight, we found out that we weren't going to be able to get a flight to Ireland until the next day. At this point I was livid. We found a hotel near the airport to stay at for the day. I needed some separation time. I sat in a bar to try to cool down. I was angry that nothing had gone the way I wanted it to go in Amsterdam. I was mad at myself for going along with her requests when I knew that it would end poorly. I'd never missed a flight in my life.

It took me the entire day to cool down, but the next morning I was ready to start fresh. We were headed to Ireland. Two of my dear friends, Rachel and Megan, were meeting us in Dublin. A couple weeks before I left, they shared with me that they were meeting me in Dublin. Initially, it was supposed to be a surprise, but they decided to tell me. They'd been communicating with Kayla to surprise me. I was so excited to see my girlfriends there.

Kayla and I met Megan and Rachel at the Brazen Pub. After a rough couple of days, it was so wonderful to see my girls. After we enjoyed some Irish beer, we headed over to see the Ha'penny Bridge. There was someone that got close to Rachel that I could tell was trying to pickpocket her. I used my body to get in the way of it happening. Rachel never realized what was happening and thought I was making it up. I was proud that I was able to save her the heartache of having her wallet stolen.

Jessica, one of the girls that I had worked with at Lush, had moved to Dublin, and she joined the four of us for dinner. While we were out for dinner, Megan spilled ketchup on herself as she was shaking the bottle. She was upset that it got all over her clothes. The waitress brought her some club soda to help get it out of her clothing. There was a sense of entitlement when she believed she should have had her meal comped because of the ketchup. I, along with Jessica, was embarrassed that we were now perceived as those Americans.

Kayla and I had been planning this trip for months before I ever knew that Megan and Rachel were coming. Kayla wanted to go horseback riding at the Cliff of Moher. Her cousin and his wife lived in the area, and we were planning to see them. This is when it got a little awkward with Rachel and Megan. It came across like I was supposed to ditch Kayla and stay in Dublin with them. However, when I asked if I was going to be staying in their room, this was not an option. This put me in a weird situation. I had just been traveling with Kayla for the last ten days and I did not understand how I was supposed to leave her. I ultimately chose to keep my original plan to stay with Kayla and her family.

We stayed at her cousin's house. He and his pregnant wife were so sweet and endearing. They drove us around so that we could see the sights at the Cliffs of Moher. They took us to a place where we would be going horseback riding in the area. They were not interested in going with us but would be back to get us. My horse had a moustache! The sights were stunning to take in as we were riding around. Checking off this major bucket list item made Kayla incredibly happy.

When we got back to Dublin, we met up with Jessica again. She introduced us to her man. We went to a party. I left with Jessica and her guy, but Kayla stayed longer. We both were leaving the next day. I was headed on my own to Scotland and she was headed back to the US. I was happy that I no longer needed to be her babysitter. When she did not want to leave, I said goodbye and let her have fun. She ended up missing her flight which made me feel better about the missed flight in Amsterdam. It made me realize that it was not me who was irresponsible.

62

I was beyond elated to be traveling on my own again. It was great to break up my solo travels by touring with Rosey and with Kayla, but I was ready to be on my own again. Whatever made my heart happy was what I was going to do.

I flew into Edinburg to see what Scotland had to offer. I did a walking tour and learned that the county was obsessed with this dog Greyfriars Bobby. We went by the cemetery that inspired JK Rowling's character's names in the Harry Potter series.

After the tour was complete, I wanted to explore Edinburgh

Castle. While I was there, a guy asked to take my picture for me if I would take one of him. In retrospect this was his ploy to spark up a conversation. He was there on business from the States. He asked if I would be interested in having dinner with him later that evening. I was semi hesitant, but he said that it was an expense account and would be going whether I was going or not. The place he made reservations was at a fancy restaurant. I find it funny that this man struggled to be alone in his own thoughts. I am sure he was looking for a booty call at the end of the night, but he chose poorly when he asked me. He was married and it was not something I was willing to do. I thanked him for the evening and wished him luck on his adventures the next day.

I had the opportunity to try scotch in Scotland, but I absolutely hated it. The beer they served was not as cold as I am used to.

There was a Lush Spa in this city, so I booked an appointment for one of their treatments. I chose the Sound Bath. It was a magical experience, different from what I thought it would be. It was relaxing to have different sounds played throughout the experience.

From Edinburg, I took the train down to York, in England. The city walls gave it a different feel from any other city I had seen so far. From York, I was headed down to Poole where Lush originated. It was a personal bucket list item to see the original shop. There was a spa there where I had booked a treatment before I'd been to the one in Edinburgh. I stayed at a bed and breakfast in the town, where in the morning I enjoyed the best breakfast I'd ever had.

The massage the Lush Spa offered was called Synesthesia. When she asked me what theme I wanted my room to have, I chose "peace." After the massage, I was able to take a shower. It was amazing to be in a Lush Spa since all the products reminded me of my shower.

I took a day trip to the city of Bath. Emily had told me about the city of Bath since she'd lived there for a while when she was attending university. I went to the Thermae Bath Spa. It was a phenomenal decision to go there. They had four steam rooms with different essential oils in each room. The pool at the top of the building looked out onto Bath. It was a perfect way to spend a day.

Stonehenge was another must see on my bucket list. I arrived as close as I could by train, then took a tour bus over to see it. You really could not get that close to it, but it still was stunning to see. Truly an awe-inspiring moment.

I stayed in Brighton and took the train into London. When I got into London, I took the hop on hop off bus. This way, I was able to see the main attractions to check off my list. We passed by Buckingham Palace, Big Ben, Westminster Abbey, the London Eye, the Tower of London, and more.

Another friend of mine who I knew from the Jaycees, Gabrielle, was in London when I was going to be there. We used to get together for sushi as we talked about our experiences with grief. We planned to meet up close to the Tower of London. We hugged each other tightly and headed to catch up over a beer and dinner. Gabrielle was someone I always admired because her soul was so gentle and kind in the most nurturing way. I was glad we were able to connect before I headed onto the next city.

I took the train from London over to Brussels. What I loved about Belgium was the beer, which was potent and tasty. By far the best beer I'd had on my journey. I always asked for a domestic beer when I was in each country. Some people are foodies, where I'm one who loves a good local beer.

I checked out a place called Mini Europe. What was fun about this place was there were miniature mockups of many of the cities I had been to. Some of the things I got to see again were the Eiffel Tower, the thermal baths in Budapest, Big Ben, the leaning tower of Pisa, and the amphitheater in Kourion.

The Atomium was one of the tourist spots that I went to see. It was somewhat interesting, but more was one of those things that you do because you are there. Created for the World Fair in 1958, it is a landmark with various spheres connected by tubes. Inside there are escalators that connect the different spheres. It was entertaining, but not that worthwhile.

I was not a fan of the culture in Belgium. Most of the cities I had been to, I felt safe, but in Belgium the men had no issues with doing catcalls as women walked down the street. A man was following me, and I ducked into a casino to help me lose him. Overall, I was not that impressed with Belgium – other than the beer.

I needed to see the *Manneken Pis*, which is a statue of a little naked boy peeing. It was not something you needed to stare at for too long, but it was funny. I headed over to the Grand Place which is the main square. There I found vendors selling waffles and chocolate. It dawned on me that I was in Belgium, so duh, Belgium waffles. Of course, I needed to try them. They were phenomenal. There were plenty of chocolate shops to buy whatever your heart desired. Ok, so in the end there were two things I liked about Belgium: beer and chocolate.

63

I was excited to revisit to Spain since it was the first place I had ever traveled overseas. Now as an adult, I would be able to see it through different eyes. I arrived in Barcelona first. The hostel was close to the Casa Batllo by Gaudi. I didn't need to tour the house since seeing the outside, I knew it would not be of interest to me.

I went to see the views from Montjuic Castle which was a military fort back in the day that looked out to the Balearic Sea. Afterwards, I walked by the Olympic stadium that hosted the 1992 summer Olympics. I easily passed by the art museum without even questioning going inside. The grounds around the museum had lavish waterfalls and beautiful fountains which was all I needed to see. I passed by a bull fighting stadium. There wasn't an opportunity to see a live event, but I wasn't sure if I would enjoy one anyway, other than checking it off my list. I walked past The Sagrada Familia by Gaudi but didn't go inside.

The World Cup was happening as I was traveling so I watched it with all the other guests in the hostel. In the dining room, I eavesdropped on the three girls next to me. Their conversation was about scandalous sex, so it held my interest. I do not have a poker face, so they brought me into the conversation. One of the girls, Sarah, was incredibly friendly. They were heading out for the night and invited me to join them. Before I knew it, it was 5am.

I headed over to San Sebastian, a stunning location with a beach in an alcove. I wanted to go swimming in the water, but I didn't want to leave my personal items unattended. Fortunately, there was an American couple that were willing to watch my things for a moment.

The next city on my itinerary was Madrid. I spent a couple hours hanging out in a park under a tree. I'd been thinking about the firefighter and my expectations from him. I wanted more from our relationship, but it never was going to be. I was struggling to come to terms with it never being what I wanted. Sitting on the grass in the shade was a good way to calm me down.

While in Madrid, I wanted to see a flamenco performance. It was these sorts of cultural moments I preferred, rather than spending time walking around museums or cathedrals.

I did a day trip over to the town of Toledo. The city was surrounded by ancient walls. Upon arriving, I was able to feel the ancient vibe of the city. Toledo had a slower pace to the city of Madrid, which endeared it to me.

As I was taking a photo at one of the gates, I tripped and fell. My phone flew out of my hand. When I picked it up, I saw that the screen was shattered, and I couldn't see anything on the phone. I was worried about how I was going to do anything for the remaining trip. My phone was my essential tool for everything. I used maps to get everywhere, a train app to know when I could get to the next city, camera to capture the moment, and so much more.

Not knowing what to do, I decided to walk over to the fire department. The firefighter had asked me to get him a patch from the fire department there, and said he'd happily send over one from Toledo, Ohio. As I made my way over, I realized I was bleeding from the fall that I took. Not only was I crushed that I damaged my phone, but now I was starting to see I was physically hurt, too.

When I made it to the fire station, I didn't see anyone there. A man eventually appeared, and I asked him if he spoke English. He didn't, so he went to get his coworker. Jesus spoke little bit of English, so we used an app on his phone to translate to each other. I typed out how my friend was a firefighter who worked in Toledo, USA, and he wanted a patch of their department. He would mail him one back if I could have their address. He noticed my leg and had Gustavo get a chair for me to sit in while he cleaned my scrapes and bandaged them up. If I was going to fall and hurt myself, it was a good thing I was headed to a firehouse! Jesus returned with a patch and a couple of shirts that said bomberos ("firefighter" in Spanish) on the back. I showed him my phone, and he typed that he could take me somewhere to get it fixed.

After I was cleaned up, Jesus drove me over to a shop that was able to fix the screen on my phone. I thanked Jesus for helping me – he was my hero of the day. The shop told me they were able to fix it. When I heard the price initially, I thought it was only going to cost me 10 euro. After it was good to go, I realized that it was 100 euro. It didn't matter how much it cost because I was reliant on it. I headed over to the train station to go back to Madrid, and I spent the rest of the day drinking away my pain.

I flew over to Lisbon, Portugal. I'd wanted to visit since we learned about it in my mom's social studies class. I took a walking tour to learn more about the city. One of the things I hadn't realized was there was a massive earthquake that happened on All Saint's Day in 1755. It had been devastating to the town between the fires and tsunami that were a result of the earthquake. But, after the destruction, they recovered and rebuilt the town. I feel like there's a lesson in there somewhere.

64

I passed through Cologne, Germany and took the train to Lucerne, Switzerland. Lisa had recommended the city to me. The town was surrounded by water and mountains.

There was a tour which included rides on a boat, train, and gondola. The boat ride was on the beautiful Lake Lucerne. Swans were swimming in the lake, and a covered bridge went across a portion of the lake – it was picture perfect. When I got to the train station at Alpnachstad, there was a long wait for the train, so I sat on a bench drinking a beer listening to musicians play. The train was a cog wheel train which happens to be the steepest in the world. It is about a 45-minute ride going almost straight up the mountain. The views are out of this world. Once I made it to the top of Mount Pilatus, I explored and took in all the scenery. As I was climbing the mountain path, I heard someone in another language speaking and then the words "flip flops" came out of his mouth. It made me laugh that he was talking about me. Little did the man know but I hiked most locations in my flip flops, so it was not that big of a deal – and if they broke, I could fix them with a paper clip if I had to!

The cable car had a check point halfway down. There were different adventures you could do. I wanted to go on the toboggan run. As I was on the toboggan run, there were cows chilling, grazing the grass. It was Switzerland after all, so it made sense that there were cows on the side of a mountain. The second part of the gondola took me down to the city. It was one of my favorite days on my journey since I hadn't planned much.

As I was making my way to the Glacier Express, I stayed in Bern for the night. It was a stunning city, but I did not connect to it the way I had Lucerne. The water in Switzerland felt as if it was clean and fresh with a slight hint of green to the water. I made my way via train to Zermatt where I would be starting the train ride through the Alps.

Getting to Zermatt alone was such a stunning journey with majestic views that I wondered if I wasted spending extra on a train ride through the Alps, but as soon as I boarded and saw the full-length windows, I knew it was worth it. We passed by so many waterfalls on the journey. There was water everywhere in the form of rivers, lakes, waterfalls, and creeks. Even the cemeteries were beautiful. The Alps were plush and green, being summertime. At the beginning of our ride, it was incredibly sunny. However, as we made our way through the Alps, it started to get foggier and foggier. I am sure it continued in its beauty, but it became harder to see it. My destination was St. Moritz.

The rain had stopped, so I walked around the St. Moritz Lake, then I left for another long day on the train to Munich. When I got there, I realized I'd made my first faux pas in booking a hostel. There was an age restriction of 35. Since I was 36, I was unable to stay. I reached out to Sarah who I had met in Barcelona to see if she would be open to me arriving a day earlier than we had anticipated. When we were in Barcelona, she told me to come visit her in Berlin, so I'd changed my plans to see her.

During the day while Sarah worked, I decided to check out some of the sights, such as Brandenburg Gate, the Memorial to the Murdered Jews of Europe, Checkpoint Charlie, and other locations. We were going to go out after she got off work to watch the World Cup. I was excited to be able to watch the USA versus Germany game while I was in Germany. Some of her friends joined us at the bar to watch it, too. They set up a television on the patio so that guests would be able to watch it outside in the beautiful weather.

My last night in Berlin and we lived it up! We went out on the town, and I understood now why I had been out until 5 a.m. in Barcelona. I was out until 4 a.m. here in Berlin! It was fun to connect with Sarah again on this trip.

My last destination on my three-month journey was Warsaw, Poland. I had booked my flight back to the States from here. I was sad the adventure was ending, but I was looking forward to no longer living out of a suitcase. Also, to be able to sleep in the same bed sounded so luxurious.

I went on a walking tour because I wanted to see if there was anything else to learn about the city. I had visited here with my mom but didn't remember much from nine years prior. When we got to the city center, they talked about the Warsaw mermaid. The tour guide let us know that there is a legend that says the mermaid is a sister to the one in Copenhagen. I loved how my travels tied these together.

The last place I went to before going to the airport surprised me. When I saw the Chopin monument, I knew I had been here before with my mom on our Eastern European trip. Then I second guessed myself that I might be making this up since it was too serendipitous. As I made my way through the Royal Lazienki Park I saw the peacock and had no more doubt that this was the place that I saw first with my mom. I was overtaken with emotions at the synchronicity of spending my last day of my trip in the first place I saw with her on our trip. It tied it all together for me since this adventure was to honor my accomplishment of getting through the grief. Seeing this spot that reminded me of my mom meant everything. What fascinated me is that I hadn't even planned on coming to Poland until the end of the trip when I found it to be the cheapest flight back to the States. Maybe this was a God thing?

To summarize my adventure, I traveled from April to July.

Over 81 days, I visited 22 countries, slept in 38 different locations, and visited 50 different cities. I used fourteen different currencies on my journey and didn't repeat a currency until I hit my twelfth location with the Euro.

I understand that everyone has different experiences when they travel. They will love some of the cities I didn't and vice versa. My focus on this trip was to see as much as I could, and I felt I accomplished this. The people I met were part of my experience, too. I learned I enjoyed nature locations where the mountains and waters were, but museums not so much.

At moments it pushed me to my limits, but it was a great adventure.

65

When I arrived back in the States, I was slightly depressed. I was happy to be back, but the trip that I had been planning and anticipating for a couple years was over. Now what?

The very first thing was moving out of my apartment and in with Tricia. I had two weeks to move. This was a perfect blessing – my rent significantly dropped, and this meant I didn't feel the pressure to get another full-time job.

I was sad to leave the apartment. I'd been there for eight years, the longest I had ever lived somewhere in my adult life. By moving to Naperville, I started to rediscover myself and created great friendships that became my chosen family and support team. Now it was time to move to the next place.

It had been years since I'd a roommate. However, Tricia made me feel so welcome. Funny enough, her condo was a quarter mile from where I had lived in the apartment with Julia. A bonus of living with Tricia was that I now was even closer to Lush, where I was excited to get back to work.

Being back was strange, like reverse culture shock. I needed to acclimate back into the US culture which no longer seemed to agree with me. It felt superficial. I didn't know how to fit back into the box I never wanted to be in to begin with. One of my observations about living in Chicago was people's identities were wrapped up in their job title. This never aligned for me. However, now only working in retail, I struggled with believing I was being judged for not having a career.

My friendships with several of my Naperville friends felt different. There was the awkwardness with Rachel and Megan that felt unresolved. Beyond that, I was disconnected from all the happenings within the city. I was interested in seeing the world out there, more than just one town. Plus, I was struggling with finding out who I was now that my travels were over.

I made the most of my flexibility at work by traveling on my off time. Rosey was headed to Michigan, so I went to see her and her family. We had the opportunity to spend my birthday together at our childhood entertainment location where we could ride bumper cars and play arcade games. On the visit, I spent time with my grandma. The family reunion was happening right up the street, so I stopped by after my visit with my grandmother. It had been years since I had seen several of them, so I was happy I was able to attend.

Prior to heading to Michigan, I went to see the firefighter. I spent the day with him and his best friend. This was the first time that I started to take the blinders off. He had always said his best friend was the most positive person, but I listened to her bitch the entire time I was there. We didn't spend any quality time together since we went to a movie rather than talk to one another. I sat through the whole movie angry, which was unfair to him and me. When I shared after the movie how angry I was, we ended up parting on bad terms. I was perfectly content with being the "bad person" so I left, not caring if he thought it was my fault. It was time to take a break from him for my own mental health. It was clear as ever that we were never going to be romantically involved.

I went to Cabo San Lucas with a friend to celebrate her birthday. For all the times I had been to Mexico, I never saw the same city twice. When I told a girlfriend that I was going there, she pointed out that I was going places on a whim which were other people's once in a lifetime trips. It made me happy that I had given myself permission to do what I wanted. It was sad to think that so few explore the world.

I'd wanted to go to Vancouver, British Columbia since I was a child. I'd become obsessed with the province when I wrote a report about it in the fourth grade. I was excited to be able to finally go see it for myself. There also was a Lush factory in Vancouver, and I'd asked my new manager if I could get a tour inside.

When I landed, I took a ferry over to Victoria which is located on Vancouver Island. I was mesmerized by the shades of blue of the water and sky. I took countless pictures – being on a boat out in a gorgeous natural setting was my happy place. When I got to Victoria, I walked around the city after I dropped my stuff off at the hostel. I loved hostels now because it made sense to not waste money on a fancy room you didn't really spend much time in – I'd rather be out seeing the sights! I walked over to the Fisherman's Wharf where I saw a lighthouse at the end of a long pier. The sun was starting to set so I captured some amazing photos as I walked out to the end of the pier. The energy I was experiencing was the most calm and peaceful I had been since I had gotten back from Europe.

I saw an essential oil shop that I wanted to check out. From my experience with the products at Lush, I knew some of the benefits of essential oils. As I was shopping, I needed to use the restroom, so the employee told me where I needed to go, which was outside in a different part of the shopping complex. I smelled incense coming out of a shop which reminded me of the summer I lived in Jenni's friend's house. This drew me into a store which was full of crystals. Several of my coworkers from Lush were obsessed with crystals, so I decided to give them a try. I bought a few crystals and then headed back to the essential oil shop to purchase some items there, too. This moment started my journey with both crystals and essential oils.

Adventure was on my mind for this trip. I decided to go both on a whale watching tour and ziplining. We saw several whales on our tour. Being on the water was pure bliss. This trip was my first experience going ziplining and it was exhilarating to fly through the trees. I thought I would be nervous, but it fed my adventurous soul.

I saw the view of the city from the Vancouver lookout. It was breathtaking. One of the spots I could see was Stanley Park, a place I had wanted to go for years. It was fall and the leaves were starting to turn. A few of the trees were red, which is my favorite color to see in the leaves. I rented a bike so that I could ride around the whole park. There was a statue called a Girl in a Wetsuit. It was inspired by the image of the Little Mermaid in Copenhagen. It was awesome that I was able to see all three of the statues in one year!

I was excited for the Lush factory tour to see where everything was made. I was given a shirt and a hair net before they let me learn how to make a few of the items. It was a little bit before the Christmas holiday, so they were making a new few items I hadn't seen yet. I made a few bath bombs and got covered in glitter when I was making one of the holiday bubble bars. Overall, the opportunity to make bath bombs and see how the company ran from the inside out was a phenomenal experience that I was thrilled to be able to share with customers on the shop floor.

I went to a Vancouver Canucks game. When I got to the arena, I realized that my seat was at the top of the building. There was no one sitting behind me, which was a perk. The Canucks ended up winning the game. The trip to British Columbia was exactly what I needed. I was able to do all my favorites on this trip.

Once I got back home, Brian came back to visit. We went

downtown to check out Lincoln Park Zoo. Shockingly, I hadn't been there until he came to visit. We met up with my cousin Jodi from my dad's side afterwards. It was a true joy to have both sides of my family there. It was lovely and I felt honored to have this time with him.

A friend Valerie and I went to Toronto to watch the Red Wings play at their arena. We went to the hockey hall of fame museum – yeah, I know, I hate museums, but since it was about hockey, I enjoyed it. We stopped by Niagara Falls on the way back, which was breathtaking. You could feel the rush of the water falling from where we were standing.

I enjoyed exploring new places and having new adventures closer to home, but the holidays were approaching, which was always a difficult time of year.

66

The third holiday family-less was challenging. While the first and second years had their problems, there was something about the third year that made it the worst. I understood my new normal, but I was angry that I was still feeling all the emotions of grief and hadn't yet gotten to a place of acceptance. I remembered a woman from the grief group who had said the third year was her hardest, too.

If I opened to people, they would tell me, "You're not alone." This didn't help me in the slightest. I know they meant well, but what they were doing was minimizing my pain. They were not listening to me. They were trying to fix me, and I never asked to be fixed. I wanted to be seen and heard.

All I wanted was someone to just say, "Yes, it sucks." This is how I would have felt seen and heard. However, this would mean that someone would need to sit in the uncomfortable space of grief with me. Since most of my peers weren't in the same space, it was hard for them to show up this way for me.

Tricia invited me to spend the holidays with her and her family. It helped that she hosted them in our place. Her mother even bought me a Christmas gift, so I didn't feel excluded. It was thoughtful, but gifts are not my thing. Since my last moment with Todd was exchanging birthday gifts, I would get weird whenever people gave me gifts. While I was physically spending time with them, I still felt as if I didn't belong, like an outsider looking in. I couldn't change how I felt. I hadn't enjoyed the holidays since being a child, so I was ready for the season to be over as quickly as possible.

I tend to hold my breath from October to January. It is my cycle in the year where the grief is at its peak. My parent's birthdays, Thanksgiving, Christmas, Dad's death anniversary and my mom's death anniversary are all in this time period. I hadn't really realized the tension I felt during these few months. It wasn't depression, but in ways, it felt like it. Each year is different – some years are incredibly challenging and others, I get into the thick of this time period before I realize I have stopped breathing.

I went out to catch up with a friend as she was in town for the holidays. When she simply asked me how I was doing, I started to sob in the middle of a busy bar. I'd had this sense of, "What now?" since I had returned to Chicago. Trying to see how she could help, she asked me when I was happy. I thought about it and told her it was when I was traveling in Europe. She questioned why I didn't go back. It was in this simplistic question that I decided I would head back to Europe. This was the time to go, as I had nothing holding me back. Emily, my former Lush manager, had told me about a hike when I was first headed to Europe. It never fit into my plan, but now I'd be able to create another adventure around this pilgrimage called the Camino de Santiago.

67

Kayla asked me if I'd be interested in going to Costa Rica in January. Enough time had passed since our trip in Italy that it sounded like it would be something we could do again. My passport was expiring soon, but I could squeeze one more trip with it.

The hostel was super luxurious, with hammocks and a tiki bar for the guests! We started the trip in La Fortuna. Since it was close to the Arenal Volcano National Park, there were various adventures we could do within the area. The first day we ziplined and relaxed at the hot springs. There even was a water slide within the place.

One of my must dos for the trip was to go white water rafting. I knew that my brother wanted to go white water rafting on his camping trip before his accident, so I was excited to finally do this in honor of him. During the tour, there was a cliff we could jump off into the water. This terrified me, but I wanted to jump through my fear. Pura Vida is the theme in Costa Rica, which means "pure life."

We took a bus to the border. This is what I call the difference between vacationing and traveling – sometimes when you're traveling, you have to go with the flow and rough it! The bus was packed, so we were standing in the aisle until seats became available. The roads had so many potholes that the bus shook most of the drive. It was a dirt road for most of the ride up to Nicaragua.

When we arrived in Peñas Blanca, we almost didn't enter the country. They have a strict policy about not letting you in if your passport will be expiring within six months. Luckily, for some reason they let me into the country.

On our way to the beach at San Juan del Sur, the cab driver let us know that Survivor filmed here. While there, we chartered a sailboat. My favorite part of the boat ride was watching the sunset over the Pacific Ocean.

We headed back to La Fortuna where we had a reservation to stay in a treehouse. There were coffee and tea delivered to our porch every single morning. For breakfast, we headed over to the open dining space where benches were set up so we could watch the wildlife and various birds that were hanging out. The owner called it our nature television.

During the day, we booked a few more adventures. Rappelling down waterfalls was an absolute blast. Then we drove the ATVs through muddy puddles. The guide led us to a hot spring to clean off and relax for a moment. We wanted to see the La Fortuna waterfall, so we went horseback riding to see the waterfall and the hanging bridges.

When we tried to get our transfer back to the airport, we almost missed it because Kayla wanted to get food. She needed to run for us to catch our flight home. Kayla and I still butted heads a little bit, but we were continuing to work on our frictions through communicating better with one another. Overall, it was a great trip.

PART 3

68

This next trip to Europe had a different feel than the previous one. This trip had a mission. I was going to be hiking the Camino de Santiago. I talked to Emily about her experience and what I could expect with my journey. She recommended a book called *A Pilgrim's Guide to the Camino de Santiago*, by John Brierley. I was planning on starting the Camino April 1st. However, I went two weeks early so I could see the northern lights in Iceland.

I landed in Reykjavik and rented a car to go around the entire island on my own. However, when I put in the reservation, I put in for a manual car versus an automatic car. I realized this when I got in the car. I had never learned how to drive a stick shift, so I knew that I needed to change cars immediately. This came at a heftier cost, but one that was necessary if I was going to be able to drive around the island.

My first destination was in Akureyri which is located at the northern part of the island. While I was driving, the jet lag and the time difference were catching up to me, so I pulled over and took a needed nap on the side of the road. The drive was picture-perfect – there were so many crisp blue lakes surrounded by snow covered mountains. I kept wanting to stop and take photos of the scenery. I finally got to my hostel in Akureyri. There was a bar in the building, and it was a great place to get to unwind with other travelers.

If you drive a little bit outside of the city, there is an area called Myvatn. The Myvatn Lake was huge and there were different breathtaking areas surrounding it. You could smell sulfur in the air. There was an area you could walk around to see the bubbling gas, which looked like grey mud, that was coming up to the surface. In other areas, you could see the steam shooting into the air. I'd never witnessed such a thing before, how the earth was displaying its majesty. I went into the Myvatn nature baths. It was like the Blue Lagoon but had less tourists, which was fantastic. It was a wonderful way to relax, with the beautiful scenery surrounding the baths.

I headed over to the area of Krafla to see the Viti crater at the top of the lava fields. As I was making the hike up the mountain, I needed to stop to catch my breath. I was giving myself a hard time since I knew I was headed out for a month-long hike in less than two weeks. The steep incline was kicking my ass. My calves would start burning, so I would turn around to walk up backwards. I finally got to the top of Ziti crater, where the water was frozen over but still stunning to see.

I headed over to see a couple of waterfalls since they are my favorite natural landscape. As I was leaving the parking lot to take the path to the waterfall, I slipped on a patch of ice. Both of my feet flew out in front of me, and I landed on my left elbow. I was in immediate pain, concerned that I might have done some serious damage to my elbow, given how it was throbbing. I wanted to see Selfoss, which is said to be the most powerful waterfall in Europe, and I wanted to enjoy this moment, but all I could feel was the pain shooting from my elbow.

When I got back to the car, I was unable to find the keys. Panic started to hit me as I was in the middle of a country where I had no one to rely on. I took a breath to calm my mind. It occurred to me that I needed to go look where I fell to see if the keys had fallen out of my pocket when I landed on the ground. Luckily, I was able to see them peeking out of the snow that was covering the ice. I drove back to my hostel and used my right arm to steer as my left arm was throbbing in a way that I could never have imagined. I was unable to put my arm on the armrest since every time my elbow touched it, I was screaming out loud in pain.

I found my supplies to try to help with the pain. I put on an arnica cream which is a natural anti-inflammatory. I took pain relievers and headed to the bar to start drinking to numb the pain. I took a photo of my elbow so I could see it to examine it. There was a large knot forming that was the size of a baseball. A hint of blue was showing as well. I was worried about how bad this little fall would affect the rest of my trip. While I had travel insurance, I was not interested in going to the hospital because I fell on my ass.

I was heading to the east side of the island. Shortly after I passed the road to get to Selfoss, the weather started to turn on me. It started to snow, and roads became icy. The wind picked up which made me worry the car was going to be blown off and into a ditch. I was struggling to see the road. There were grooves where cars had driven on the road, but between the wind and the new snow falling, it was getting harder and harder to make it out. I was terrified. There was nothing around me as I was driving. Not only was the land covered in snow, but also the rental car was white too. It easily was on my top three worst drives I've ever done.

When I finally made it to the guest house outside of Seyoisfjorour, I was relieved to be able to relax for the night. The building I was staying in had several beds, but I ended up having the place completely to myself. I was grateful since I needed to decompress from the drive and give my elbow time to heal. The next morning, I had breakfast in the home of the family who operated the guest house. They were a sweet family who explained Icelandic culture to me. One thing I had been curious about was why the horses were so much smaller than I have seen elsewhere. They explained that it is a unique breed of horses that are native to only Iceland.

The next morning the drive was still a little challenging since the fog was heavy, making it difficult to see while driving. I'd learned on the plane that people were flying over to Iceland to see the eclipse that was going on. As the sky started to clear, I managed to capture the tail end of the eclipse as I was driving along the coastline inlets.

I arrived at the next place I was staying the night in, Hofn. I asked what would be worth visiting, and they told me to check out this place called Hoffell. It was hot baths that were in the middle of the mountains. When I arrived, I was the only one there. You pay based on the honor system in a drop box. There were four different tubs, each one a different temperature. This was taking thermal baths to the next level! I loved the exclusiveness of this amazing experience. Not only was it relaxing, but also it was a private and unique little gem.

As I was driving, I came across Diamond Beach. If I'd done my research, I would have wanted to stop here. Instead, I was surprised at how awe inspiring it was. The black sand beach had hundreds of natural ice sculptures on it. What I didn't realize is that it was part of the glacier that had broken off and landed on this beach. I stood there amazed, staring at this unique beach, the likes of which I never dreamed of. A little farther down the road, I stopped again to explore. It had been a little bit foggy in this area, so I didn't see it until I was upon it: Jokulsarlon lagoon, where thousands of ice caps were floating on by. I passed by Svinafellsjokull Glacier, which I had been seeing for several miles before I got close to it. It is the largest ice cap in Europe, and you could get gear to hike it, but unfortunately, I didn't have time.

The hostel that I was staying at was right next to Skogafoss waterfall. I decided to climb up the side of the waterfall to get different viewpoints of this magical wonder. I went to see Gullfoss waterfall again, too. This time it was snowing when I was there. I also headed to see Geysir again. I magically stumbled upon the Vatnsleysufoss Waterfall. It was like a smaller version of Gullfoss. Seeing all the waterfalls in this stunning country was so magnificent for my soul.

The last place I went on my trip around the island was Reykjavik. I wanted to see those northern lights, and this was the perfect opportunity. This time, I went into the Hallgrimskirkja to see the views from the church. I was able to see the northern lights this time, which meant my mission in Iceland was complete. I was able to travel around the entire country and I was able to finally see the aurora borealis.

I flew over to Edinburgh to see the city again. When I was on the walking tour the previous year, the tour guide said it rained often in the city. Both times I visited, the weather was stunning with blue skies and big, white, fluffy clouds. I guess I lucked out!

As I was on my way to Cardiff, a man in a kilt asked me where I was headed. He was thrilled that I was going to Wales since most tourists do not take the time to visit the country. I visited Dolwyddelan Castle. There were all these knitted afghans on the trees that I found interesting and strange at the very same time. At a market, I bought a piece of moldavite – a crystal (technically glass) formed by a meteorite – to carry with me on my trip across Spain. I also bought a stuffed animal since I wanted something soft and cuddly to carry on my journey.

I went back to Bath since I needed to experience the luxurious steam rooms at the Thermae Spa again. I savored this experience by getting food and drinks. This is one of my favorite places to rejuvenate in the world. By the time I got to Bath, my elbow had healed. I was relieved it was not worse than a welt and a bruise.

I took the train to London to stay with a friend from college who was living with her husband on the outskirts of the city. It was wonderful to catch up with her. I hadn't seen her since my dad's funeral when she and her two best friends came to support me. The three of us went out on the town for drinks. The following day, we were able to watch the Red Wings playoff game. I had a feeling she'd have a way to watch sports from the States as she was a die-hard sports fan.

During the day, I took a trip to a Lush store in London called Lush Gorilla Perfumes. It was a specialty store with perfumes exclusive to this location. Being a die-hard Lushie, I knew that I needed to get these perfumes that weren't available anywhere else. I also made a special trip out to visit the Poole location, too. This time, I asked my manager if she could arrange a meet-up with Mark Constantine, the creator of Lush. Much to my delight, I was able to shake his hand. I ended up getting my picture taken with Mark Constantine, Mo Constantine, and Rowena Bird, the co-founder of Lush. This was an awesome moment for me. Mark even gave me a large bar of soap that he had recently created.

My mission in the UK was complete. I was ready to get to France and start the journey of the Camino de Santiago.

69

I boarded a flight to Bordeaux, France, where there was a bus that would take me to St. Jean de Pied de Port, which is where I would begin my journey to the Camino de Santiago. Also known in English as the way of St. James, the Camino de Santiago or "El Camino" is an ancient pilgrimage said to be the path the apostle James took as he was preaching the gospel in Spain. My focus was to slow life down by walking across Spain in order to face my grief head on. I anticipated it would take me over a month to hike, which would give me time to be with the pain and anguish without escaping it.

After the plane landed, I waited for my bag to arrive. I waited and waited until I was the only one still waiting and the conveyor belt turned off. Then the panic hit me. How in the world was I to start the Camino if my bag with all my supplies wasn't there? I had to report it missing. I was frantic because I was in a country where I felt uncomfortable – for some reason, I had this belief that they didn't like Americans, especially ones who didn't speak the language. The woman who dealt with me had way more patience than I would have had. There was a flight arriving at the same time tomorrow, so she said to come back then to see if my luggage arrived.

I found a hotel within walking distance and booked a room. I was over-the-top hysterical and not handling the stress well. Without my belongings, I thought I wasn't going to be able to do the Camino.

The hotel had a bar and restaurant. Being in Bordeaux country, I decided to start drinking wine. It was a perfect storm to get out of control. I had a full-blown drunken adult temper tantrum. As I hadn't eaten anything yet that day, I went to the restaurant. I was unable to get control of my emotions and continued to wail as I sat there trying to eat. A waitress tried to make sure I was okay, but I was beyond consolable, so I just cried more. I wish I could edit this out of my story since I am embarrassed by my actions, but I can own that I showed up poorly.

I messaged friends to share my frustrations, but I was completely irrational. My luggage was missing, and it felt as if it was the end of my world. I knew I needed to complete the Camino by the beginning of May since I'd booked a flight out of Madrid for then. I was unable to hear anyone's encouragement that it would work out. It was evident that I had reached my capacity for dealing with yet another setback in life. It was a metaphor for me, but I was not in a place to see the opportunity – it was only a failure in this moment.

I was overjoyed when my luggage arrived the following day. I rushed over to where the bus was departing to take us to St. Jean. While I was waiting to board, I noticed a guy had a couple of Camino patches on his backpack. One was the symbol of the shell, and the other was a blue background with a yellow arrow with the sun. Most of the people on the bus were soon-to-be pilgrims on the Camino de Santiago.

Everyone started walking to the Pilgrimage office when we arrived in St. Jean. At the office was where we received our paper passports that we would use to get stamps at the albergues along the way. Albergues were typically a large dorm room with multiple bunk beds where you would find refuge while on the Camino. After I got the passport with my first stamp, I headed out to find my hotel room I booked for the night. With the luggage delay, I missed my reservations for the first two locations. I needed to book a new place that was a little farther out of the city center.

Words cannot describe the excitement I felt as I stood at the old bridge over the Nive River. I had seen photos of this location, and it felt incredible to be officially here. Even though yesterday I had broken down emotionally, I was happy to be here starting my pilgrimage tomorrow. As I laid my head down to fall asleep, I felt a blister on my right foot. I knew that I was going to possibly get blisters while walking, but I couldn't believe I had one before I started.

In the morning, I took my time getting in a good breakfast before I started out for a long day ahead. My destination was Roncesvalles, which was approximately 25km away. I thought I was heading out rather early, but there were a few people out on the trail. I put my coat on to keep warm as there was a bit of a chill in the air.

The scenery was stunning. The sky was a clear blue with few clouds. The grass was lush and green. There were even some sheep in the fields that I walked past. Arneguy is where I walked into Spain from France. The roads started to get windy and hilly. In the distance, I could see the city of Valcarlos. It appeared as if it were up on a hill, but the pathway led us down into the woods before I would reach the town. Mostly, I'd been walking on the asphalt of the road. As I headed down into the forest, the ground was softer to walk on than the hard concrete. Walking through the woods, I saw streams, cascade waterfalls, and a small river that followed the pathway. I couldn't help but take several photos, thrilled to be out in the fresh air, on my way to the unknown.

As I started to get closer to Valcarlos, I found a place to sit and rest for a moment. A gentleman was sitting next to me, and we struck up a conversation. He was staying in the town rather than walking all the way to Roncesvalles, which was a brilliant decision. He was writing a blog about his journey and told me where I could find him. After I left him, the path became an incline, which felt as if it would never end. I realized I'd made a massive error by not stopping to eat and get refueled.

I was in the thick of hiking through the Pyrenees. I came upon a stone wall where I decided to take my backpack off, sit down and catch my breath. I had hiked up a mountain to see where Todd fell, but I hadn't been carrying an oversized bag. My bag was heavy too since I had items to carry for three months and the perfumes, which I was unable to send. I had anticipated shipping them home, but when I went to the post office, I was unable to send liquids from the UK. To make matters even worse, I made a rookie mistake by packing them at the top of my bag, meaning the weight wasn't distributed properly.

I was skeptical if I'd want to use hiking poles, but I was happy to use them to push me up the mountain. As the day progressed, I was taking more breaks to recover. I kept wondering if this shit was ever going to end. I hadn't seen anyone in hours and the sun looked as it was getting closer to setting soon. I was exhausted. I questioned why in the world I'd set out to do this. Would I even be able to do this for thirty days?

At the top of the mountain, I could see the mountains I had walked through. This showed me how far I'd walked. It was astounding and frustrating all at the same time. There were markers to let you know which way to go and how close you were to the next village. I knew that Roncesvalles was only another kilometer away. I was close, but it felt so far.

When I arrived in Roncesvalles, I went to the albergue to see if they had any more availability and happily took the last bed that they had. They asked me if I wanted to purchase the pilgrim meal for an additional fee. I was starving so I paid for it and headed up to my bed to drop my stuff off. My bed was located on the third floor which meant I slowly walked up the additional three flights of stairs at the end of a long day. People commented on how exhausted I looked.

Someone told me that a shower would make a world of a difference to me, so I gathered my stuff and went to try. Being my first night in an albergue, my expectations were higher than the reality. It was a timed shower, so you had to keep pushing the button for the water to come out. Top that off with the water was slightly hotter than lukewarm. For something that was supposed to make me feel better, it was a huge disappointment.

Since I was going to be heading to sleep right after I ate, I put on my pajamas, which were shorts and a tank top. I put on my flip flops and headed downstairs to get much needed food. I slowly crept down the three flights of stairs taking one stair at a time. I asked the desk where the dining room was and was shocked to discover that it wasn't in the main building. I looked down and knew what I was wearing was not appropriate to wear into a restaurant, but then I looked over to the steps and knew there was no way I could go back up and down again. I proceeded to the restaurant, not caring that I was underdressed.

When I arrived, there was a long line of people waiting to be seated. To try to get everyone in to have dinner, they started asking people to sit with other parties. I didn't care who I was seated with as long as I could eat. The couple started asking me question after question. I was slowly responding to them. They never got the hint that I wanted silence, so I point blank told them I was exhausted and had no more energy left to speak. I finished eating, wished them well, and excused myself to head to bed.

Before I fell asleep, I quickly journaled:

> *That was the hardest thing I have EVER done! It was painful and I didn't believe I would make it. I didn't have any moments of clarity other than everything is an uphill battle! Many times, I*

swore at God because in my life, He just has not been there. I didn't feel good the entire time. When I got to the albergue, I heard some people fell and had to go home. At least I never fell. My bag is way too heavy. My body has never felt this kind of pain before – EVER!

Beyond exhausted, I fell asleep rather quickly. When I woke up, there were very few people in the room. I learned people got up early to start hiking as the sun rises. I've never been a morning person so I knew I would never be getting ready in the dark. As I made my way out of the building, there was a table full of items left by the pilgrims. People left extra items that might have been weighing their bag down. I wished I could lighten my bag, but at least I had rearranged it so that the perfumes were no longer at the top.

Even though it was officially spring, there was still snow on the ground. I was doing my best to get excited about the second day of the hike, but mentally I was struggling. I passed the famous sign that shows you it is 790km to Santiago de Compostela. I asked another person to take a photo of me to capture this iconic spot. Then I gathered my strength and headed out for my second day of hiking.

70

As day two got off to a start, it was nice to be on the gravel path versus the road. And thankfully, it was flat! I passed by so many farms with sheep. The couple that I had dinner with the night before greeted me as they walked past. When I got to the first town, I stopped in a restaurant for breakfast. I started the pattern of having a breakfast baguette with café con leche. I typically did not drink coffee, but when I was in Europe, this was how I preferred to start my day. I dreaded the thought of getting up to put my backpack back on and walk. I checked the book which told me it was only another 3.5km to the next town.

Every time you passed another peregrino (pilgrim) you would say the phrase, "Buen Camino." This literally means "good road" or "good path." Path could mean either the physical or spiritual path. It was the way to greet one another, no matter what language we spoke. It became the greeting I used instead of the standard English hello. Along the pathway, there were yellow arrows to let you know when you needed to turn or let you know you were on the path. There were moments that I would panic if I had not seen one in a while.

When I got to the second town, I had to sit again. I headed into a bar and ordered a beer. This refreshed me so much, I had a second one, and it took the edge off the pain I was experiencing. I was wanting to do approximately twenty kilometers per day, but I decided if I were tired, it would be okay to pause. Mentally and physically, I knew that I needed to take care of myself, so I would more than likely be stopping early for the day. I saw a place in the guidebook I could stay, so I found it and knocked on the door. The woman who answered hesitated for a moment and asked how many people were in my party. I said it was just me. She let me in as their last guest for the day. Others would be arriving later as they had already pre booked with her.

She showed me the room I would be staying in. I was grateful to have my own room for the night. I took my backpack off and laid down on the bed. I was going to nap, but she came back to show me around the house. She had an accent, but I knew that it wasn't Spanish. She asked me if I smoked, to which I replied I did not. She asked if I would be willing to sit with her while she did. While we were sitting there, she shared with me that her husband would be gone for only an hour, and she needed to sneak in her cigarettes before he returned.

We had a lovely conversation. She revealed to me she was Hungarian. I commented how I had been to her country a couple times. She wanted to know if I knew how to pronounce the capital of the country. When I was able to say Budapest properly, she was impressed. When I was sharing that I stopped because my backpack was way too heavy, she informed me there is a company that picks up your stuff and delivers it to your destination. This was a game changer for me! If I could lighten my load, it would be manageable. I happened to have a smaller backpack to take essentials with me for the day. Between resting and lessening the amount I had to carry, I was finally excited to get back to the Camino.

They hosted a dinner where we were able to connect with the hosts and the other guests. This style of dinner was what I preferred, rather than going to a restaurant in my pajamas. The other guests all had a partner that they were walking with. I was happy that I had traveled the year before and knew that I prefer to travel solo. My speed on the trail was a lot slower than I had imagined it would be. Not having the pressure of needing to keep up with anyone other than myself was perfect for my own journey.

I was rejuvenated from my stay at the guest house and excited to be back at it. This was my first day where there was an overcast. When I paused to have a little break on a fallen tree, I witnessed a double rainbow. It was not incredibly vibrant, but it reminded me that there is beauty everywhere.

One of the hardest things to deal with was how hard the ground was. Roads are obviously hard. The dirt pathway is hard as well, compacted from everyone walking these same places over the years. There also were a lot of rocks. I knew I was going to need to do something to have more cushion in my shoes to absorb the impact on my feet. I knew people had prepared for the hike by walking on treadmills, but nothing can prepare your feet for how much they hurt after walking all day long on the hard ground.

There were special pilgrim meals that you could get on the pathway. I stopped for lunch, but when I walked away, I forgot one of my hiking sticks. I had been only walking with one of them, otherwise, I would have forgotten them both. When I realized that I had forgotten my hiking stick, I was way too far away to go back to get it. I had been on an incline and the thought of having to hike down and back up again was not worth it.

I approached a landslide where the pathway had collapsed. I climbed down and then needed to pull myself up the other side. I was so grateful that I did not have my full backpack, or I would never have been able to climb to get back onto the path. It was strange that there was not a way around this collapsed land.

My fourth day on the Camino happened to be Easter. While I never planned walking during Holy Week, in retrospect it ended up being perfect. I learned that several people would come and walk a portion of the Camino during Holy Week. Some people were unable to walk the entire passage, so they would do it week by week over the years. I had the honor of walking through Pamplona on Easter. I was thrilled to see the city where the running of the bulls is held. On the outskirts of the city, I paused to have lunch and a beer before continuing. Quite possibly the best Easter I'd had in years.

Outside of Pamplona, the scenery was stunning. Yellow flowers in green fields. Cerulean sky with white fluffy clouds. Seeing these lovely vibrant colors brings me a sense of calm. Whenever I saw a bench, I would take a moment to pause and rest my feet for a bit. These were great moments to reflect on my journey. Being Easter, I chose to have a shortened walk. It would give me time to tend to the blisters on both of my feet. I had packed Compeed blister care and I was going through it way faster than I had anticipated.

Every time I eased up on my mileage for the day, I would walk a longer day to make up for it. Also, the rest was necessary to give me the strength to walk farther distances. After Easter, I planned on a 26km day.

Shortly after I started the day, I came across the Alto de Perdón, which means "hill of forgiveness." This location contains 14 natural sized iron figures that made their way by foot, horse, or donkey. It is a famous landmark of the Camino path. The view looks over the

El Perdón mountain range, where there is a wind farm with 40 turbines. There was a food truck where I bought a beer, so I relaxed and took in this beautiful scenery.

As I continued the journey, I crossed the famous bridge in Puente La Reina, which translates to "bridge of the queen." Right outside of town, I felt someone's presence behind me. When I turned around, I saw a shepherd with his sheep. They were gaining on me quickly, so I stepped over to a pile of rocks to sit on while I let them pass me. This was by far the coolest thing that I had seen on the path. I was walking this ancient pilgrimage where the apostle James was said to have preached to the country, and I was witnessing a real-life shepherd with his flock of sheep. It felt as if I was in biblical times. After they passed me, I watched the two dogs that were keeping the sheep in line and on the correct course. They went into their gated pasture. I couldn't stop smiling ear to ear in this exquisite moment that I would never be able to recreate.

71

I came upon a cross with thousands of rocks lying beneath it. One of the lessons of the Camino journey is letting things go that no longer serve you or are weighing you down. To symbolize this, people stacked rocks in pyramids on different things such as the Camino markers. I had yet to lay a rock down as I had not figured out what it was that I needed to let go of. I had an idea, but it was not complete. I had only just begun this journey so I knew it would come to me when I was ready.

Any town I stopped to rest; I would treat myself to a beer. This all started that second day on the Camino when I realized that beer helped take the edge off the pain I was feeling in my body, especially my feet. Jokingly, I've called it the longest pub crawl of my life. I'd start the day with a café con leche, then any following town I came upon, I would start drinking beer. If the villages were spaced out exactly right, I would be able to maintain a slight buzz throughout the day.

Walking in April, I wondered how people were able to walk the Camino during the summertime. There were several days where it was so hot out that I imagined I would overheat in the summer. This might be why they all got up early in the morning, so they would be resting when the weather was at its hottest peak. I brought my scarf I bought in Istanbul the year prior to protect me from getting sunburned. The large rocks on the path continued to add pressure to the soles of my feet. I purchased jelly insert soles to add inside my shoe to give it a little extra cushion, but it still hurt as I navigated through the rocks and boulders.

The scallop shell is an iconic symbol of the Camino de Santiago. I've heard two different reasons for this. The first is that it is said pilgrims would use it for food along the journey. The second one was to use it as proof that you had been on the pilgrimage when you got to Finisterre. I purchased a shell so I would be able to add it to my backpack. There was a sense of pride having it on my belongings.

At the albergue I was staying at, I noticed a woman that I had seen on my very first day right outside of the Pilgrim office in St. Jean. I heard that you meet different earthly angels on your journey. When I originally saw her, I hoped our paths would cross again. We talked briefly in the albergue.

My new friend was from Australia. We were heading out of the village at the same time, so we decided to start the day together. When we walked into the city of Estella, we stopped at a deli to get items to make lunch. Right after the deli there was a crystal shop. The translation of the shop was "health art." I was called to buy a necklace of blue kyanite. I had no idea what it meant but discovered later it helps support authenticity and weight loss. It was a Taurus stone, which I didn't realize, and I would be walking the second half of the Camino in the Taurus moon!

We found a grassy knoll to sit down to have our lunch. As I was looking at the map on my phone, I saw a thing that said "Vine Fountain." I pulled out my Camino book and realized that this was said to have free wine, and it was close by. I was excited to hear such a thing existed and felt lucky that this was the location we had chosen to sit outside. When we finished eating, we headed back to check out this place called Fuente de Vino, which means "fountain of wine." Who knew there was such a beautiful gift available for all the pilgrims? I happened to have a plastic water bottle that I filled up with wine. It was a wonderful treat to have this wine on my journey.

After we left there, the Australian girl asked if I minded that she went ahead as I was on a slower pace. I was ready to have time alone. I was slightly buzzed and enjoying the beauty of the landscape.

When I arrived in the city, I was staying in the same albergue as the Australian girl. This location had a dinner provided for all the pilgrims, and they gave us a miniature book of John. The workers were on a mission to serve those who were making this pilgrimage. As I was getting ready in the morning, I was putting makeup on. A woman sitting across the room started laughing. She didn't speak English, but I was able to understand that she was laughing at how I was putting on makeup and she was putting on Band-Aids for her blisters. It was a great observation since I really did need to take better care of my feet rather than worrying about how my makeup looked!

I was now most certainly in wine country. Most of the fields that I passed by were vineyards, rather than farmland. There were different regions along the path, and it was great to see the landscape changing. I came across a little pop-up restaurant. A man who was at the same albergue I stayed at the night prior was sitting at a picnic table. He started giggling as I was eating. He openly shared he was still laughing about the perfumes I was carrying with me on this journey. I got that it was funny, but how funny he found it rather annoyed me. I was no longer complaining about it, so I didn't get why it really was any of his business. As I made my way back to the path, there was a shoe on top of the stone marker leading the direction. Inside the shoe were some of the yellow flowers I was seeing in the fields. The platform also had a couple stones on which someone had drawn the British flag.

I stayed overnight in Torres del Río which had a church like the one in Jerusalem called Santo Sepulcher. I headed to Jerusalem after the Camino, but I never realized the two buildings were connected.

Right outside of Torres del Río, I came across a place that Emily texted me about the night before. I had been messaging her throughout the trip to see if my experience was different than hers. She asked me to leave a message for her at this location when I came upon it. Her timing ended up being perfect. The area was a sea of messages written on paper that were placed under large rocks. It was a place to ask the path to bless your journey. I wrote out her message and placed it under a rock. I started walking away without leaving one for myself, but an inner voice told me to turn around and leave one. This is the message I wrote: "Time to let go of control and allow the good to come to you. Trudi." Then I added at the bottom, since I knew there was more that needed to be said: "Time to release all your grief upon the Camino, for it will allow you to let go fully and live joyously. Trust in the positive energy!" I took a picture of it so I could look back on it once I completed my journey.

As I was en route to get to Logrono, I saw a spray-painted picture of a shell with the words "Buen Camino." It was on the opposite side of a tunnel I walked through. I took a photo and vowed that if I finished this journey, I would get this as a tattoo.

When I got to Logrono, I stayed an extra night to have a full day of rest. Knowing I would be here for two nights, I found a hotel room so I would be able to have privacy. I got a massage and laid around watching television on my phone. I realized that for me to complete the Camino, I needed to implement rest days. I knew that this meant that I would need to take a train to make up for my off time. I was not certain exactly what this would look like, but I knew that somehow it would all come together.

72

After my day of rest leaving Logrono, I was going to do 29.1km, my longest day thus far. I started with a café con leche in the morning and each little town I passed, I would order a cerveza grande (large beer). This day, each village was perfectly spaced out. By the time I got to the next village, I would use the restroom and order another beer.

Benches around scenic views were my favorite moments in the day. I would pause to take a break and drink in the beauty of nature. I took a break from listening to audiobooks and put on an EP I had of David Nail. One of his songs eventually became my theme song on this journey, called "The Sound of a Million Dreams." I would listen to it on repeat for hours – it helped calm the voices in my head. Whenever I hear this song, it always takes me back to the path.

There were multiple days in a row that were utterly picturesque, with the three colors of white, blue, and green mixed together. Depending on which region I was walking through, there was the addition of yellow from the wildflowers.

After multiple days of sunshine, it rained for several days. At least when it rained, there was a little bit of give in the ground to soften it. But one day, I'd had enough of walking in the rain. I headed into a bar to ask for a cab take me to my next destination. Initially, I felt bad for giving up, but I'd forgotten this was my journey. If I wanted to order a cab, I could order a cab. There was nothing wrong with asking for help when I needed it.

My second rest day was in the city of Burgos. The hotel had the thinnest walls, and I could hear noises all night long. I managed to find an American pizza place for lunch on my day off. I wish I could say it was good, but strangely, I missed the pilgrim meals. Since I was in a big city, I went out to the bar to feel like a normal person, rather than a pilgrim. The hotel had laundry service so my clothes could be cleaned by a machine rather than having to wash it by hand.

Upon leaving Burgos, the transportation company didn't take my bag. This meant that I was going to have to carry it for the day. I was so annoyed since it was raining and I had gotten used to not carrying it all day long. Typically I would have walked longer after a day of rest, but it ended up being shorter than I'd anticipated. The next days, I walked longer hikes to make up for this shorter hike.

I started climbing up a mountainside where there were switchbacks to help break up the incline. I took multiple breaks as I was walking up the mountain. At the top, there were benches to sit to recover. As I was walking on the plateau, I could see people way ahead of me. Suddenly someone grabbed my right arm which made me scream out loud. When I turned around, there was no one there. I was shaken, but I believed it was my mom's spirit that grabbed me. I did not tell anyone other than Emily since I did not think anyone would believe me. The reason I believe it was my mom was because it was my right arm that had been grabbed. When I was born, there was nerve damage done to my right shoulder. My mom always wished there was more she could do for me to have a fully functioning arm.

Becoming infatuated with crystals at the end of 2014, I decided that I would have a crystal of the year for 2015. I chose rose quartz since I wanted to focus on self-love. It was after I felt my mom's presence that I found it synchronistic that here I was, walking the Way of James with my crystal being rose quartz. My mother's name is Rose, and my father's name is James. I never planned it, but it was meant to be. They were with me my entire journey.

The firefighter's dad had been diagnosed with cancer and his health had progressively gotten worse. He'd asked me to please pray for his dad. While I was on the walk, I went into one of the chapels to say a prayer for the firefighter and his father. I knew he was stressed out taking care of his father and knowing he could lose him. After all the harsh things I'd said to him about not understanding my grief, I knew he was close to understanding the anguish you feel when you lose a parent. For all the times I had lacked compassion for him, I felt it now.

By the time I got to Fromista, I knew I would be taking a train from here to Leon. When looking for a part of the path I could skip, I chose an area that was flat and considered to be the dullest part of the journey. I would be skipping a little over 100km of walking by using the train. With adding in the necessary rest days, I needed to make up this mileage. My flight out of Spain had been set, so I knew when I needed to complete the Camino by. It was hard for me to put my pride to the side, but I knew that it needed to be done. Plus, taking the train was a part of my journey.

Finally in a major city, I headed over to the post office to mail the perfumes and other excess items home. When I was at the post office, I looked down at my right foot to check on the blister that was not going away. I had been putting Compeed on it to the point I had to replenish my stash. My leg surrounding the blister was bright pink. This made me immediately worry. I went to a pharmacy to buy more Compeed and see what their thoughts were about my foot. When I showed the lady, her face said it all. She went to get another person to look at it whose reaction was even worse.

Since they didn't speak English and I didn't speak Spanish, she used her computer to help translate it. She told me that I needed to go to the emergency room as it was infected. I was afraid of this. There was no way I was going to the emergency room. I went to my hotel room to examine the items I brought as my own first aid kit. I had two essential oils, lavender and tea tree. I chose them since I knew you could put them directly on your skin. Lavender and tea tree are both antiseptic and anti-inflammatory. I would be watching it closely, but I knew that they would keep it clean and heal it. I decided to trust in natural remedies, rather than spending my precious time in an emergency room.

73

As I headed out of Leon, I noticed a statue of a pilgrim in the Plaza San Marcos, so I had my photo taken by it. A little farther outside the city limits, I came across a little park that had trees and benches. I took out my palo santo that I had brought with me. Palo santo is a holy wood with a beautiful aroma which you can use as an incense. It also helps to clear your energy field. I was getting farther along this journey, and I wanted to start to figure out what I was here for. This place called me to clear out whatever was around me. Knowing that it can be hard to catch the palo santo on fire, I had brought a little tealight candle to assist me in getting it burning. This was a sweet moment, taking in the beauty of the trees and the blue skies.

I started to itch my leg. When I pulled up the pants, I saw five bug bites on my left leg. I was not sure exactly what this was. When I asked someone, they shared their suspicion was that it was bed bugs based on the way they were clustered on my leg. I now needed to wash and dry all my belongings as soon as I could to ensure any possible bugs I picked up were killed. There weren't many dryers in Spain, but I lucked out because the albergue I was staying at had one.

One day after it rained heavily, I observed multiple people putting crumpled newspaper pages into their shoes. I learned that this was a trick to dry out wet shoes. The newspaper soaked up the moisture, leaving your shoes drier in the morning rather than being slightly damp. I was grateful for these useful tips!

My second angel arrived later in the trip. I was having a bad day. I started talking to a man who came upon my path. This was his second time walking the Camino. I couldn't wrap my head around the idea of anyone choosing to do this again after knowing how challenging it was. He listened to my complaints, and his reaction was why I call him my second angel. He said, "I know that you said you are complaining, but all I hear is your laughter about what has occurred. Maybe, just maybe, it is not as bad as you are telling yourself it is." It was another turning point for me. Rather than focusing on my blessings, I was focused on every little thing that was not going exactly as I wanted it to go. This meant that I was continuing to have these things show up. It really wasn't an awful experience – in fact, it was magical. I was able to spend every single day being in nature!

We had started talking when I was trying to find out where I was on the map. Turned out that I'd taken the wrong path. There were two options people could take, and I wasn't headed towards where my backpack was being taken. We had lunch together and then I got a cab to take me over to the correct path so I could get to my destination for the night.

I saw so many interesting things on the pathway. Incredibly tall haystacks. Little cemeteries with raised vaults. Acres of little yellow wildflowers, striking with the bright blue sky. One place I walked into had a talking parrot!

When I stayed at an albergue close by, I checked to see how my foot was doing in the healing process. While it was still pink, it had faded to a lighter shade. The essential oils were helping! I reapplied my oils to keep on the path to recovery.

Further on down the path, it started to rain heavily. I needed to take refuge under a tree as I was nowhere near a town. I looked down at my shoes, which were caked with mud. Now I understood why all the albergues made you put your shoes in a designated space by the entryway!

As I was grabbing dinner one night, I met the husband of an Australian couple that I would continue to see along the remaining path. I'd been told that you would see people come and go at your pace along the path. I didn't realize that these two individuals would be in sync with me for the last quarter of the Camino.

I didn't stay in Astorga but appreciated the beautiful cathedrals and other vast buildings as I walked through the town – one of the bigger towns on the journey. Outside the city limits, I saw a man-made cross that was built in honor of someone. When I went to investigate, I noticed it was for someone named Trudy who was pictured with a tiger! She'd passed away in 2011. I had seen other memorials on the Camino and wondered what the significance was. – if they had died making the journey or if they just loved the Camino. I assumed that it was on the pathway, but I never found out for sure.

Just past the town of Puente de Panote, I walked by a place that had lots of crosses woven into the fence. It was a little overwhelming, how many crosses there were here. I wasn't sure what the significance of it was, but it was stunning to see. That evening, I stayed in a hotel room with a bathtub – bliss! There was a television in the lobby that had Rick Steves playing. It made me smile to see him on the screen. My foot was healing by leaps and bounds with the lavender and tea tree. I was pleased that I chose a natural resource to allow my foot to heal while I continued the path.

I made it to Cruz de Ferro, a famous location on the journey. This point is 1,504 meters (4,934 feet) above sea level. There is a simple iron rod with a cross at the top and a pile of rocks that have been left here over the years. I wasn't ready to leave my rock yet, as I still hadn't figured out what I wanted to let go of.

However, the irony is not lost on me that this would be the day I would start to put together the reason I was on this pilgrimage. It was a dreary day as I walked through the mountains. There was a purple shade on the mountains in the distance. It more than likely was wildflowers, but they blended in the haze with the sky. This area I was walking reminded me a lot of the place where Todd had died. The hint of purple – my mom's favorite color – made me feel there was a purpose in walking through this terrain.

One of the things my guidebook told me was where I was gaining or declining altitude. I knew the beginning part of the day, I'd be going on an incline. Then I would be headed down the mountain. What I had not thought about was how the conditions would make going down the mountain incredibly hard on the knees with all the rocks. Halfway down the hill, I met my third angel, Tessa, who asked me how I was enjoying this hike. My exact response was, "This fucking sucks." To which she responded with, "It's so wonderful to meet a fellow American." This made me laugh – I'd met people from all over the world, but it's nice to meet someone from your homeland.

We slowly walked down the mountain together and started to get to know one another. When we approached the town of Acebo, I told her I needed to eat. Of course, I ordered a cerveza grande and the pilgrim meal. She had a Coke and chips. I shared with her why I was on my journey, the story of my brother, my parents, and my loss. This was the beginning of me putting it into words. She was done for the day and was staying overnight in this town. I had a few more towns to go by the time I was reunited with my backpack, so we left one another with a "Buen Camino."

Leaving Acebo, it was a steep, rocky, downhill hike. I carefully went from one rock to another. The rocks were slippery, and it seemed as if it was steeper than the mountainside I had just left. I took each step slowly since I was not interested in falling.

The conversation about my grief of my family I'd just had with Tessa was playing out in my mind. I let it percolate inside for the next several days while I was trying to make sense of it. I hadn't realized yet that I take a moment to process deep conversations. It was helpful to be in an area that reminded me of the hike in the Smoky Mountains.

I laughed out loud when I saw that the path I needed to climb was uphill though huge pockets of mud. I would take a step and then slide back. I wondered if I was going to be able to get up the hill to rest for the night.

I was messaging my mom's friend who had befriended me. She was having the hard conversations with me about how I was reacting to others who were trying to be encouraging. She pointed out that I was never given the tools to face everything that had been presented to me, so I'd learned to grit my teeth and muscle through it. This was my normal. She also gave me one other thing to contemplate as I was out on the trail: God knew that my family could survive Todd's death. My mom could survive my dad's death, but she could never have survived losing me. I'd never looked at this from this view. It was something to ponder.

After a yoyo of weather from rainy to sunny, I finally realized what I was here to face. I spent my childhood trying to live up to the memory of Todd after his death. He'd become a saint in our family dynamic. Once he died, he could do no more wrong. Only the good memories of him remained. It had been a lot that he was incredibly smart and athletic. However, once he died, I spent my life trying to live up to this idea of him. I was destined to fail, to always be not good enough. I was somewhere on the mountaintop of Alto do Riocabo when I finally put my rock down. It might have only been a rock in size, but it had been a boulder in my heart that I released that day. The pathway was turning a different direction, so this felt as if it was the perfect location to leave it. I felt like a weight that had been holding me down had been released. As I walked away, I was smiling and feeling a sense of freedom that I'd never experienced before.

Within 3kms later, I saw Tessa. I was so excited to see her again, and we spent the rest of the walk talking about what had happened in the last four days for each of us. We came across a restaurant where we split a steak. I know that this does not sound nearly as glorious as it was to us at this moment. The entire Camino path, when you would order steak it was a thin slab of sliced meat. Our steak was almost an inch thick. We both were staying in Sarria that night. I was taking a rest day the next day, but we had a wonderful night getting ice cream. I loved how my conversation with her started the process of releasing my rock. Then seeing her once I released it was the best Camino gift I could have received.

74

Sarria was the turning point of the Camino. Your passport credentials needed to have a minimum of 100km to qualify, so this typically was where people would start if they wanted the certificate for completing the Camino. This meant that the number of people on the trails were a lot more than I had seen the rest of the time I was walking. Also, I would not have another rest day until I got to Santiago de Compostela.

I spoiled myself with fancy meals on my day off, at least fancy in comparison to the meals I was eating on the trail. I went out for a hamburger and fries for lunch. For dinner, I ordered a steak. I normally don't eat this much red meat, but I was craving it the last several days. The rest of the time, I relaxed by watching television shows. It was strange to be watching tv for a large portion of the day as I really didn't watch too much of it on my travels. However, it was nice to take a break from the path and be mindless for twenty-four hours.

I could tell that releasing that rock really shifted my entire being. I was lighter and freer. I was finding joy in this journey. It had taken 26 days to release what had been weighing my soul down for years. I had not known what I came on this journey to do, but I was grateful that I had trusted the process. There had been moments when I was complaining to Emily about how hard it was, and she told me I never needed to do this path. If I was miserable, I had the choice to take a train and do something else. I was thrilled that I stuck it out and found what I had been looking for.

Walking got easier. I looked forward to getting up and starting my day of adventure. As I was walking through one particular spot, I took the photo that is on the cover of this book. The moment I took the picture, I knew it would be on the cover of a book I would write in the future.

The town of Portomarín had the most stunning entrance. There was a staircase that you needed to climb to take a bridge over the river. While I was getting a bite to eat, a woman told me that she met someone who said that had met another pilgrim that was going from bar to bar, drinking beer. I had to laugh, and I said it was me.

I met an older couple from the United States who didn't always walk together but would meet up at certain spots. It was nice to walk with the wife for a moment to learn about each other. I was starting to realize that while I loved that I did this path on my own, I was finally opening to talking to people as I walked.

I passed another couple that had Canadian and United Kingdom flags on their backpacks. As I struck up a conversation with the woman, Angela, I learned that the man was her brother-in-law. He lived in the United Kingdom with her sister, while she resided in Vancouver Island, Canada. Her brother-in-law wanted to hike the Camino, but his wife was unable to make the journey, so she had recommended Angela to hike with him. So, here they were. It was a lovely meeting, but I kept walking and passed them.

My mood all the way around was better now that I released my burden. When it was raining, I was still joyous. I was starting to see how this path was like the journey of my life. The first portion was the hardest three weeks of my life. Now that I was in the home stretch, it was so much fun to just get up and walk. I was embracing it that walking was all I needed to do for the day. What an amazing moment in my life, to only walk.

I had stopped at a restaurant to grab lunch. As I exited, I walked out to someone screaming my name. I turned and saw it was Angela, the Canadian. Initially, I had no idea who she was. I had been more focused on her Canadian flag than I had on her face. She shared she was smashed and grabbed onto me while laughing hysterically – for not remembering her, I now would never forget her!

We met up again later and walked together for kilometers. We shared our stories and climbed a steep incline together. It was nice to be included in their little circle. I had been sharing my frustrations I was having with my family. I'll be honest – I don't remember what it was other than being super angry about it at the time. When we arrived at the place they were staying, I joined them for a couple of beers. Since I had farther to walk, I needed to head out after a couple of drinks.

As we hit the 100 km marker, I was so excited to see that we were in the home stretch. This meant that I would be completing this walk in less than a week. At this point, I decided to release another rock. This one was in honor of the firefighter. The last year of constant arguing or starting fights was so depleting of my soul. I placed a triangle black rock on a kilometer marker, and I released any attachment to him. It felt freeing to let the firefighter go from my heart.

When it rained, my hair had a natural wavy texture to it. I'd brought several buffs with me, and they'd come in handy, but lately I was using them as a headband. My hair was looking fabulous – actually, I was looking fabulous overall! I was glowing from the inside out. I'd never known what was going to happen on this journey, but it was working out for my best good. I'd wanted to release the grief, most of which stemmed back to releasing what I had taken on after Todd died.

I met up with Angela and her brother-in-law again. We

stopped at a bar and had a few more drinks. I was loving every moment with her – we couldn't stop laughing. Every time I said the f word, which was often, she flinched. But when we were drinking, she wasn't bothered by it. She invited me to come see her on Vancouver Island where she lived. We exchanged emails so that we could stay connected, but sadly, I never saw them again.

My final day was going to be less than 20km to walk to Santiago de Compostela. I was thrilled that this day was finally here. It happened to be a full moon evening. I texted Emily, and she pointed out that I was aligned with doing big things around the full moon.

As I started the hike, I was all alone to reflect on this journey. I decided it was the perfect opportunity to speak to each one of my family members. I started with Todd since he was the first one to die. His death had the biggest impact on the trajectory of my life. As I was talking to him, I reflected that he would have been jealous that I got to experience this. I loved that we both shared an adventurous soul. Next was my dad. I teared up when I felt the overwhelming sensation of how proud he would have been of me walking as far as I had. He was always my cheerleader and admired my strength. When it came to my mom, she would have wondered why I walked so far. I laughed out loud knowing this was my reflection of my mom. She had always questioned me when I was training for the marathon so it made sense that she would do it for the Camino. I'd come on this journey to deal with my grief head on. To be able to have this sincere moment with my family was the completion of this journey.

It started to downpour which led me to getting drenched, but fortunately it stopped and I was able to dry out a bit. I happily took my photo by a tall pillar just past the 13km remaining sign. I noticed that the Australian couple was right behind me. We walked and looked at Monte do Gozo which means "hill of joy." It's a religious sculpture that sits on a hill. Apparently, you can see the cathedral from here, but I didn't know this at the time. Since we walked at a similar pace, we decided to walk into the city together. It started to downpour again. This time it was raining so much harder than it had earlier in the day and I was now soaked for the second time. We came upon a city sign that said Santiago de Compostela. Shortly after this moment, we got separated as we found cover from the rain.

When I got to the Santiago de Compostela Archcathedral Basilica, I had thought I would feel this magical moment. I did not. It was so disappointing. However, this same thing happened at the end of the marathon. It's all about the journey rather than the destination.

Afterwards, I headed over to take my pilgrim passport over to the Pilgrim's office to get a Compostela, which is a certificate saying that I met the criteria. They used a different spelling of my name on the certificate, which was Gertrudem, for making the journey. I headed back to the Cathedral. I stood in front of Santiago de Compostela Archcathedral Basilica with my backpack, my scallop shell, and my Compostela. I was grinning ear to ear knowing that I accomplished my goal of making the entire journey on my own.

I dropped my bag off where I was staying. I was meeting up with Tessa for a celebration dinner. Another friend she met on the path was going to be there, too. This dinner was way more luxurious than I'd had in days! While we were talking and laughing, my Australian friends walked in. She'd heard my laugh and came in to see me. She'd just gotten her hair done and felt completely refreshed. They joined us to celebrate our individual accomplishments.

We took several photos of us raising our arms in victory – what an amazing accomplishment we all completed! I walked 664.8 km over the course of a little over a month! We said our goodbyes to one another and I went back to get some sleep before I grabbed the train to Madrid in the morning.

75

I took the train to Madrid, where I spent a rest day before heading over to Switzerland. After spending a month in Spain, I was ready to move on. I flew into Geneva. I was not going to be staying here long but wanted to walk around a little bit so I could check it off my list as a city I visited. I headed over to see the flower clock. From what I read, there were over 6,500 flowers used to create the large clock. I had to check out the Jet d'Eau, which shot water up over 400ft into a lake. The lake was beautiful that day and I took a little stroll before heading to the train station. The sky was bright blue with white fluffy clouds – it was a picturesque moment.

I took the train from Geneva to Lauterbrunnen. I'd been told I must go see this town as it was the most beautiful place in the world. The train ride was just as stunning as the Glacier Express trip I had taken last year. When we got to Interlaken, I was approached by an attendant who told me that I needed to pay more to get all the way to Lauterbrunnen. He was understanding and told me that I had time to jump off the train to pay at the station versus the upcharge he must enforce. I was nervous jumping off the train while leaving my stuff onboard. However, I was able to get the additional ticket needed for the train ride.

Even though this country is stunning, I couldn't imagine it getting even prettier – but it did. When I stepped off the train in Lauterbrunnen, I honestly felt as if I'd walked into a fairy tale. The village is set in a stunning valley surrounded by cliffs, on one side of which are green, luscious grassy fields with houses. There are snow-capped mountain tops off in the distance. Off to the side is this unbelievably gorgeous waterfall that you can hear from the train station. This was the most stunning place I have ever set my eyes on. Think

Sound of Music ambience.

I took the cable car up to the highest lookout point to see the mountains and the valley below. I took so many photos of the mountains, enchanted by the mixture of blue and white in the setting – the different shades of deep mountain blue and the baby blue skies, the streaks of white clouds dancing through the sky with the snow on the mountains. The top location was Piz Gloria. At this altitude, we were in the clouds and at times, above them. It was spectacular being as high up as most of the mountain peaks around us. There were three mountains dominating the scene here: Eiger, Monch, and Jungfrau. Jungfrau was the tallest at 4158m. This was another one of those moments when I knew I was seeing true magic in the universe.

As I descended the mountain, I stopped in Murren a bit further down to walk around. I loved the view of the mountains above and the valley of Lauterbrunnen below. There was a train on the mountainside, but it wasn't working. I also got off at Gimmelwald which was even further down. There I found The Honesty Shop which was an unattended self-service place. It looked as if it was still closed for the season, but I still thought it was a great concept. When I got to the bottom of the valley, I walked back to the center of the village and soaked in all the views. Everything was so magical, I wanted to breathe it in.

Speaking of breathing, the air was so clean! The water was a different shade than I was used to seeing. I immediately wanted to move here to retire. There is no way that you can be in a bad mood living in such natural beauty! The waterfall was gorgeous to listen to and see. Throughout the valley, you could hear the peaceful sound of the water falling. Cows were chilling in the fields as I passed by them. As I made my way back into town, I passed by a cemetery. Even this was aesthetically pleasing with the symmetry of the graves and flowers decorating them.

I decided that I was going to hike up the one side of the cliff at the recommendation of someone working at the hostel. Having just hiked across a country, why not hike up the cliff? I started out going through a neighborhood until it led me to a dirt path. There was a red arrow showing you which way to go. It made me laugh as I was used to following yellow arrows for the last month.

There were several switchbacks to help with getting up to the higher altitude without just climbing straight up. I paused often to catch my breath and wondered if I was in shape to do this. Being persistent, I kept with it. I loved seeing all the waterfalls that you couldn't see from the main valley. It seemed as if these smaller waterfalls would eventually lead to Staubbach, the largest waterfall in the valley. I'd seen that there were over 72 waterfalls in the village of Lauterbrunnen!

I came upon a little wood cabin with a bench outside of it, so I sat to rest for a moment. The views were spectacular of the trees and the village across on the other cliffside. I bought a sandwich from the grocery store to have for lunch. While I was in Switzerland, most of my meals were enjoyed outside as I took in the natural beauty.

This hike I took up the cliff was a 1000m (3200ft) incline. When I was researching to find out how tall the hike was, they all were labeled as difficult hikes. This made me feel better as I had a harder time with the hike than I thought I would. When I looked up to see how many stories that is, I learned this would have been equivalent to me walking up to the 103rd level of the Sears Tower twice. Seeing that makes me realize how strong I am!

I went paragliding while I was there. I met my tour guide in Murren. Then we walked up a tiny path of switchbacks that must have been created for all the paragliders. It was questionable for a moment if we were going to be able to go, as bad weather was rolling in soon. We took off right before it was called off. It was strange to run with someone as we jumped off the cliff to paraglide down into the valley. This was such a rush, and the views were incredible! I loved this way more than skydiving.

I headed to Lucerne to relive the ambience of the village again. When I arrived, there was a firefighter thing happening in the downtown area. I had to laugh to myself about how it made me think of the firefighter. I did the same tour as last year, where I rode on a boat, took a train up the mountain, and the gondola back into town. I needed to ride the toboggan run again! When I got to the top of Mount Pilatus, I walked into areas I'd not been to before, such as the caves. My GoPro fell and tumbled a little way down the side of the mountain. There was grass where it fell, but it was not a walkway. I was going to go get it, but I had on flip flops, of course. I took one step out and was a little uneasy with my balance. A man stopped me and told me he would get it. I was so grateful to him for stepping in to retrieve it. I really didn't want to lose the photos I had taken but hadn't downloaded yet.

Next on my adventure, I headed to Croatia. I wanted to get to Croatia the year before but didn't have enough time. After I dropped my stuff at the hostel, I was ready to explore Split. I headed towards Marjan Hill where there was a park I wanted to walk through. By walking up this way, I was able to see the panoramic view of the city and the Adriatic Sea. There were moments in the park that reminded me of the Camino walk. However, the view of the sea was a major difference from the Camino. There was a lookout that had a cross, with the Adriatic Sea in the background. The white cross with the bright blue color of the sea made for a perfect picture.

I wanted to see Dubrovnik, too. I took a quick trip by bus to see the city. The bus briefly went through Bosnia. The view alone was worth the effort heading down to Dubrovnik. When I got to the city, I was asked if I wanted to take the *Game of Thrones* tour. I hadn't really been watching much tv in the last several years, so I didn't know what *Game of Thrones* was. Instead, I headed into the old city of Dubrovnik.

While I was there, I decided to take a boat tour. The Adriatic Sea was a clear beautiful blue, reminding me of the Mediterranean

Sea around Cyprus. The boat even had a glass bottom, too. The waves made the trip a little more brutal than I'd wanted, but it was worth it for the view of the city. There were parts of what we saw that reminded me of the Greek Islands.

On my flight into Basel, my luggage got lost again. I was irritated since I was headed to Zurich to catch my flight to Cyprus. After I arrived in Zurich by train, I was contacted that my bag came in on the next flight. I'd wanted to sightsee around Zurich but decided to make the round trip to grab my luggage rather than waiting for it to be delivered to Cyprus. This time when my luggage went missing, I didn't flip out like I did in France. I was annoyed, but I handled it way better. I think that shows growth!

76

Cyprus was such a refreshing part of the trip. I was able to relax during this time. It was the perfect break to spend time with one of my dearest friends, and it was wonderful to see her kids again. Her daughter had become even more of a selfie queen than I was!

This week was a slower pace than it had been in other trips to see Rosey and her family. We went out for dinner often. We headed to the mountains to meet up with Rosey's in-laws. They also hosted a barbecue at their home. I learned that halloumi is a cheese that tastes phenomenal when grilled. Pairing it with the sausage on the grill made it even better.

Rosey and I headed to the beach to get some sun at Ayia Napa. The beach was closer to her home rather than taking a long drive across the island. I attended another one of her girls' nights where I met a few more of her friends that I hadn't met the last time. It warmed my heart to see Rosey's life in Cyprus and how she had found her own group of sisterhood friends.

Somehow, I was there for Eurovision for the second year in a row. However, this time it was a rather boring show. I was told that this was a typical Eurovision. We did get to see Conchita Wurst perform again.

Rosey took me to a crystal shop in her area. There was a glorious tree in the entryway made of rose quartz as the leaves and amethyst as the base. I was in absolute awe. I purchased a celebratory piece of pyrite for completing the Camino. Pyrite empowers you to take action to manifest your desires.

I had the opportunity to go to the Turkish side of the island. I'd been to Cyprus twice, but I'd never been over to the northern side of the island. The northern part of the island had been invaded back in 1974. Rosey's husband had never been to that side since it was a sensitive subject to Greek Cypriots. I needed my passport to cross onto the Turkish side. It was awful that there was a divide on such a small island.

When I walked over, I immediately saw the abandoned storefronts and homes that must have been left unattended since the invasion. There was a wall separating the two countries. This area reminded me a lot of my time in Istanbul. I checked out both the open market and a mosque then grabbed lunch before walking back to the Greek side of Cyprus. It was a short stay over on the Turkish side of Nicosia, but it was interesting to see.

I was going to Israel to explore the cities of Tel Aviv and Jerusalem. I hadn't bought my flight out of Israel as I wanted to see if the price would go down. However, when I was trying to check in for my flight, this was a huge issue. It was a big no-no to not have your flight booked for leaving the country. I needed to contact Rosey to come back to the airport to help me. I was a nervous wreck and couldn't get my phone to connect to the Wi-Fi to get the flight. Once I finally booked the flight out of Israel, they were able to check me in.

Going through the protocols to board a plane to Israel was nothing like I thought it would be. I was flat out told my luggage wouldn't be able to make it on this flight. They needed to inspect it thoroughly and they didn't have enough time to do this. I waited in a back room for a female security agent to do a full body search of me. It took a good 20 minutes for one to arrive. It was questionable if I was going to make the flight. After I was cleared, another agent and I ran through the airport to get to my gate. I heard my name being called over the public announcement system that it was the last call for me to board. The gate was at the farthest point in the terminal. I barely made it and was seated in the very last seat on the plane. I learned that I needed to make sure my next flight was booked when flying into a highly secure country. As I sat there, I realized that I felt the safest I have ever felt flying anywhere. I never realized it was an underlying fear I had.

When I landed, I immediately went to the missing luggage counter to give them the information of the hostel I was staying so they could deliver my bags. This was the third time I didn't have my bags – I was becoming a pro at missing luggage! At least this time I knew that it wouldn't be there, so I didn't even bother to wait. The agents at the counter were the kindest by providing me with a package that included pajamas, dental essentials, and other toiletries. It made me wonder if this was a normal occurrence that they had these ready for people. I was grateful to be given these items to help me until all my stuff arrived.

The girl who was staying in my hostel room ended up being the coolest person I'd ever met on my travels. She inspired me by being fearless in places she had traveled. When she shared her bucket list, it included specific experiences she wanted to have. We started talking and I shared that I almost missed my flight trying to get into the country. We headed out for lunch, and we shared our traveling stories. She was from the UK but had been living in Syria with her partner. Listening to her made me realize how sheltered my life was.

While I was in Tel Aviv, I got the word from the firefighter that his dad had passed away. I was saddened to hear the news of him losing a parent. However, what I noticed was that releasing the rock had made a difference for me. I was sad for him, but I was unwilling to cross over the boundary I had created for myself. I didn't need to fix him. This told me I had truly let go of his influence in my life.

The woman I befriended in Iceland on the brewery tour was from Tel Aviv, and she connected me to her group of friends. I ended up going out with one of her friends to a bar. This was a fascinating encounter. While I'd always heard about the turmoil in Israel, it was another thing to listen to someone who lived the experience. I was grateful to have this encounter to show me how privileged my life had been growing up where I did.

After my favorite traveler left, I befriended another girl that was staying in the room and we went to relax at the beach together. She shared how she booked this trip to get away from the troubles in her relationship with a married man. I was able to sympathize with her as I'd been in a similar situation in college. It made me wonder why so many of us girls fall for married men. I had compassion for her. I could tell it was never going to work out for her but knew she wasn't ready to hear this yet.

We spent the day together walking along the coastline all the way up to Old Jaffa. There was such history mixed in with the stunning coastline. We paused to have lunch. I was loving the Israeli food. Later in the evening as we had dinner, a protest passed us by. I wasn't worried about my safety, but I found it fascinating to witness.

I loved the vibe of the city. Several of us from the hostel headed over to the bar to enjoy the nightlife. This was one of those fun moments of meeting new friends from all over the world for an evening of partying.

I went to Jerusalem via bus. When I got to there, I saw several men with curls on the side of their heads. I learned that this hairstyle is typical for Orthodox Jews. As I made my way to the Old City of

Jerusalem, the energy I was feeling within my body intensified. I am not sure how to describe it other than it was the most intense energetic feeling I've had anywhere in my life. It made me think that it was due to all the history here.

When I came across the Western wall, I didn't realize what it was. I was confused as to why there were so many people walking backwards. When one of my friends shared with me the spots they saw in Jerusalem, I realized that it was the famous wall. I laughed at myself for not realizing. However, what I appreciated about this moment is that it shows I walk into anywhere with an open mind and no expectations.

I headed out of the Old City and came upon massive tombs spread out over the side of a mountain across the road. There were several tombs that were larger in size. It was a moment of awe to see in person. One of the large structures was said to be the Tomb of Zechariah. I went to the Mount of Olives, I walked around the Garden of Gethsemane, and I found the place where it is said that the Virgin Mary was buried. This was amazing, witnessing the rich history of the beliefs I was raised with.

I did one a tour throughout the city of Jerusalem. I learned so many cool things, but the thing that stood out to me the most was when the tour guide said that St. James' head was allegedly. buried on the Armenian side in Jerusalem. He talked about how there is a famous pilgrimage through Spain where his body is buried. It became a full circle to have done the Camino and then to be here in Jerusalem!

Seeing Damascus Gate got me really giddy for some reason. It was thrilling to me that I was walking where Jesus had walked. I learned how the city is broken down into four quadrants of Jewish, Muslim, Armenian, and Christian. There was a mosaic map of what the city looked like during the days of Jesus. Part of the street dated back to the 6th Century AD!

I went to see King David's tomb. It fascinated me that it was divided between men and women being able to see different sides of the tomb. The room of the Last Supper was another location I found interesting. There was a Chamber of the Holocaust along with a synagogue for martyrs of the Holocaust.

I took a tour into the tunnels under the city. The history was intriguing. Seeing the size of the stones used to build the wall and thinking about how they were able to do it without equipment was mind-boggling.

I took a public bus out to see Masada and the Dead Sea. The Dead Sea is the lowest place on Earth. Before heading up to see Masada, I watched a video where they told you what the area was. It is a village at the top of a plateau overlooking the Dead Sea. There were black lines in the rock structures to show where the original buildings were and what had been built to show what it looked like back in the day of Herod.

The Dead Sea was a highlight as I was so excited to be able to swim in the water. I was enthralled with the fact that I kept bouncing up that I started splashing around and having fun with it. There was a woman near me who seemed bothered that I was enjoying myself because she scolded me for splashing around. It did dampen my mood for a moment, but I moved away from her to continue to enjoy my experience. I thought it was so cool that you could see the salt gathering at the edge of the water. When I was getting ready to head back to Jerusalem, the sun was starting to set behind Masada, with beams of light shining down like on a Christian inspirational poster.

When I got back to the Old City of Jerusalem, the Festival of Lights was going on. I was so excited that I was here to witness this. All the gates around the city had different lights. It was wonderful to walk around to see the different settings for each individual gate. The best light, though, was the full moon in the sky.

Before I left the city of Jerusalem, I wanted to check out the Holy Sepulcher. I went to the place where there was an altar of the crucifixion. I saw the rock of Calvary which was encased in protective glass. When I was in the Holy Sepulcher, I witnessed a service going on where people were receiving holy communion. I ended up partaking since this is said to be the exact location where Jesus Christ was crucified. It was a unique opportunity to participate in communion which represents the body and blood of Christ through His sacrifice.

When I arrived at the airport to leave Israel, I got there three hours ahead of time to have plenty of time to get through security. For as early as I felt I had gotten there, I didn't have much time in the airport before boarding. I was thrilled I'd been able to visit Israel on my own.

77

The final leg of my trip was spending time with friends. First, I headed to Berlin to meet up with my friend Sarah that I had met last year on travels. Sarah asked me if there was anything I wanted to see while I was there. However, I only came to Berlin to spend time with her.

On my way to see Jessica in Dublin, I had a six-hour layover in London. My manager had just been there to see a new Lush store in Oxford. She told me that if I could make it happen, I needed to see it. The store was massive with three levels.

When I got to Dublin, I decided to tour the Jameson Distillery. While I was in a restaurant, two guys that had to be from America came in. They were those stereotypical guys who had their green "Kiss me I'm Irish" shirts and a bottle of Jameson that they had just purchased. It made me chuckle to myself to see them nerding out on a trip to Ireland.

Jessica had been in the theater scene so when we were hanging outside of a bar in the alley, she kept saying hi to so many people as they walked past. She said that Dublin was a big city, but it really was rather a tight community. Then the night got strange. I saw someone high on heroin or some other heavy drug that unsuccessfully tried to steal a wallet. Then another guy tried to steal someone's phone. It was all topped off with a drug deal. My little sheltered eyes watched this all in horror, wondering where in the world I was. Neither Jessica nor her boyfriend seemed worried, so I didn't worry either, but this was not your typical experience of Dublin.

I flew back to North America but went to Canada instead of the United States. The women's World Cup was being held in Winnipeg, Manitoba. Several of the girls I had played soccer with were going and I decided to join them. We all wore American flag stretch pants when we went to see the USA team play Sweden. It was fun to see Swedish people who were wearing their country colors as well.

That tattoo that I told myself I would get if I completed the Camino? I got it two days after I returned home. I got my first tattoo when I was 33 years old – an Irish trinity symbol, known as a triquetra, with the words faith, hope and love around it. By each of those words, I have the initials of each of my family members. My brother was "love" since he showered me with protective love. My dad was "faith" because he was a man strong in his faith. My mom was "hope" since she exemplified it as the recipient of the kidney transplant. The tattoo was all in black ink. When I got my second tattoo of the scallop shell with the "Buen Camino" phrase, I decided this one would have a pop of color to represent how I am vibrant and full of life.

Coming back after this second trip was way different than the year prior. Between walking the Camino and seeing all the other areas, this trip fed my soul the way that I thought the first trip would have. I knew that I had done what I needed by letting so much go on the Camino path. I didn't struggle with the fact that I didn't have a full-time job. I was satisfied that I was working at Lush only. I knew that eventually I would figure out what was next, but I was not as interested in hurrying to find out, since I was finally at peace with myself.

78

Back in the States, Courtney decided to have her bachelorette party in Nashville. Courtney's sister, Meg, was there. She'd moved to Denver, Colorado a couple years earlier. She shared that when people ask what you do, they mean for fun and not for work. It was in this conversation I knew I wanted to live there. I had always struggled with people in Chicago who seemed to identify as their job. I honestly couldn't care less what people did at their jobs. I texted my cousin Brian to see if he would be open to the possibility of me moving in with him for a bit, and he said yes. That July day, I decided that I would be moving to Denver by October.

When I shared with Angela that I was going to be moving, she told me that she knew I always wanted to live somewhere else. I hadn't realized this, but it made me happy to hear that it had apparently been in my plans all along! Most people thought I would be moving to Nashville based on how often I traveled there. While I loved the town, I had no interest in trying to make it in the entertainment industry. Colorado seemed to be a better fit since I would be able to travel around the state without having to get on a plane.

A couple weeks after the bachelorette party, Eric Church was the headliner for the grand opening at a new amphitheater built downtown. He was going to play a special two-night acoustic show. It would be worth it to drive to see him perform. Since Blake lived in Nashville, he attended the first night with me. The concert happened to fall on my brother's birthday.

Blake had a driver so we could head to the city without worrying about drinking and driving. We were catching up about our trips to Europe and what had happened for us both since then. We'd always been comfortable with each other and able to speak openly. It was prior to the concert and in my conversation with him that I accepted that I'd found a way to turn my family's death into a new life for myself. I was able to live life on my terms rather than needing to live up to anyone else's expectations. This was a powerful moment for me, having this realization. I confessed how I'd fallen in love with myself on my journey over the last two years. While I missed my family deeply, I was happy that I had grown into the strong independent woman that I was. I loved that I was able to follow my heart rather than needing to play by the rules that had been set by my parents.

While I came there for the concert, I got so much more in my conversation with Blake. He had been there for me that night in Paris when I was struggling. To see him a year later when my whole life had shifted was what I needed. He gave me the space to be me without any agenda. I was grateful for this time to be able to know I was finally exactly where I was meant to be.

For my birthday, I headed out to a state park called Starved Rock to go hiking. I have done this over the last three years. Knowing it was going to be my last one as a resident of the state, I asked all my friends who wanted to go. It was so fun to see friends from all of my different circles, such as my Jaycee friends, church friends, Lush friends, and friends of friends. Tricia and her dogs came with me to hike as well.

On what would have been my parents 44th wedding anniversary, my cat Circe died. She had stayed in my friend's grandma's house as her pet since the year prior. Circe had a great last year of her life living with her. I felt awful about the grief my friend's grandma was now going through. In a way, it was poetic since Circe was my last tie to the Chicago area. I knew it was time for me to move.

I headed to Michigan for my 20th high school reunion. It ended up being a blast since everyone asked me about my travels. I had heard that reunions are hard on people, but that was not my perception. If there is a gap between where we are and where we wish we were, then it can lead to undue pressure. Being comfortable in my own skin made it great to see people I hadn't seen since we graduated years earlier.

After the reunion, I went to spend the day with my grandma. I wanted to have quality time since I wasn't sure when I would be back to visit with her. We had such a lovely conversation. She shared with me how she never understood what my mom had been through until she had lost Grandpa. It was nice to hear her utter these words since I knew it always bothered my mom that no one understood the pain that she was experiencing. I cherished this time with her since it was raw and real.

After our conversation, I fell asleep in my grandpa's recliner. When I awoke, I noticed my grandma was quietly playing her word search game while I slept. I was grateful that not only did we have a deep meaningful moment, but also she allowed me to rest in her presence. It is one of my favorite moments with her.

Before I left, I took a selfie with my grandma. She even asked if this was what a selfie was. I was so glad that we had this time together. She shared her wisdom and told me to make sure I was doing all the things I wanted to while I was still young. I told her that I was working on it.

79

Since I was going to move, I knew that I would be putting my notice in with Lush. This made me sad, walking away from this place that had connected me with the best individuals.

I had one last hurrah as a goodbye party. At the party, one of my friends bought me a book so people could leave me goodbye messages. A former personal trainer took the time to wish me luck on my journey which was touching as I had not seen him for several years.

I hired a moving company to get all the items from my storage unit and Tricia's condo. This made it real that I was on my way. I said goodbye to Tricia's dogs and went to Angela's house to stay the night before I headed out early in the morning.

Driving out to Denver was rather uneventful. I had gotten up early so that I could make the drive in one day. It was a long day, but I was happy when I got to my cousin's house since I knew I was finally home.

I wanted to start fresh in Colorado, to start a new chapter in my life. The previous 38 years had been all about grief. It was time to create a life I wanted to live. I felt I was never going to meet a guy in Chicago but felt I was destined to meet someone in Colorado. I felt led here. It was scary to start over, but it would have been scarier to stay exactly where I was at. I had transformed way too much through my travels to stay in Chicago where I no longer fit in as a person. I was going to need to embrace the quiet time as I had to create my world in this new environment.

80

The job search took longer than I thought it should, but I finally ended up getting a job through one of the temp agencies I was working with. A little over a month of being in Colorado, and I had gotten a job. I was so excited! However, I was going to be paid hourly through the temp agency rather than being a full-time employee as I had been used to. After 19 months and 2 days, my sabbatical was officially over. I was a working woman again.

I went to Chicago for Thanksgiving. It was great to get to see various friends on the trip. I spent Thanksgiving with Lisa and her family as I had over the last several years. It was rather soon to return, but it was nice to see those I had missed.

Now that I had been working and bringing in a steady paycheck, I decided that I wanted to start working out again. I found a gym that did high impact circuits. Becoming focused on my health, I started going to the 6 a.m. class before work. I have never been a morning person, so it was a big deal for me to get up early to go.

I was still interviewing with other companies, since I was ready to have a full-time job. I wanted to move out of my cousin's house but needed a full-time job to do so. For some reason, I was being turned down for all the jobs I interviewed for. I was getting frustrated that I could not get full time employment. Then out of nowhere, the company I had been a temp employee at offered me a full-time position.

I finally could look for an apartment. I found a place that was close to my cousin. It had an amazing bathtub and a huge living room space. The moment I walked in I knew it was the perfect place for me. A week after I landed full time status, I was moving into the apartment. I was so thrilled that after two years of living at other people's homes, I officially had my very own place.

81

My grandma took a fall in the garage which started a domino effect in her health. She ended up needing to be moved into a rehab facility. I spoke to her a couple times when she was there, but these were hard conversations for me to have. She openly spoke about wanting to die. I am not sure if she talked to the rest of the family this way, but it was hard for me to process this.

My grandma chose to stop eating in her final days. While it bothered me that she chose this, it was her choice, not mine. The two strongest women I knew in my life were my mom and my grandma, my mom's mom. But at the end of their life, it felt as if their will to live was gone. While I know it is not my place to judge either of their choices, it saddens me that this is how I perceive it. It does not take away what they meant to me since it was not their whole life.

We knew it was getting to the very end of my grandma's life. My cousin Jenni was going over to the rehab facility to see her and informed me that I could speak to Grandma, but she was no longer able to talk. I wanted to tell Grandma how much I loved her and thank her for being such a wonderful influence in my life. Jenni called me and held her phone up to Grandma so she could hear me. I said everything I wanted her to hear from me. When I finished, my grandmother, with every ounce of strength she had left, managed to say, "I…love…you." Instantly, I bawled. Jenni was startled that she spoke.

Those were the last words my grandma ever spoke. The strength she used to show me she loved me meant everything to me. She had witnessed everything I had gone through with losing Todd, my dad, and my mom. I am not saying I was her favorite because I genuinely believed she loved us all equally, but I do believe she had a soft spot in her heart for me after watching me endure all the grief that I had experienced.

Her funeral was the last of my family. I'd been to my brother's, my dad's mom, my dad, my dad's dad, my mom, my mom's dad, and now finally my mom's mom. All of this by the time I was 38. Yes, I was blessed to have all my grandparents around me. However, I experienced all out of order deaths. You expect the older generations to die before the younger generations. In my family, it went backwards.

Brian and I flew back to Michigan for my grandma's funeral. At the funeral, we sang the song, "How Great Thou Art." I smiled as I sang the line, "When Christ shall come with a shout of acclamation and take me home, what joy shall fill my heart! Then I shall bow in humble adoration and there proclaim 'My God, how great thou art!'" It filled my heart knowing this was what my grandmother wanted. It was such a unique experience to be happy for someone who had died. She was with God and her loved ones now.

82

As I continued to work through my stuff with men with the help of a counsellor, I felt incredibly content on my own. I realized that I had spent most of my life needing validation from others. A friend reflected to me that I seemed happy. I took this as a huge accomplishment since it was true. I was happy. I had no issues having a self-care day where I made sure that all I did was please myself. I could be without needing other people's validation. I was doing it for myself now.

Slowly, I was building a social life. My friend Kristy held events at different breweries around town. It was nice to catch up with her, check out some new brews, and meet some of her friends. She attracted interesting dynamic people. One of them was someone who performed in the theater world in Denver. I was excited to have an in on different areas to see productions and see her perform. I was missing going to the theater.

One night, Kristy was having a party. The theater girl was there with her new boyfriend. They were sharing the story of how they met online. She talked about how she just cut to the chase and asked to meet immediately. When they did, everything fell into place. It inspired me. I boldly stated I knew love was on the way. I wasn't sure when I was going to meet him, but I knew it was coming soon.

I decided it was time to try online dating again. I logged on to a profile I'd already created to look at the history of who had checked me out. The first guy I saw happened to be wearing a hockey jersey. I peeked at my four mandatory checkpoints: height, Christian, attractive, and can type without using all caps. He met my criteria, so I sent him a message. We started to chat back and forth. After a while, he said he was going to be gone for a little bit as he was going out to run. While he was out, I started reading his whole profile. Typically, I didn't waste my time reading people's profiles. As I was reading it, I thought to myself how this guy was a perfect match for me on paper. Being inspired from the conversation at Kristy's party the night before, I decided to ask him if he was interested in meeting up. We decided to get together the following evening.

We met at a sports bar halfway between our homes. I learned that Fran and I had a lot in common. We both loved hockey. He was adventurous and had gone traveling after his mom died. He'd been to a Stanley Cup Final Game Seven. Also, he had been to all the hockey arenas – something I was trying to accomplish myself! We worked in the same field, but on different sides of it. We drank and got to know one another. When I went to the restroom, I realized that it was way later than I realized. We'd been talking nonstop for four hours! It had felt as if no time had passed.

As if I did not think we had enough in common, when we walked out to our cars, I saw we both drove the exact same vehicle. It was shocking to see how similar we were. Fran gave me a hug and we went our separate ways.

I was excited that this had been such a fun and easy date. It was as if I'd known him forever. Rather than butterflies, I had a huge sense of comfort. The following afternoon, he sent me a text asking if I would be interested in going to a baseball game that night. I was thrilled at being able to see him again, and this sounded like a perfect Tuesday night.

It was another magical date, continuing to get to know one another better. We walked around the stadium and hung out by the forest area on the back side of the park.

Our third date was the next night where he came over to my house to watch the season finale of a reality show I watch. I was surprised that I had spent three evenings in a row with this guy – it was like he was already becoming my boyfriend!

The next several days, I had other plans so I knew that I wouldn't be seeing him. I was going to a country concert on Thursday, and Friday I was headed down to Mesa Verde National Park which was another place my brother had seen.

When I got back home, Fran and I met for dinner. I'd missed him. It all seemed rather quick, but we decided we were exclusive within a week of meeting one another.

I headed over to Fran's place to hang out for the evening. He'd bought me red roses and I was blown away with how he was a gentleman on all fronts. We talked more and I wanted to pinch myself as he seemed too good to be true. Both of us had been married before and neither one of us had kids. Also, both of us had a feeling that we would meet someone when we moved to Colorado.

Fran and I agreed to get a partial hockey package together. What was funny is that I thought the tickets were rather cheap because I had been used to Chicago prices, and Fran thought the tickets were expensive since he was used to Arizona prices. Either way it was fun to have a common interest to enjoy together. I'd always wanted to be a season ticket holder, but never in a million years did I think it would be for the Colorado Avalanche!

We started to do different hiking adventures together. I was overjoyed that I had found a man who loved hockey, hiking and was my age. I had met my partner in crime.

We went over to Brian's house for Fran to meet my family. He was trying to fit in, so he took off his pants since I had told him my cousin always hangs out in his boxers. As Fran was dropping his pants, my cousin's son walked into the room. I was laughing hysterically since Fran was freaking out that he did not have anything except his boxers. When Brian came into the room, he joined him. They got along well which made me so happy.

For Thanksgiving, he went to visit his family in Arizona. He sent me roses, letting me know he was thankful for having met me. I appreciated the thoughtful gesture, and ended up traveling to Arizona to spend Christmas with him. I met his dad, brother, and the rest of his family, including cousins and aunts. I passed the test with meeting the family.

We went to see the Arizona Coyotes so I could see another arena while he watched his team play. We headed down to his favorite place, Sedona. He wanted to show me the Chapel of the Holy Cross. We went inside and Fran lit a candle. It made me want to light a candle for Todd, dad, and mom. I went to take a picture of the three candles and Fran was sitting in the background praying. I loved this photo. It really said everything I needed it to say.

He took me over to a crystal shop where I looked around a lot longer than I think he expected. As we were leaving, it was snowing outside. This was not a normal occurrence and was his first time seeing snow in Sedona. We went back over to the Chapel of the Holy Cross so he could get pictures of it snowing in the background. He was thrilled with the snow until he started to make his way back to his dad's house. I was nervous and I was trying to be patient with a man who had no clue how to drive in the snow since he was used to hot weather. It was wonderful to meet everyone and spend my first official holiday with Fran.

83

Fran and I continued doing different adventures on the weekends. We planned a whole weekend for his birthday in Buena Vista which is out west in the mountains. We stayed at an Airbnb that had a hot tub. We went dog sledding and snowmobile riding. The house we stayed at had a stunning view of the mountains. It was a nice trip to celebrate my boyfriend's birthday.

On Valentine's Day, he texted me to see if I would be available for dinner. I had asked if he'd made a reservation, and he said that he had. I was impressed that this guy had gotten a reservation on Valentine's Day. I asked where we were going, and he told me it was a surprise. About ten minutes into the drive, I figured out where he was taking me and told him I knew where we were going. I ended up being correct that he was taking me to Casa Bonita.

Casa Bonita is a restaurant that has been featured on South Park. All I'd heard was that the food was disgusting, but the entertainment made it worth it. When we arrived, there was a couple in front of us and the guy said, "What better place to spend this romantic day than watching cliff divers!" I expressed my shock as I had no idea what was inside. The food was gross, but we were able to watch the cliff divers from our table. While it may sound fancy, the cliff divers were young guys who would dive into the pool down below. It was definitely a unique experience. It was actually the perfect place for Fran to take me for Valentine's Day since I laughed the entire night. He'd been nervous that taking me there may have offended me, but I got how incredibly silly my man was. He was good for me.

I'd started selling supplements through a multi-level marketing company for a bit after someone at the gym recommended them. Through the company, I was encouraged to attend a personal development course. While I was waiting for the meeting to start, I saw a girl named Katie that I'd met before. We sat and got to know one another since the person who invited us was late. By the end of the introductory meeting both Katie and I signed up for their next program to attend.

The personal development course promised us transformation. I was not sure what this meant, but I was getting that I needed to take responsibility for my own actions. The easiest way to try to explain it is that when an event happens, we create stories about what happened based on our past experiences. Due to the meaning we place on them, we tend to repeat the same thread of stories, a vicious cycle predetermined by past life circumstances. What we don't realize is that we automatically added the meaning to fit our own narrative. However, all that happened was an event. The meaning is our own interpretation. Each person has their interpretation of what happened based on their own life circumstances, but that does not mean it is true.

The biggest thing that came from this was that I wanted to clear up how things were left with my ex-husband. I had no idea how to get in contact with him other than to reach out to my former mother-in-law. When I reached out, she was skeptical as to what I wanted. I let her know I was ready to clear the air with him so we could both forgive the hurt we caused one other. She said she would reach out to him and see if he were open to this.

When the ex-husband reached out to me, it was awkward at first, but I apologized for making him out to be an asshole. I never took responsibility for my part in the relationship and that was not fair to him. He stopped me to apologize for lying and leaving abruptly. It was a real honest moment that left me happy. I was able to walk away from that conversation without any hatred towards him any longer. By the end of the call, he asked me if it would be okay if he texted me every so often. I had no issue with it and was happy that we were able to leave the hurt in the past.

By the end of the course, I signed up for the next one offered, which would be in a couple of months.

Afterwards, I found a new sense of calm that hadn't existed before. When I went to work after attending it, I laughed at how I created all these stories about everything. I was able to see for the first time how much I was limiting myself by being captive to fabricated stories that brought no benefit and instilled fear within myself. What a huge relief it was letting go of the thoughts I created about others' opinions of me! After attending this seminar, I was able to sleep soundly as the voices in my head had quieted down. Little did I know that this was the true start of changing my life in a way I had never imagined.

84

We kept exploring Colorado. We also checked different sporting events, including a Detroit Red Wings game. This tested our relationship. Fran openly made fun of Detroit. I did not find it funny. We made it through the game, but for the betterment of our relationship, I never need to see the Detroit Red Wings with Fran ever again.

My friend Tessa was getting married to the love of her life. When we met on the Camino, she and her girlfriend had ended their relationship. After she returned, they got back together. Tessa asked me to be one of her bridesmaids. She was getting married just outside of Fort Lauderdale. Fran came as my date. Getting to witness Tessa marrying the woman of her dreams allowed my Camino journey to come full circle. She had talked about wanting to get back together with her girlfriend, and now she had and was marrying her. I caught the bouquet – the first time in my life I wanted to catch it.

Fran and I danced the night away. The booze was flowing and by the end of the night, I was feeling wonderful.

We were getting to a point where Fran and I knew we wanted to move in together. I was interested in buying a place, rather than renting. The rent in Colorado was so high that it made more sense to buy a place to start building equity. He wasn't as certain about buying, but I was ready to lay down roots in Colorado. Finally, I was in a place to buy a home. I had been given my inheritance from my mom's parents and I knew that it would be used for a down payment.

At the beginning of April, I started to look at houses. The second day of looking for a house, I found one that I thought would be perfect for Fran and me. I put in an offer, and it was accepted.

Fran got to have his first experience with me at an Eric Church concert. The seats were where hockey players would sit, so we had our own little cup holder for the entire concert. I drank a lot during the concert, so he got to see the whole experience.

I went to my second weekend of the personal development course which was an advanced course. This was an expansion on what we learned from the first weekend. This one focused on how we as humans repeatedly show up. While we think we are making new choices, we really are continuing to run on the same program. Meaning we react the way we do because we interpret everything as we always do. We see the world how we want it to fit into our narrative.

This course was different from the first one since we were placed in groups. Katie was there with me for the entire weekend but was in a different group. While I watched her have huge breakthroughs, at the time I really didn't think I had any. However, I actually I took away something huge: I realized that I needed to quit my job, since I was tolerating something that was not feeding my soul and, in fact, was depleting it. However, as I was in the final stages of closing on the house, I knew that I had to wait to quit my job. While I thought it was not a big thing I took from the course, it was in fact a huge thing.

I closed on the house on a Friday. The lease for my apartment was not up until the beginning of July, but I loved that I was going to slowly be able to move into the house. Fran and I went shopping for bedroom furniture and ended up buying a bar with a bar back to go into the basement. It was the first piece of furniture delivered into the house.

I handed in my resignation letter on Monday to my boss. She was a little bit shocked. I told her that I wasn't going anywhere so I could help with the transition and training a new candidate.

Since I had the house, I knew it was finally time to get all the belongings out of the house in Michigan. I had stored everything in a room that was not bothering Steve or his family. I wanted to have my dad's recliner and my parents' kitchen table in the new house. I flew back to Michigan to pack it up so it would be ready for the movers.

Tricia came into town to visit with one of her dogs. We had a nice visit where we went to dinner with her dog relaxing on the patio. Tricia and I headed up to the mountains to go for a hike and to check out the town of Breckenridge.

Right after Tricia's visit, Fran asked me if I'd be interested in having a dog. I'd wanted one a year prior, but the timing felt right now. I also would have his help since he'd had dogs before. Tricia's dogs were there the only dogs I'd ever around been around. One of his coworkers sent him a picture of two dogs that she was fostering. One girl was tan and white with piercing blue eyes. The other was a black and tan mix. We decided to adopt them. They were litter mates and we wanted them to stay together. We went out to buy all the supplies we needed for these two sweet babies.

We were trying to figure out what we wanted to name them, and eventually we landed on Aspen and Estes as they were Colorado locations. Originally, he wanted to name them Phoenix and Sedona, but we went with Colorado names as we met in Colorado.

Aspen was mostly black with tan spots. Estes was mostly tan with a white belly. Aspen started to take the dominant role, but Estes had her moments. I made it known to them that I was the alpha. Other than lack of sleep, they were the best pups. I was starting to build my own little family.

85

In the personal development program, they had a "future" meeting. We would discuss what I wanted to create for my life in the future. The two things I wanted for my future was to marry Fran and find a job that I loved. I didn't know what this job would be, so I said I wanted to help people. This is when my coach asked me if I had ever thought about becoming a life coach. It hadn't been something I'd ever considered. At the end of the meeting, I was happy that I had done this course to set the stage for creating my future.

I had been working a job for a couple of months, but it didn't work out and I was let go unfairly. I was shocked and worried. Mostly it was a concern about feeling as if I needed this job. I was desperate to be employed. I was supposed to talk to my coach the day I was fired, but I texted her to cancel. She encouraged me to contact her when I was ready.

I called her the next day and we got to action. I remembered our conversation about possibly being a life coach. I wanted to move forward with this. We set up an action plan for me to research three to six different schools to find the right one for me. When I completed the process, I decided to go with Institute for Professional Excellence in Coaching (iPEC) which was starting the next week.

Shortly after I started with my peer coach, an accident happened. I had been taking the girls to the dog park. It had become their favorite place on earth. We would get a pup cup, which is whip cream, then head over to the spacious fields for them to run and play in. It was a nice day in December, so I took them to the park. When we were there, Estes and Aspen ran over to the lake to get water. Since Estes was a little bit timid, she stopped before the opening in the ice. However, Aspen's paw hit the water and she nosed dived into the icy water. I started to scream her name and crawled to the opening. I had witnessed it in slow motion, but there was nothing I could do to stop her from falling in. After about five seconds, she popped up further out in the water and started to swim towards me. As she got closer, she was getting tired. She had never swum before, so I was proud of how well she did.

I pulled her out of the water and dragged her to the side of the lake and screamed for help. When no one came to help, I picked her up, then a man walked over to help me. He took Aspen from me, and we headed towards the entrance. She started to make gurgling noises which made me think she was coughing up the water. We walked as quickly as we could to the car. Estes stayed by my side the whole time. He laid Aspen on the backseat of my car and Estes jumped into the front seat. I went to grab my phone to call Fran, but realized it was in my coat pocket. I had put the coat around Aspen to try to warm her up. When I went to get the phone, I saw that her eyes did not look like her eyes.

I was frantic when I called Fran. He said that he would look for a vet for me to go to. I looked for one too as I was driving. It wasn't safe, but I was desperate to find a place to take her. I called the closest one to the park. I was beyond hysterical the whole drive there. It took what felt like forever to get to the facility. They came out and grabbed her to try to save her. However, I am fairly sure she had already been gone for a while. I let Fran know where I was. He came over, too. I felt guilty even though it was an accident. They allowed us to go down to say goodbye to her before we left. Fran asked if I could call someone to help me drive home. I tried Brian, but he did not answer. I then called his neighbors and they helped us out. I cried the whole ride home. I was devastated.

Fran took my car to go get cleaned. While he was waiting, he saw a dog that looked exactly like Aspen. Fran broke down telling me this. He felt it was Aspen letting him know that she would be alright.

Those first couple days Estes went back and forth between Fran and I to comfort us. Taking her out for a walk by herself broke my heart. I was grateful that Estes was intimidated by the water, so she did not fall in too.

One of the best gifts I had was I had my student coach. I reached out to her to let her know that we had lost our dog in a drowning accident. I wanted her to know before we had our call since I was more than likely going to want to be coached around this. More importantly than being coached, I wanted her to hold the space of grief with me. I had been through so much grief in my life that I knew some people struggle in the uncomfortableness of these moments.

In February, my iPEC training was in Denver for the second session. I was determined to show up differently than I had at the first one. I wanted to gain a lot this weekend which meant I needed to break out of my shell.

This session was primarily coaching. There were a few highlights from iPEC's core principles that were covered, but mostly we worked on our coaching skills. Being vulnerable enough to learn my strengths and weaknesses in my skills as a coach helped shift my confidence. The honest feedback only gave me the ability to strengthen my skills.

After the third and final training session, I needed to record a coaching conversation to ensure that I was following the guidelines of the ICF. One recorded coaching conversation felt as if it was good enough to be transcribed. However, when I got the results, I did not pass. I was crushed and felt like a failure. I learned that it was not that I did a poor job coaching, but rather I did not hit enough markers to qualify in my certification.

After a couple of months of coaching my butt off, I sought out the avenue to retest. I was paired with an iPEC coach to see if I was able to pass. While I was on the call coaching him, I felt good about how it was going. He was unable to confirm on the call, but he hinted that it went well. A few days later I found out I passed and qualified to be a certified professional coach.

I realized most people don't ask for your credentials, but it was necessary for my own confidence to go through the proper channels to be certified in the industry. Having the CPC behind my name does not mean much to some people, but it means everything to me. I was ready to start helping people navigate through their own struggles so they, too, could have a life that they loved.

It was recommended to me that as an entrepreneur, I should hire a coach. I was unsure what the benefits would be, but quickly started to understand. It was an investment. A large investment. I even cried ugly tears when I realized that I was committing to myself in a way I'd never done before in my life. I made myself a priority. The number one priority. It shifted my mentality.

I'd been committed to my own growth throughout the years between counseling, graduate education, personal development, and life coaching school. Now I was open to being coached. I thought my mindset was in a good place. However, my first conversation with my coach let me realize I wanted someone to validate me. I'd been told for years that I was strong and resilient. I wanted to hear the praises from him, too. He wouldn't do this since he knew it was a disservice to me. I needed to learn that everything comes from within. He restored my power by giving me the ability to choose my own beliefs. I committed to a two-year coaching relationship which ended up being the absolute best investment I've ever made. I learned that I am the creator of my life.

86

We went to Arizona for the weekend to visit Fran's family. When we landed, Fran's dad picked us up at the airport, then we headed out to Sedona to stay the night. I had known that it was Fran's favorite place, and I had a feeling that he was going to be proposing to me. I was so confident that this was the reason for the trip that I had gotten my nails done. If he was proposing, I wanted my nails to look good in the photos!

We went on a hike. I thought he was going to propose at the Chapel of the Holy Cross, so I was confused why we were hiking. We chose to do an off-road adventure tour. It was great to be able to be driven around seeing all the beautiful locations off roads in Sedona.

After the tour was over, Fran wanted to find sweatshirts for us since it was colder than normal in Arizona. The shops did not have any sweatshirts for sale, but he found a couple of Baja style pullover ponchos. We headed back to the hotel so that he could ask them where a secret location was. He wasn't telling me what we were doing since he wanted it to be a surprise. It was dark by the time our car lined up with others. I finally found out we were going to a stargazing event. With the temperatures so low, I was grateful for our ponchos.

They took us to an area with about sixteen other people. We were given chairs and blankets to keep warm. There was a telescope and the guide was telling us about the constellations in the sky. After he gave us the background information, we were invited to look at the stars he was talking about. Stargazing in the middle of Sedona was special to me. It was Fran's favorite place, and I was fascinated with the energy vortexes. After it had concluded, Fran pulled me over to the side and got down on one knee. Before he could even say anything, I said yes! After I said yes, he awkwardly said, "Will you marry me?"

We went back to the car where I kept saying, "We're engaged!" We both laughed that I had said yes before he even asked me. As we were pulling out of the parking lot, we saw three deer standing on the side of the road. I felt this symbolized my family being there, so I asked him to pull over so I could take a photo of them. Our engagement picture was taken back at the hotel with our ponchos on. Fran got me the most beautiful morganite engagement ring. I wanted morganite since it symbolizes divine love.

We had an engagement party at his dad's house the following night. His dad joked he was happy I said yes, otherwise it would be an awkward night. Everyone came over to congratulate us or officially meet me. It was great to meet so many of Fran's friends and family.

After we got back from getting engaged, we wanted Estes to have a playmate. We went over to his coworker's house since she had a couple of dogs she was fostering again. Both puppies played with Estes. It was adorable. We fell in love with one of the two dogs. Estes had made it known who her sister was going to be.

The rescue would number their dogs every year. As we were watching them all play, I noticed the collar on the girl we fell in love with had a number that I thought was similar to the numbers the girls had the year before. When I got home, I looked to see if I was correct. The dog we wanted to adopt ended up having the number after Aspen's! Aspen was 807-17 and now our soon-to-be puppy was 807-18. It was a sign!

We decided to name her Sedona. Sedona and I were kindred spirits from the beginning. The two girls played together, but it took a couple of days for them to cuddle together. They are now the best of friends.

87

Since it was a second marriage for both of us, I hoped we would get married privately. However, Fran wanted to have a wedding. My compromise was that it needed to be in Colorado since we met here. Then people could choose if they wanted to show up or not.

I didn't want to wear a wedding dress. Hearing this, Fran asked me if I would be open to wearing hockey jerseys. I thought it was a perfect representation of us. Our "save the date" notices were the back of our team's hockey jerseys with the number to display the date of the wedding.

I had seen an RSVP online where it said that if you don't respond by a certain date to bring a sandwich and a chair. I thought this was hysterical. I showed it to Fran, and we knew we would do something like this for our invitation. We used that line but changed it to a lawn chair and a side dish. Also added was a line that said, "Our feelings will not be hurt if you say no! You'll actually save us money, so thank you!" The responses were, "Accepted with pleasure," "Accepts but feels forced," "Declines with regret," and "Honestly, I don't want to come." People who got me and Fran found it funny.

Renee and her parents, Aunt Karen, Uncle John, several of my dad's brothers and sisters, my cousin Jodi and Patric, Robin, Tessa and her wife – so many people from different parts of my life were coming. I was ecstatic to have their love and support.

Several people were helping us to have our special day. Fran's friend Dan married us. Brian walked me down the aisle. Erik was our photographer for the wedding. The girl's foster mom was going to walk both Estes and Sedona down the aisle as our ring bearers.

Initially, I had wanted to have the reception in a bar since we were going with a sports theme, but Fran vetoed this. We chose a place on a botanical garden. Even though it was still wintertime, getting married outside was beautiful. Our reception was in a large log cabin with two fireplaces. The location was only 15 minutes from our place.

Our wedding attire was our favorite teams, the Arizona Coyotes for him and the Detroit Red Wings for me. On the back of the jerseys, we had "Groom" and "Bride" where the last names usually are. Our numbers were 3 and 17 for the date.

Aunt Nancy arrived in town early and assisted me on running errands. It was special to have this moment with her before everyone came into town. She shared that she was happy to see me getting married. I told her that I believed that while most people were happy for the bride, I felt as if people were overly happy for me since they had seen my journey of losing everyone. She acknowledged that this was true.

On our wedding day, Tricia was my support to ensure everything went smoothly. Fran and I had decided that we did not want to have a bridal party, but I asked Tricia to give a maid of honor speech.

It was a beautiful March day. His side of the family were cold since they were used to a warm climate. My side of the family was warm since they were still in the thick of winter. Everyone was able to wear whatever sports attire they wanted so to me, it was the perfect climate.

Brian and I walked down the aisle to a song Eric Church had written for his wife at their wedding. We had Dan wear a Colorado jersey to represent where Fran and I had met.

I'd been told that there was going to be a special vow after we exchanged ours. I was nervous since Fran can joke around and I didn't know what to expect. However, it ended up being the sweetest gesture. Fran serenaded me with a verse of the song, "Keep on Lovin' You." The guests had been handed a sheet of paper to sing along with the chorus as a surprise for me. I laughed when everyone started singing. Some guests even stood up to sing it.

When the girls walked down the aisle, they were pulling to reach me. Even they were wearing jerseys – Estes had on a Buffalo Bills jersey while Sedona wore a Detroit Red Wings jersey.

The ceremony was a perfect blend of us along with Christian tones to it. We had a unity cross that we assembled during the ceremony. The outer portion is to represent the strength of the man, the inner portion is to represent the beauty of the woman, and the nails holding it together are a representation of God.

We had a remembrance table, which I'd been calling the "dead person's table" to those I thought would be able to handle my brutal honesty. We paired the photo of our loved one with their favorite team's jersey. Fran's mom had an Arizona Coyotes jersey, his uncle had an Arizona Diamondback jersey, and one of his best friends had a Minnesota Wild jersey. Todd had a Detroit Tigers jersey; my dad had a Detroit Red Wings jersey, and my mom had a Trinity Lutheran Warriors jersey. We added a photo of Aspen to the table as well.

This day was so special to me. Not only was it my wedding day, but it was a day celebrating with those that I loved, and the start of my new family. I'd moved to Colorado to start that next chapter of my life. And here it was. One of my favorite days ever.

88

Life has not been easy. At times, it hurt like hell. However, I never gave up. Somehow, I managed to take a step forward every single day. It doesn't mean that there weren't setbacks, because there were. I am a fighter. I am resilient. I am focused on the journey.

Moving to Colorado was necessary for me. I was intentional

about starting a new chapter in my life beyond grief. I focused on creating a life I wanted to live. It gave me the opportunity to examine my world. I was able to slow down and see what was for my greatest good. This meant that relationships which no longer served me would be eliminated from my life. In turn, I minimized the drama. My life became peaceful.

These things did not happen instantly when I moved to Colorado – they started to show up when I became active in the personal development world. While I ended up leaving the multi-level marketing company, I was grateful for the path it led me on.

Throughout my adult life, I smoked weed and drank alcohol. While I stopped smoking weed before the end of my first marriage, I continued to drink. Overall, I would say that I drank socially, but there were times where I used it to cope. It was heavier after my mom's death. However, I can say now that I have done a lot of personal growth, I don't really drink anymore. I'm not saying I never drink, but it's way less. I don't need it anymore to hide from my feelings.

There was a strong internal pull to move to Colorado so I could find my family. I never believed that I would meet a man in Illinois. Little did I know that Fran would have the same feeling. However, we both knew on that first date that we'd met someone special. I've heard that you just know when you meet them. I never believed it. I thought it was bullshit. However, I knew. It was easy. I'd never experienced that before. Not that every moment with us is easy. It's not. But it's different than any relationship I've ever been in.

Fran is my family. I know without a doubt that my parents and brother would have loved him. I know they are smiling down on me and the life I've created. I know they all are proud of who I became on my journey to find myself once all the grief settled. Better yet, I am proud of who I am today. I am my favorite transformation story.

Afterword

Writing this memoir was a lot harder than I expected it would be. However, this is usually the case with me. Repeatedly throughout my life, I have thought things would be easy. Two examples that come to mind are the marathon and walking the Camino. I jump into life without any expectations until I get into the thick of it. Then the story of how difficult it is starts to replay. I talk about how I am all about the journey, but the truth is I only appreciate the journey when I get beyond it. Reflecting on the experience is when I finally see the value.

Writing about Todd's death was incredibly confronting on various fronts. Not remembering it meant I needed to research it to share it in a way that made sense. What fascinated me was that I was able to see it from an adult point of view whereas all my recollections have been from a child's perspective. It made me sit with the emotions. Once I finished writing about the aftermath of his death, I felt a sense of healing. I felt more comfortable speaking up to share my truth.

As I was writing, I cried about every little thing. A few of my sisters from my sisterhood reminded me the tears wanted and needed to be expressed. Once I stopped suppressing these feelings by allowing them to flow, my younger self was given permission to release emotions that no longer served me. I could hold space equally for knowing my loving parents did the absolute best they could and knowing they could have done better. These two statements no longer needed to contradict one another, but rather, they could be true at the exact same time.

I developed a narrative at some point in my childhood that I wasn't good enough. Insecurity was a large part of my identity that I created after Todd's death. My insecurities run throughout my life, which I was able to see in a new light as I wrote this memoir.

The largest thing that was stirred within me while writing this was the anger I have towards the church. I realize it was a different time. Mental health is finally starting to be openly talked about now, but back then it was rarely discussed. However, I feel my family was told to cope by relying on faith alone. To me, that was a misjudgment. Putting faith in God was not a bad thing, but for it to be the only thing was not enough. We had a sudden traumatic loss which deserved the respect of a professional helping us through the grief process. I've heard the phrase, "God doesn't give you more than you can handle" more times than I can count. This makes me twitch, since it minimizes my experience and the need to process.

I have a personal issue with how the church handled my family. The accident happened through an outing they hosted. I am not placing blame since it truly was an accident. However, it feels to me that by managing our family internally, it allowed the church to sweep it under the rug. My parents may have been against getting any outside help other than a church affiliated grief group. Once again, I wish someone would have addressed the elephant in the room by telling us we needed more than God. It was too interconnected, with my mom working at the church and school and my dad being a lifetime member. My family was used as an example of how you must put your faith in God during life's hardships. Not saying the church did not help, but more should have been done.

I no longer believe in the faith I was brought up in. That doesn't mean that I reject it either. It means I continue to seek my own understanding of God and what my relationship looks like with Him. It is a personal relationship. I believe that everyone has a right to choose what is right for their own personal beliefs.

When I was in the personal development program, it was the first time I understood the loving God I'd been taught about in my youth. I was grateful to be enlightened since I had always been bothered that it felt as if I was not getting it right. When I took out all the judgment and shame, I was able to see God in a new light.

Acknowledgments

Fran Fries – thank you for loving me and being my family. I love you!

Renee Boelcke – thank you for more than I can ever say. Your friendship has meant everything to me. Even if time passes without us speaking, I know that we have each other's back no matter what. I was blessed the moment you followed my family into our dorm room.

Tricia Dimitropoulos – thank you for inviting me to be a part of your family. I value your love and support beyond words I can ever express here. Never stop sending me pictures of the girls.

Katie Rutherford – thank you for being on this incredible transformational journey with me. I appreciate you! Love you forever!

Rosey Ioannou – thank you for your lifelong friendship! I love having you in my life even if you are half a world away from me.

Robin Fisette – thank you for being positive even when I may have not wanted to hear it. I am grateful to have you in my corner forever.

Deena Scheiber and Amy Edgington – thank you for reading as I wrote my draft. Thank you for reading all the details that have now been edited out. I appreciated all your feedback.

Nicola Humber – thank you for your love and support throughout the year to write my very first book.

Unbound Press – thank you for connecting me to the editing genius of Jesse Lynn Smart and the design genius of Leah Kent! I am eternally grateful to the both of you for helping me get this into the world!

Steve Janke – thank you for being a light in my life when I needed it most. I am grateful our paths crossed when they did.

Simon Crowe – thank you for serving me and not pleasing me. You have forever changed how I look at the world. Thank you for all the love and the support and believing in me.

Rockstar Sisterhood – thank you for holding space for me as I cried. Thank you for the encouragement you gave me as I was confronted while writing the memoir.

Thank you to all who shared their perspective surrounding Todd's death. It helped me be able to piece it back together to share it as authentically as I could.

About the Author

Trudi is a life-after-grief coach. Her superpower is her ability to let you be seen and heard by listening deeply and tapping into her intuition. She loves to connect women back to their inner power so they can be their best selves. She lives in Colorado with her husband and their cherished dogs.

Trudi can be reached at **www.adventureafter.com**

www.ingramcontent.com/pod-product-compliance
Lightning Source LLC
Chambersburg PA
CBHW021429080526
44588CB00009B/470